Obedient Unto Death

Obedient Unto Death

A Panzer Grenadier of the Leibstandarte-SS Adolf Hitler Reports

Werner Kindler

Translated by Geoffrey Brooks
Foreword by Charles Messenger

Frontline Books, London

Originally published in German in 2010 as
Mit Goldener Nahkampfspange
Werner Kindler – Ein Panzergrenadier der Leibstandarte.

This English edition first published in 2014 by Frontline Books

an imprint of Pen & Sword Books Ltd,
47 Church Street, Barnsley, S. Yorkshire, S70 2AS
www.frontline-books.com

For more information on our books, please visit
www.frontline-books.com, email info@frontline-books.com
or write to us at the above address.

Printed and bound by CPI Group (UK) Ltd, Croydon, CR0 4YY

Typeset and designed by M.A.T.S. Leigh-on-Sea, Essex

Contents

List of Plates

Foreword

There is no doubt that Werner Kindler was a very brave soldier and was probably very lucky to survive the war. He was also clearly a dedicated member of the Waffen-SS and appears to have retained his Nazi views throughout his life. True, Kindler had cause to be hostile towards the Poles. His family lived in the so-called Polish Corridor, which Germany had had to surrender to newly independent Poland after the First World War, and, as ethnic Germans, suffered. He therefore welcomed the German invasion of Poland. He then found himself in the SS Totenkopf, with whom he did his military training before joining the Leibstandarte, which had originally been formed as Hitler's personal guard. He entered Russia with it at the beginning of July 1941 and remained with the division until the very end of the war. Three spells on the Eastern Front, northern Italy over the time of the Italian surrender to the Allies, Normandy, the Ardennes counter-offensive, Hungary, and finally Austria provided the author with a wealth of combat experience.

Kindler claims that Hitler launched a 'preventive war' against the USSR because it was poised to strike at Germany and cites an article in Pravda of June 2001 and a book by Viktor Suvorov, *nom de plume* of Vladimir Rezun, a Soviet army officer who defected to the West in 1978. Rezun wrote a number of books claiming that Stalin intended to attack and was supported by a number of German and Russian historians. It was, however, a total myth in that, largely as a result of Stalin's purges, the Soviet Armed Forces were in no fit state to launch any form of attack and were still undergoing drastic reforms resulting from their poor showing against the Finns during the winter of 1939–40. Their posture in June 1941 was solely defensive.[1]

When we get on to the actual fighting and what it was like, Kindler says little about his own feelings and experiences. The only aspect that he does recount in detail is the medals and other awards that he earned. In particular, he details every day that counted towards his Close-combat Badge. It is difficult not to believe that he was what the British

FOREWORD

called in the Second World War a 'gong hunter', although he does also recount the awards won by his comrades. Otherwise, the book is more a history of his battalion, 3rd Battalion, 2nd SS-Panzer Grenadier Regiment, which he calls the APC Battalion. His ultimate hero is its commanding officer, Jochen Peiper, who time and again displayed extraordinary leadership and tactical flair, qualities which he would take with him when he was promoted to command 1st SS-Panzer Regiment, also in the Leibstandarte and under which Kindler's battalion often fought.

What is revealing is the author's views on general aspects of the war. The Russians are guilty of atrocities against German soldiers, but there is no mention of those perpetrated by the Waffen-SS and the German Army. He has little regard for Germany's enemies, except perhaps the Western Allies' air power, but Allied bomber crews are dubbed 'terrorists'. Unconditional Surrender meant the adoption of the Morgenthau Plan, which aimed to strip Germany of all its industry. This, indeed, was Allied policy until more realistic measures were adopted at the July 1945 Potsdam Conference and the German propaganda machine made much of it during the last months of the war. Kindler, however, goes one further, claiming that the intention was also to literally emasculate the German male population. When it comes to the December 1944 Ardennes counter-offensive and, in particular, the Malmédy Massacre, he claims that Peiper and his men were forced to make false confessions. As for himself, he was not at the scene since his sub-unit was providing security for the battle group's supply echelon. As to who did carry out the murder of the US soldiers, Kindler offers no explanation. Finally, he noted that morale plummeted when Hitler's death was announced.

What then to make of this book? Some will view Kindler as an arrogant and cold-blooded warrior, who delighted in combat. Others may consider him as a man displaying intense loyalty to his country. What his writing does reveal, however, is something of the mind-set of the Waffen-SS soldier, whose fighting spirit was largely forged from the very close bonds which existed among his officers and their men, bonds much closer than those in the Army. Add in National Socialist indoctrination and one begins to understand what motivated them to continue to fight with the same intensity long after the prospect of ultimate victory had vanished.

Charles Messenger

Preface and Translator's Notes

The author Werner Kindler was a Volksdeutscher, a person of German race and blood who by political circumstances had a bond, whether desired or otherwise, to the foreign country in which he was born and dwelt. In 1920, West Prussia became Polish territory by virtue of the Treaty of Versailles, and Werner Kindler was born there in 1922. It was Hitler's avowed intent that all these expatriate Germans, and the former German territories of which Germany had been dispossessed after the First World War, should return to the Reich. Although West Prussia was reincorporated into the German Reich in 1939 by conquest, the author was technically ineligible for the Wehrmacht, and so was conscripted into the Waffen-SS.

His memoir is the story of the ensuing six years of his life during which time he became one of the most highly decorated non-commissioned soldiers to serve in the German armed forces. He first saw frontline action in Russia in 1941 as a machine gunner, and was then selected for 1st SS-Panzer Division Leibstandarte Adolf Hitler (LAH). He remained in it until the end of the war.

Eighteen million men served in the German armed forces in the Second World War, and only 630 of them were awarded the Close-combat Clasp in Gold. The author was one of them. This statistic bears witness to the high value of this decoration, for which the soldier was required to have confirmed in his service record book (Soldbuch) fifty close-combat days. Accordingly this decoration could only be won after years of bitter fighting and privation. By October 1944, when the recording of his close-combat days was discontinued, the author had already amassed eighty-four confirmed days. He eventually received the award on 1 April 1945.

Werner Kindler served in Russia, Italy, Normandy, in the retreat across France and Belgium, in the Ardennes campaign, in Hungary and finally in Austria, where he sank his APC in the River Enns and surrendered to American forces on 10 May 1945, with the Soviets in hot pursuit. By then he commanded a company of the Leibstandarte in the rank of Oberscharführer (sergeant), and besides the gold Close-combat Clasp he had been awarded the German Cross in Gold, the Iron Cross First and Second Class, the East Medal and the Gold Wound Badge, having been wounded six times in action. Although short-listed for the Führer's personal bodyguard, by choice he eluded selection in the summer of 1944, preferring to be at the front.

The detailed material in this book was compiled over twenty-five years, from 1985 to 2010. Many conversations ensued during this period with Kindler's former company commander Otto Dinse and platoon commander Bernd von Bergmann, and veterans of his erstwhile companies. Names, dates and other information are based on official files such as the war diaries of 2nd SS-Panzer Grenadier Regiment and operations reports: also field-post letters from men involved, diaries and notes and replies to queries. Works of reference consulted were Rudolf Lehmann's history of the LAH Division (Munin Verlag) and P. Agte's biography of Jochen Peiper, commander of the Leibstandarte's Panzer regiment. Other contributions were made by the author's former battalion commanders Paul Guhl, Jupp Diefenthal and Georg Preuss. Much information was also supplied over the years by Erhard Gührs, Willi Pluschke, Erich Strassgschwandtner, Rudi Knobloch, Karl Menne, Fritz Thier, Erich Schöbel, Günther Wagner, Kuno Balz, Günter Gaul, Rudolf von Ribbentrop, Herbert Rink, Gerhard Stiller, Heinz Meier and Wilhelm Schermeng, to all of whom the author extends his grateful thanks.

The presentation is bereft of unnecessary commentary so as not to reduce the documentary value of the book as the faithful reporting of a soldier's personal experience. The intention is that the book should follow the guidelines laid down by the historian Leopold von Ranke that historical events must be researched and then reported free from ideological interpretations and told '. . . as it actually was'.

In the translation of the main text of foreign works, it is the publishing practice to use British equivalent ranks. These can only be approximations. The three ranks of the private soldier encountered in the Waffen-SS and used in this book were:

SS-Mann: Entrant
SS-Sturmmann: Trained Grenadier
SS-Rottenführer: Leading Grenadier. The Rottenführer was given responsibilities much greater than those of the British lance-corporal, but the Rottenführer was not an NCO. In the Waffen-SS the lowest NCO rank was full corporal (SS-Unterscharführer) and it was necessary

to pass a training course at Unterführerschule to obtain the rank. Only in the last few months of the war does it seem that, as was the author's case, for the fighting units at least this requirement was occasionally waived.

The NCO ranks used by Kindler were:

SS-Unterscharführer: Corporal

SS-Oberscharführer: Sergeant

SS-Hauptscharführer: Senior Sergeant

SS-Stabsscharführer: Staff Sergeant

The Officer ranks most frequently used by the author were:

SS-Untersturmführer: Lieutenant (junior grade) shown in the text as 2/Lt.

SS-Obersturmführer: Lt

SS-Hauptsturmführer: Captain

SS-Sturmbannführer: Major

SS-Obersturmbannführer: Lt-Colonel

Standartenführer/Oberführer: Colonel

Brigadeführer: Brigadier

A few abbreviations are used in the text where the frequency of their use has justified it:

APC = armoured personnel carrier

LSSAH (Leibstandarte SS Adolf Hitler) or LAH, the same thing

OKH = Oberkommando des Heeres – Army High Command

The Translator

Introduction

On 20 December 1939 the Infantry Assault Badge (Infanterie-sturmabzeichen) was introduced, for which a soldier qualified after participating in three attacks on different days. As the war went on and the fighting became more bitter on the Eastern Front and in North Africa, the burden on troops fighting in the most advanced sectors of the frontline became ever heavier. Attacks became a constant feature, but now included close-combat skirmishes in which soldiers fought man-to-man using close-combat weapons such as pistols, submachine guns and entrenching tools.

Therefore on 25 November 1942, the Führer and C-in-C of the Army instituted the Close-combat Clasp (Nahkampfspange) as 'a visible sign of the recognition of those soldiers fighting man-to-man with cold steel and close-combat equipment'.[1] The OKH implementing regulations of 3 December 1942 prescribed that: 'To count as a close-combat day, the qualifying soldier must have seen "the whites of the enemy's eyes". i.e. he fought the opponent man-to-man to the final decision using close-combat weapons'.[2] From the outset, the Close-combat Clasp was to be awarded in three grades based on the number of officially-recognised close-combat days: fifteen for the bronze clasp, thirty for the silver and fifty for the gold. An exact individual conformation of the number of days, with each date and location, was required, confirmed by the unit commander with his signature and service stamp. The opening day was retroactive to 1 December 1941.

Since there had been no register of close-combat days of this kind before 25 November 1942, but only confirmed assault days to qualify for the Infantry Assault Badge, it was decided, 'in order to give prominence to numerous proven long-serving frontline soldiers' that those men who had been in action on the Russian Front without a break since 22 June 1941 would be eligible for fifteen close-combat days for fifteen months served, ten close-combat days for twelve months and five days for eight months. The same rules regarding confirmation applied.

1

After November 1942 the confirmed close-combat days had to be confirmed at regiment, or the respective reconnaissance unit, pioneer battalion and so on as applied for by the company commander and these then came down to the units in daily orders. The company commander would identify which of his men had been involved directly with the enemy on these close-combat days and would enter their entitlement on a certificated tabulated form pasted into the Soldbuch (soldier's service record book). The soldier would thus know precisely how many close-combat days stood to his credit. The close-combat days continued to be differentiated from the confirmed assault days for the award of the Infantry Assault Badge.

The exceptionally high standing which the gold clasp had in Germany can be seen from the fact that it was an award which Adolf Hitler desired to make personally, so as to see and know the man.[3] This differed from the award of the Knight's Cross, frequently performed by Hitler in the Führer-HQs, but occasionally he would be represented by Himmler or Guderian. However, some gold clasps were awarded and distributed within the divisions before the publication of the Führer-order, and so there is an unknown but relatively small number of gold clasps which cannot be accounted for.

Undoubtedly the Close-combat Clasp enjoyed the highest recognition amongst front soldiers. If you met a grenadier who wore the silver clasp, you knew at once that he had been involved in hand-to-hand fighting with the enemy on at least thirty occasions and had come through. The few soldiers who had survived fifty or more close-combat days stood head and shoulders above these.

The award was won on pure merit, and could not be earned as the outcome of a single successful attack, but only through months and years of proven individual clashes beyond the foremost front, and it was a decoration reserved for the frontline soldier. In making the register entry it was necessary to confirm that the man in question had actually been involved in this or that attack. On 26 March 1944, OKH drew attention once more '. . . that in the calculation of close-combat days – corresponding to the Führer's founding decree – an especially strict yardstick is to be employed in order to maintain the high value of the Close-combat Clasp'.

Because of the nature of the fighting at the fronts it was clear that only a few soldiers would be able to win the gold clasp, for which fifty close-combat days had to be confirmed. These soldiers would be accorded special recognition and attention by the Reich, and as from

August 1944 it was laid down that soldiers who had been awarded the gold clasp could be recommended directly for the German Cross in Gold.

Furthermore upon awarding the gold clasp it is to be ascertained if the conditions of the award of the German Cross in Gold apply. This will generally be the case, since the count of fifty close-combat days represents a quite especial proof of worth over a long period of time. The Führer has agreed that the holder of the gold Close-combat Clasp can be recommended for the German Cross in Gold without further cause to be shown.[4]

As a result, some divisions acted accordingly and recommended their men holding the gold clasp for the German Cross in Gold without further ado. This was not the procedure in all units, for not all holders of the gold clasp received the German Cross in Gold.

In contrast to Knight's Cross holders a further measure of welfare was provided exclusive to holders of the gold clasp. They were to be removed from direct frontline operations for at least a year to attend training schools for their weapons branch. A number of NCOs and men were transferred into the Führer's escort brigade at the end of 1944 and withdrawn from their units before the Ardennes campaign. Hitler also ordered that holders of the gold clasp and their dependants were to receive the same care and welfare as holders of the Knight's Cross.[5]

For my unbroken service over a period of twelve months on the Russian Front from July 1941 I was awarded ten close-combat days. The other seventy-four confirmed days all occurred during my service with 3rd Battalion, 2nd SS-Panzer Grenadier Regiment LAH. I have made an entry in bold in the text where any activity in which I took part on one of these days finds mention, otherwise the days are summarised at the conclusion of each relevant chapter.[6] The last close-combat day credited to me, by when I had already been notified of the impending award to me of the gold clasp, was on 12 October 1944. Other panzer grenadiers in the APC battalion had confirmed close-combat days in Normandy, the Ardennes, Hungary and Austria.

Chapter One

From a Farm in Danzig into the Leibstandarte-SS Adolf Hitler

I was born on 15 July 1922 at Kottisch in West Prussia, the first son of farmer Otto Kindler and his wife Elisabeth. He had served the Kaiser in the First World War as a soldier on the Düna. I grew up on the family farm with two sisters and a brother born in 1928. Kottisch, founded in 1818, lay in the Preussisch-Stargard district of West Prussia. Geographically it lay west of the Vistula and south of Danzig. Amongst others, the town of Preussisch-Stargard and Dirschau fell within the region governed by the great Baltic port of Danzig. Kottisch was a small village, half-gutted by fire in 1888. When I was a boy, the village had thirteen independent German farms. Shortly before my birth, my West Prussian homeland was severed from the territory of the German Reich and ceded to Poland under the victors' dictates of the Treaty of Versailles. From 1920 Poland exercised full control over West Prussia. Three-and-a-half million Germans therefore came under Polish domination whether they liked it or not. West Prussia now formed the so-called 'Polish Corridor'. This was the former part of Germany, now Polish, through which one was obliged to drive in order to get from Germany to the German province of East Prussia. The great Hanseatic port of Danzig was now controlled by the League of Nations.

In 1931 Germany estimated the presence of 1,018,000 persons of German racial stock in the Polish sphere of influence. As a result of the prevailing pressures, at the census 277,000 persons had preferred discretion to claiming they were Germans. Since Poland had been given West Prussia in 1920, over three-quarters of the original German population had left, and the remainder were to be oppressed and ousted in a long campaign aimed at forcing them to leave.[1]

By 1924, by means of liquidations, expropriations and compulsory purchase, Poland sequestered 510,000 hectares of land, to which by 1939 they had added another 1.2 million acres through so-called 'agrarian reform'. A whole string of laws and decrees, the worst being the notorious 'Frontier Zone Law', was created to dispossess and expel the Germans or deprive them of their legal rights. German miners and employees in Upper Silesia subsisted on meagre incomes, and in thousands of cases faced starvation. Men of the Hela fishery, established for centuries, suffered similarly.[2]

I grew up on the parental smallholding. Our family was cut off from the great economic and generally improving tendencies in Germany. From 1928 by Polish law I was obliged to attend the Polish village school at Kottisch, from where I went to German secondary school in Preussisch-Stargard until 1938. Germany under the Hitler regime considered it a matter of overriding importance to return to the Reich those Germans expatriated beyond its borders, and to reincorporate the occupied regions severed from the Reich by the Treaty of Versailles. In 1938 Austria and the Sudetenland were annexed to Germany. Tension with Poland over the West Prussian Corridor and the Free City of Danzig grew. In 1939, the German Foreign Ministry suggested to Poland that the time was now ripe for Germany and Poland to come to a general agreement over all existing problems. The German proposals were as follows:

1. The Free City of Danzig should return to the German Reich.
2. An extraterritorial autobahn and extraterritorial multi-track railway line would run across the Corridor.
3. In the Danzig region Poland would be given an extraterritorial highway or autobahn and a free port.
4. Poland would receive marketing guarantees for its products in the Danzig region.
5. The two nations would recognise and guarantee their common frontiers or the mutual territories.
6. The German-Polish treaty would be extended by ten years to twenty-five years.
7. Both nations would add a consultation clause to their treaty.[3]

Poland rejected all these proposals outright and ordered a general mobilisation, relying on the British guarantee of 31 March 1939 for support, and on 3 September 1939 Britain and France declared war on Germany.

In that calamitous summer of 1939 I celebrated my seventeenth birthday on 15 July working on my parents' farm. The Polish attitude had become more hostile. Polish radio and newspapers were stirring up feelings against the Germans again. On 26 June 1939 a Polish newspaper published a letter showing Poland's territorial claims. After the Polish attack on Germany, the new Polish border would extend from Bremen through Hannover, Fulda, Würzburg and Erlangen, cutting Germany in half. A Polish 'Western Border Union' (West-markenverein) circulated a huge number of maps and postcards showing those parts of Germany to be annexed to Poland.[4]

Because of this agitation, Germans were attacked and killed in West Prussia and other regions. Especially from August 1939, larger numbers of Germans began to be kidnapped by Poles and murdered. German schools were closed by the Polish authorities. My own village escaped these attentions, although elsewhere Fräulein Maisohle, one of my sister's teachers, was killed. As I recall personally, in Preussisch-Stargard only a few kilometres away, several German businessmen were taken away and murdered.

Up to 21 August 1939 about 70,000 Germans had fled the state, but the terror even spilled over into German territory. Polish mounted units made repeated cross-border forays into German territory, killing farmers in East Prussia and torching their farms. For their protection the 57th Artillery Regiment was brought up from Königsberg to Garnsee/Neidenburg in East Prussia. On 26 August 1939 a party from the German regiment intercepted one of these Polish raiding groups returning from such an incident on German soil and killed forty-seven of them.[5]

In the late summer of 1939 the pressure intensified, and after the Polish mobilisation my father had to find somewhere to hide his horses, wagons and coachman. In order to escape the Poles I went into the forests. The war began on Friday 1 September 1939. With my friend Siegfried Sell I cycled to Dirschau and next day came across an SS-Heimwehr Danzig MG post on one of the Vistula bridges. Finally, the first German soldiers! On 3 September troops of the German Wehrmacht liberated nearby Preussisch-Stargard.

In the middle of the following week the population was called upon to protect West Prussia. Men aged from seventeen to forty-five years were to report. I was amongst them and, under the direction of German police units, assisted in street patrols, guarding the municipal building and Preussisch Stargard prison. No uniform was provided but I was given a green armband with the word Selbstschutz ('local militia') on it to wear on my civilian clothing, and armed with a 98-carbine and a 7.65mm pistol.

On 6 October 1939 Poland surrendered unconditionally. This cancelled the local provisions of the Treaty of Versailles and West Prussia was reintegrated into Germany. My home village of Kottisch was renamed Gotenfelde and fell once more within the jurisdiction of Preussisch-Stargard which, from 26 November 1939, became part of the newly-formed Reichsgau (Reich administrative district) of Danzig-West Prussia.

During my short tour of duty with the West Prussian militia, at age seventeen on 13 November 1939 I was called up at Kloster Pelplin and sent to Prague for four weeks' military training with 6th SS-Totenkopf-Standarte (SS-Colonel Bernhard Voss). At Prague-Rusin I met colleagues I had known in the Danzig militia.

This particular unit was the first of the Totenkopf-Standarten to have been set up in wartime. I went into No 9 Company, still in civilian clothing. The training at Prague was harsh. We were sworn in by SS-General August Heissmeyer on 16 December 1939 at the Heinrich Himmler barracks, Prague-Rusin.[6] This is the oath we took:

> I swear to thee, Adolf Hitler,
> As Führer and Chancellor of the Reich
> Loyalty and bravery!
> I pledge to thee and to those placed by thee in authority over me
> Obedience unto Death
> So may God help me!

Two days after taking the oath I was transferred to No 2 Company, 13th SS-Totenkopf Standarte (SS-Colonel Klingemann) at Linz. My company commander was SS-Captain Fritz Holwein. We were 250-strong and composed mainly of men from Preussisch-Stargard, Dirschau and Karthaus. In February 1940 a rooting-out left only thirty-six of us in the company. All the others were discharged, most to be re-conscripted later.

We had harsh, intensive winter training in Upper Austria equipped with Czech weapons. I did not finish an NCO's course. On duty one day the Company visited Hitler's parents' house at Leonding. In March 1940 the regiment moved from Linz-Ebelsberg to Vienna-Schönbrunn into barracks previously occupied by 1st SS-Regiment Der Führer. In Vienna my company commander SS-Captain Holwein took over the 6th NCO Training Company and was replaced by SS-Lt Hans Opificius. He was a much-liked commander who visited the men on many weekends with his two children. He lived with his family in Vienna. That April I got my first spell of home leave with my family in West Prussia.

In May 1940 they transferred me again to No 4 (MG) Company/13th SS-Totenkopf-Standarte to train on the heavy MG 08. At Vienna one of my instructors and also my gun-captain was SS-Corporal Hans Fuchs, a businessman and reservist from Franconia alongside whom I was to serve until 1944 in the same company. Another instructor was 40-year-old Professor Eckert who taught me how to make the best impression on NCOs and officers. On 15 July I celebrated my 18th birthday.

The 13th SS-Totenkopf-Standarte was disbanded on 15 August 1940. We held an ironic burial ceremony in the presence of its officers. My next drafting was to Holland, into the reorganised No 4 (MG) Company, 4th SS-Totenkopf Standarte, made up in the main of men from the same unit previously known as Ostmark. 1st Battalion was at The Hague, 2nd Battalion at Groningen and 3rd Battalion at s'Hertogenbosch. They put 4th (MG) Company in the Leopold School on the fishery dock at Scheveningen. Here I did infantry and weapons training in the sand dunes. We had only old MGs and the water-cooled heavy MG 08. For a change, we did turns of duty as coastal defence against expected British raids and we also blew up drifting mines by firing at the detonator horns. Unit welfare was outstanding, a hallmark of the admired battalion commander 'Kapt'n Schuldt'. However, men up to eighteen years of age received no coffee, only milk and cocoa on Sundays; adults got morning coffee. In September 1940 occurred a high point in my service when I stood honour guard over a week for former Kaiser Wilhelm II, exiled to an estate at Doorn, and I did guard duty on three occasions for the visits of Göring to Wassenaar.

It was at this time – August 1940 – that Waffen-SS Command was formed and the Totenkopf-Standarten were absorbed into the Waffen-SS. The average age in the Standarten was high. To reduce it, the older reservists were released and the younger men transferred into the lower numbered Standarten 4 to 11 inclusive while the others were disbanded. The surviving Standarten then reorganised along the guidelines set for the motorised SS-infantry regiments, and in September 4th SS-Totenkopf-Standarte was also motorised. I spent a whole month at driving school and obtained my Class I and II licences. I was taught about vehicles and engines, repairs and oil-changing and got to know all the vehicles in service.

The year 1940 drew to its close. The Netherlands Reich Commissioner Artur Seyss-Inquart attended the Yuletide festivities of our No 4

Company. In February 1941 our regiment arrived by train in the Warsaw district of Mokotov. On 25 February we removed our Totenkopf collar patches and sewed on the SS runes: our unit was now known as the 4th SS Infantry Regiment (Motorised), and in May attached to 2nd SS-Infantry Brigade (Motorised). Thus I completed an 18-month period of training under what amounted to peacetime conditions; I was an infantryman competent to handle the light and heavy MG, and able to drive all manner of road vehicles. This training would stand me in good stead later, and now a major change was to occur in my military fortunes.

In May 1941, the companies of the 4th SS-Infantry Regiment paraded for inspection by officers of the Leibstandarte Adolf Hitler who had arrived in Warsaw from Wischau. Together with others I was selected for transfer into the LSSAH. That was the last I ever saw of the 4th SS-Infantry Regiment (Motorised).[7] I joined the ranks of the Leibstandarte at Wischau that same month and became a member of the most famous German unit. By virtue of its military achievements the prestige of this strengthened regiment was on a level with the Prussian Guard units of earlier centuries, whose famed predecessors included the Guard Regiment of Foot, the Garde du Corps and the 1st Life Guard Battalion of the 15th Guards Regiment. As a further parallel to the Leibstandarte it is valid to mention that the most elite Prussian regiment, the Garde du Corps, founded in 1740 in squadron strength, fulfilled the role of personal bodyguard to Prussia's king Frederick II. This corps, like the Leibstandarte, was composed of tall volunteers and was held in special regard in the Reich. Frederick the Great and the Prussian kings who succeeded him always had the privilege to be commander-in-chief of this regiment. Yet the Garde du Corps was by no means just for parades and bodyguard duty, for it fought with great bravery at Hohen-friedburg in 1745 during the Second Silesian War. Furthermore in all subsequent battles, and in the German Wars of Liberation, including the legendary People's Battle at Leipzig, the Garde du Corps proved itself outstandingly as heavy cavalry.

The Leibstandarte Adolf Hitler was in the direct frontline at the outbreak of war in 1939. It was still not a division although it was made up of four infantry battalions, a heavy weapons battalion, an SP-gun battery, a company of self-propelled 4.7cm anti-tank guns, an artillery regiment (two batteries), a pioneer battalion, reconnaissance unit, flak unit, signals unit and supply. After operations in the Balkans in the early summer of 1941, the LAH relocated to Bohemia and Moravia. In the Brünn/Wischau area it received reinforcements including its own 4th Battalion from Berlin, previously the Guard battalion of the Leibstandarte there. Of the five companies comprising 4th Battalion (Nos 16–20 Companies), only Nos 16 and 17 Companies had gone into the field as originally composed, while Nos 18, 19 (MG) and 20 (Heavy) Companies had a nucleus of Leibstandarte soldiers but also men from various other units, particularly specially-chosen men from the 4th, 8th and 10th Infantry Regiments. Therefore the 4th Battalion of the Leibstandarte in its personnel structure may be considered new with effect from June 1941.

As a trained machine-gunner, in May 1941 I was transferred to No 19 (MG) Company/4th Battalion under SS-Captain Hans Meiforth who had begun service with 4th Battalion LAH in the summer of 1933. I was placed in 3rd (Heavy-MG) Platoon (SS-2/Lt Rudolf Möhrlin). A minority of the personnel of this company came from the Leibstandarte, but in the main from other units as for example No 12 (MG) Company of the 10th SS-Infantry Regiment from Cracow. Even Möhrlin came from the 8th Infantry Regiment. It was here that I was drilled in the MG 34.

No 19 (MG) Company, 4th Battalion LAH

Occupants of the Principal Posts from June 1941, Beginning of Russian Campaign

Company commander: SS-Capt. Hans Meiforth (fell 14 April 1942) then SS-Lt Georg Bormann

Runners: SS-Leading Grenadier Fritz Jacobi: SS-Corporal Dressler

Medical Orderly NCO: SS-Corporal Figura

(Acting) CSM: SS-Sergeant Joachim Thiele (with LAH since June 1933)

QM: SS-Sergeant Hoffmann

1st (Heavy MG) Platoon

Platoon leaders: SS-Lt Erich Otto Thomas (fell 12 July 1941)

SS-Lt Georg Bormann:

SS-Ensign Joachim Kaden

2nd (Heavy MG) Platoon: SS-2/Lt Hans Scharna (from 6th SS-Regiment Germania November 1938, fell 12 July 1941)

3rd (Heavy MG) Platoon: SS.2/Lt Möhrlin: SS-ensign Otto Bölk (fell 15 July 1943)

4th (Mortar) Platoon: SS.2/Lt Max Trampler (from 8th SS Infantry Regiment, fell 11 March 1945 at Kis Bajou as SS-Captain and commander, 3rd Battalion, 35th SS-Panzer Grenadier Regiment)

My comrades in the Leibstandarte were on average younger than in the Totenkopf Regiments. I had come into an intact community of young Germans from all corners of the Greater German Reich. Berliners and Viennese, Brandenburgers, East and West Prussians alongside Saxons, Bavarians, Franks, Tyroleans, men from Kärntner, Central Germans and Sudeten Germans now were all our battle companions. Separatist and provincial rivalries, together with the schism between Catholic and Protestant, the main evil in the thousand years of German history, had been overcome. In the Leibstandarte, national origins and class had been largely extinguished.

Chapter Two

Russia 1941–1942:
My First Ten Close-combat Days

On 22 June 1941 Germany unleashed a preventive war against the Soviet Union. The Bolshevists under Stalin had decided long before to attack Germany. The first stage of the objective to conquer the world for Communism was to be realised in Europe. The official Russian newspaper *Pravda* confirmed on 11 June 2002: 'Long before 22 June 1941, Stalin was preparing a war of aggression against Germany.'[1] All of the preparations made by the Soviets for the great offensive in the years before were close to completion in that fateful summer of 1941.

The territorial demands, invasions and seizures by the Soviets, the evidence of major Soviet troop build-ups on the other side of their western frontier, their economy and armaments production, all these spoke volubly for a war against the Reich, and Germany decided to confront the threat before the Soviets spilled across the border. In the summer of 1941 it was time to put that eighteen months of first-class military training to good use. Confident in myself, my abilities and having the carefree way of youth, on 2 July 1941 I mounted my vehicle and drove it into Soviet Russia. This was the day when the Leibstandarte entered the war against the Soviet Union. Before night fell, my battalion commander SS-Major Willi Janke was fatally wounded at Olyka. SS-Captain Günter Anhalt stepped up to replace him.

My duties in the initial period were limited to aircraft spotting from the orderly clerk's lorry. After a short while they gave me a captured Soviet Ford lorry to drive. Still in July 1941 I was transferred as machine-gunner No 3 in the heavy MG section of SS-Corporal Hardt after Wipfler fell ill. The Leibstandarte broke through the Stalin Line against bitter resistance, and I fought at Kiev, where on 12 July SS-Lt Erich Thomas, commander of No 19 (MG) Company, met his death.

I was nineteen years old on 15 July 1941. With the Leibstandarte I obtained my first promotion to full private (SS-Sturmmann). In the years of training in the Totenkopf-Standarten nobody had been considered fit to promote. In August 1941 I was involved in the fighting to seal the encirclement at Uman. In my first attack holding a rifle in August I received a splinter wound to the right knee. It seemed so insignificant to me that I declined a field dressing and medical attention.

The LAH moved forward, and on 17 August 1941 set up a bridgehead over the Ingulez, taking the Black Sea port of Cherson two days later. In a Ukrainian village one of the inhabitants began enquiring of us from which areas of Germany we originated. It surprised me to discover that the man was a German from my own village, and had been a friend of my father. In the First World War he had been taken prisoner by the Russians, settled there after his release and so had been classified in Germany as 'missing'. His joy was unlimited to be amongst Germans again. Occasionally I acted as a courier, for which I used a captured horse.

Between 21 August and 7 September 1941 the LAH rested near Bobrinez. In September SS-Ensigns Joachim Kaden and Otto Bölk came to No 19 (MG) Company. Bölk was made my platoon commander. On 9 September the LAH crossed the Dnieper and followed the coastline of the Sea of Azov eastwards. After pursuits through the Noga Steppe and the attack on the Crimean access road near Perekop, LAH fought in the Melitopol area. While under heavy pressure at Wessyoloye near Melitopol, my heavy-MG platoon under SS-Ensign Bölk lost seven men dead and fifteen wounded on 1 October, amongst them nearly all the section and platoon leaders. At the time I was the sole ammunition runner and kept the entire platoon supplied. Amongst those who fell were SS-Corporals Hardt and Töpfler, and SS-Private Griser.

Shortly afterwards we took Mariupol and between 12 and 16 October 1941 the LAH forced a crossing over the river Mius. On 17 October the Division attacked Taganrog. At 0530 hrs 3rd Battalion set out over level, open country, Nos 12 and 13 Companies leading, Peiper's No 11 Company drawn out behind. When sections of the leading companies crossed the railway embankment upon von Hornisten's signal at 1100 hrs, two platoons of Soviet tanks appeared suddenly from Taganrog. The 3.7cm anti-tank gun of SS-Private Fruth stopped them, but 3rd Battalion, lacking cover, suffered heavy losses from artillery, anti-aircraft fire and MGs. The situation was extremely critical. Many of Peiper's men sought cover in a trench running at a right-angle to the railway line. The trench came into the field of fire of a wagon of an armoured train. These men were killed.

Jochen Peiper SS-Colonel
b. 30 January 1915 (Berlin) d.14 July 1976 (Traves, France).

Awards:
Knight's Cross 9 March 1943.
German Cross in Gold 6 May1943 as SS-Major commanding 3rd Battalion, 2nd SS-Panzer Grenadier Regiment of SS-Panzer Grenadier Division LSSAH.
Oak Leaves 27 January 1944.
Swords 11 January 1945 as SS-Lt Col commanding 1st SS-Panzer Regiment.

Full details of his career are set out in the biography *Jochen Peiper – Kommandeur Panzerregiment Leibstandarte*.
6 January 1935 Entered military, passed out SS Officer School, Braunschweig.
1 April 1936 Commander, No 3 Platoon, No 2 Company LAH, subsequently Staff, Reichsführer-SS.
4 August 1941 Returned to LAH.
4 October 1941 Commander, 2nd Battalion LAH.
14 September 1942 Commander 3rd Battalion, 2nd SS-Panzer Grenadier Regiment, converted in November 1942 into APC battalion.
9 March 1943 For his endeavours at Kharkov awarded Knight's Cross.
6 May 1943 Awarded German Cross in Gold.
21 July 1943 After Kursk awarded Tank Destruction Badge
1 September 1943 Awarded Close-combat Clasp in silver.
20 November 1943 Commander, Panzer Regiment LSSAH until end of war.
27 January 1944 Awarded Oak Leaves
11 January 1945 Awarded Swords.
Peiper was one of the most charismatic and intelligent officers of the Division. In all his units he was recognised and esteemed as an outstanding personality and mentally adept officer. The men of his units felt secure and responsibly protected under his leadership. He stood trial at Dachau after the war for allegedly ordering the so-called Malmédy massacre and was condemned to death by the US tribunal. The sentence was commuted to life imprisonment and Peiper was released from Spandau on 22 December 1956. He was murdered in his home in France by arsonists in 1976. The perpetrators were never caught.

Battery commander Albert Frey found himself in an anti-splinter trench near a stationmaster's house not ten metres from the tracks. When finally he established radio contact with the field-howitzer battery, it had to aim indirectly and failed to damage the armoured train. The virtually defenceless SS men remained exposed to the fire of the latter and continued to sustain losses. Finally Frey managed to bring one howitzer and an 8.8cm Flak into a position with a clear field of fire and registered hits. The train began to burn and several individual wagons exploded. This got the attack moving again and by evening the LAH had taken Taganrog. In my Company SS-2/Lt Scharma was seriously wounded and died in the field hospital at Taganrog on 22 November 1941. During his last month he was awarded the Iron Cross 1st and 2nd Class.[2]

On 20 October the Leibstandarte attacked to the north-west and reached Ssambek before the advance bogged down on the 23rd. According to an order from Corps, LAH had to set up a defensive line 28 kilometres long 'for reasons of supply'. In the weeks following, the exhausted officers and men of the Leibstandarte sheltered on the cold steppe, filthy and lousy in holes in the ground, for there were no villages around. At night, the temperature would fall to minus 20°C. The enemy kept our heads down with artillery while his scouting parties and raiders probed our security. SS-2/Lt Max Trampler of my Company was wounded: SS-Lt Georg Bormann replaced him as commander of 1st Platoon.

On 17 November 1941 we began our attack towards Rostov, and the next day reached Krasny Krim. On 19 November 1st and 3rd Battalions attacked Ssultam Ssaly from the south east while 4th Battalion arrived from the north east, and our company took the town. 3rd Battalion reconnoitred, reporting strong field fortifications this side of Rostov, particularly protecting the airfield. On 20 November the Leibstandarte attacked Rostov along the Don and captured the airfield.

In a bold stroke, No 3 Company (SS-Captain Hein Springer) succeeded in capturing the great railway bridge over the Don undamaged. Street fighting went on day and night, armed civilians also joining in. Thus Rostov, gateway to the Caucasus, fell into our hands. The mopping-up operations lasted throughout 21 November while 3rd Battalion LAH secured the Don west of the bridge. Unfortunately Rostov was too exposed to be held. The Soviet thrust against the northern neighbours of the LAH towards Mariupol threatened to cut off III Panzer Corps, as a result of which the Corps and LAH pulled back to a waiting position on the other side of the river Mius. As of 31 October 1941, the four platoons of my No 19 (MG) Company had been whittled down to three officers, nine NCOs and fifty-one men, the strength of one platoon.[3]

On 1 December 1941 the Division withdrew from the Mius sector and

15

in icy temperatures dug in at Ssambek. Trenches, earth bunkers and accommodation were excavated under great hardship in the hard-frozen ground. The territory held by friend and foe alike was an open expanse. The Russians maintained their grim, relentless attacks against our defensive line but never broke through. At the outset my No 19 Company was fighting them off ten to twelve times per day. In this winter refuge at Ssambek the Leibstandarte spent the following months.

I now had six months of almost uninterrupted warfare in the vastness of Russia behind me. Kiev, Berdyansk, Mariupol, Rostov, Ssambek – these were the milestones of my first year of fighting. I had a wound and had faced Soviet soldiers face to face in combat and survived. For this I was later awarded my first ten Close-combat Days. I had proved myself in the ranks of the Leibstandarte for which, on 17 December 1941, twenty-four men of my company including myself received from the hand of our legendary divisional commander, Waffen-SS General Sepp Dietrich, the Iron Cross 2nd Class.

After that we spent the next six months immobile in earth bunkers and snowed-in infantry trenches. I spent Christmas with my company in bitter cold. On 27 February 1942 I was awarded the Infantry Assault Badge in bronze. At that time I was No.1 gunner on the MG 34. Our exhausted company remained facing the enemy in trenches and bunkers until 2 June 1942. On 14 April my company commander Hans Meiforth was shot dead while leaving the bunkers occupied by his men at Warenovka. The commander of No 1 Platoon, SS-Lt Georg Bormann, took over from him. At the beginning of the year almost all No 1 machine-gunners in the winter refuge were sent on an NCO's course, their places being taken by their No 2. I did not go. I was transferred from No 1 machine-gunner on Duffert's gun to Bussacker's gun in the platoon of SS-2/Lt Bölk.

The shrunken company was now made up of two heavy-MG platoons: No 1 Platoon (Bölk) and the other commanded by SS-Ensign Joachim Kaden. How heavy the losses sustained by No 19 (MG) Company in the first year of the Russian campaign had been can be seen from the bare statistics. One company commander and two platoon leaders had fallen and despite receiving reinforcements on three occasions, when disbanded at the end of June 1942 the company had only forty-eight survivors including catering and supply. In the winter refuge there were only seven heavy MGs on hand instead of twelve, and only three men now served each gun instead of the usual five or six. The mortar platoon had no mortars. On 1 July 1942 I was promoted to SS-Leading Grenadier (Rottenführer).

With effect from 3 July 1942, the Leibstandarte moved to the Stalino area where the major reorganisation was begun. On 5 July six existing infantry battalions were combined into two regiments: re-equipping and rearming would take place in France. Between 12 and 26 July 1942 the Division relocated by rail to Paris. On the 29th of the month, Field-Marshal von Rundstedt, Commander-in-Chief West, took the salute at a march past including the motorised Leibstandarte.

We were to be transformed into a Panzer Grenadier Division and for this purpose early in 1942 Panzer, anti-tank and SP-gun battalions had been set up in Germany. The artillery regiment had been increased to four batteries and the two infantry regiments were each made up of three battalions, with the corresponding regimental units. The summer weeks saw hard battle training for the men and the newly arrived reinforcements.

On 15 July 1942 I celebrated my twentieth birthday. On 25 August I received the award of the Ostmedaille. In the setting up of the two Leibstandarte infantry regiments, 4th Battalion LAH became 3rd Battalion of 2nd SS-Infantry Regiment, which consisted of Nos 11 to 15 Companies inclusive. My former No 19 (MG) Company was now No 14 (MG) Company (SS-Lt Georg Bormann) in 2nd SS-Infantry Regiment LAH.

Chapter Three

I Become a Panzer Grenadier

On 5 July 1942 all rifle (schützen) regiments throughout the German armed forces were renamed panzer grenadier regiments. The tradition of the grenadier goes far back in history. In the newly created term 'panzer grenadier', first we have the concept of 'panzer' (armour), a word dating from the early twentieth century embracing a new mobile form of warfare for defence and attack and which symbolises at the same time the close relationship between firepower, armour and mobility. The second word is of French origin, derived from 'grenade', and was in use in the seventeenth century. Grenadiers were especially valuable, strong soldiers who in battle could hurl a grenade into the enemy ranks.

Grenadiers were introduced in Brandenburg in 1676. From 1740 they fought as elite units and proved themselves as special intervention troops. Frederick I, from 1713 king of Prussia, had six battalions of grenadiers as household guards. The Regiment of Dragoons Freiherr von Derfflinger was honoured with the name 'grenadiers of foot'. Even in those times they combined mobility and firepower, the milestones for the modern panzer grenadier to follow. Therefore the dragoons and the cuirassiers were the forerunners of the panzer grenadier. Armed with a carbine their weaponry enabled the dragoons to fight as infantry on foot while the horse gave them more mobility than the infantry.

Initially soldiers wore a felt hat with a broad brim. This interfered with the action of throwing hand grenades and so the 'grenadier's cap' was designed: a high cap, rather like an extended nightcap fitted with a brass shield on the front. It became the trademark of grenadiers at the time.

The idea of strengthening the cavalry of earlier centuries by very mobile infantry and unconventional weaponry can be found in all major campaigns in the field to the present. Frederick the Great often transported infantry by wagon in order to provide his cavalry with the necessary support.

A German armoured vehicle of the First World War took with it up to twenty footsoldiers to provide infantry protection for the panzer should it become unserviceable in action. Although the use of hand grenades in war had become less common at the beginning of the eighteenth century, grenadiers continued as elite troops. In Prussia until 1919, the 1st and 2nd Battalions of the Guard were designated grenadiers and elsewhere there were regiments of grenadiers. Since German grenadiers of the past had helped win great victories, in 1942 the German leadership decided to combine the name 'grenadier', rich in tradition, with the word 'panzer'. Thus 'panzer grenadiers' came into existence.

General Heinz Guderian, designer of the modern panzer arm and panzer tactics, planned the setting-up of the panzer grenadiers, and therefore both the panzer grenadiers and the panzer divisions fell in his jurisdiction as Inspector-General of Panzer Forces. Guderian's pioneering idea was to provide advancing panzer groups with support. Until then they had lacked mobile infantry, pioneers and artillery. Guderian recognised: 'Panzers can only be fully effective in the framework of the modern army if they are considered the principal arm, assembled in divisions, and coupled to fully motorised support arms.'[1] Thus the modern panzer grenadier evolved from the erstwhile infantry, becoming equally fast support for the fast panzer groups. A new kind of armoured vehicle was needed to keep pace with the panzers and, upon successfully breaking through the enemy defensive positions, engaging the enemy both from a vehicle and on foot. As a result the armoured personnel carrier (APC) was born.

On 5 July 1942 the rifle regiments of the German panzer divisions were renamed panzer grenadier regiments, although only about 25 per cent of the panzer grenadiers had armoured vehicles in the course of the war. The rest were merely motorised but mobile. In order to distinguish one from the other, panzer grenadier units equipped with armoured vehicles were indicated as such in the unit title as armoured (German abbreviation: 'gep.'). Since I served from this point on with the APC battalion, all of whose vehicles were armoured, I have dispensed with the abbreviation.

On 14 September 1942 Jochen Peiper was appointed commander of 3rd Battalion 2nd SS-Panzer Grenadier Regiment LAH.[2] Former SS-Leading Grenadier Günter Gaul of No 12 Company remembers this event thus. 'When he took over 3rd Battalion, there was a huge whirl of activity. He would surface amongst the companies in the morning and supervise the daily programme. We had exercises and square-bashing. Thrilled we were not.'[3] Peiper introduced extensive field

19

training involving the whole battalion. Even the company commanders had to play along and if they failed to meet Peiper's expectations he would put them right, sometimes with the men looking on. 'The men were much impressed by the similar treatment handed out by the commanding officer to officers, NCO's and men alike.'[4] His former regimental commander, SS-Lt.Col Fritz Witt, wrote of him: 'In character, clear and clean, reserved. Observes in a caustic manner, harsh and even cynical in his criticism. Leadership in battle calm and reflective. In training level-headed and gets into the spirit of the thing. Tactically thinks and acts clearly.'[5]

Peiper's Battalion HQ was located at Verneuil-sur-Avre west of Dreux in a small mansion in parkland behind the market square. My No 14 Company was at École de Roches, the others as follows:

No 11 Company – Chaise Dieu du Theil, east of L'Aigle.
No 12 Company – Town centre, Verneuil, quarters in a hall.
No 13 Company – At Les Ventes, later in the school at Verneuil.
No 15 (Heavy) Company – Chennebrun.

We received new Steyr vehicles and in September 1942 the motorcycle reconnaissance platoon (SS-2/Lt Georg Preuss) was reorganised and equipped with twelve BMW R75 machines with sidecars. The platoon courier had a solo machine.

Peiper commandeered his old friend from his pre-war company, SS-Lt Paul Guhl, who was instructing at the SS-NCO school Lauenburg, as company commander. At first Guhl had to combine his duties at No 11 Company with the NCOs' course at Dreux.[6] SS-Lt Otto Dinse, with the battalion since 1941, remained as adjutant. This small wiry officer from Hamburg was a capable and well-liked adjutant known throughout the battalion.

For the entire 2nd Regiment, August and September 1942 were taken up with work in the field, training in platoons or sections.[7] The exercises for 3rd Battalion's motorcycle platoon under 2/Lt Preuss were often linked to visits to the numerous chateaux around Dreux, L'Aigle and Verneuil. The young Danziger liked to talk with the French nobility and he would be often seen in friendly conversation with French clergymen and ordinary people in the villages they drove through.[8]

On 14 October 1942 a second panzer half-regiment was added to the existing one so that the Leibstandarte became a panzer regiment, and the division was thus a panzer division. Towards the end of that month,

Company and Battalion exercises were intensified. On 1 November 1942 Peiper's Battalion held a sports day which remained a pleasant memory for everybody despite the rain. With effect from 24 November 1942, the LAH was reclassified officially as a Panzer Grenadier Division, and on the same day was ordered to set up an APC battalion, determined by SS-HQ to be 3rd Battalion of the former 2nd SS-Panzer Grenadier Regiment.[9]

A new and more onerous task now devolved upon Peiper: to transform a motorised infantry battalion into an APC battalion. The battalion was renamed 3rd Battalion 2nd SS-Panzer Grenadier Regiment LSSAH and its companies incorporated per instructions valid for APC companies. Because an APC battalion had no MG companies, my No 14 (MG) Company was disbanded before Christmas and most of its personnel less myself made up the new No 14 (Heavy) Company. There was no No 15 Company in the APC battalion. A heavy MG platoon and mortar section of the former No 14 (MG) Company were allocated to Divisional HQ.[10] SS-Corporal Werner Schiller (Iron Cross First Class) went to the regimental HQ with most of 2nd Platoon.

So now I found myself in No 12 Company, 2nd SS-Panzer Grenadier Regiment with 4th Heavy Platoon (SS-2/Lt Otto Bölk again). My company commander was SS-Lt Lux Westrup (Iron Cross First Class) who had previously led this company in Russia as No 17 Company LAH from the autumn of 1941. From now on the battalion consisted of Nos 11 to 14 Companies inclusive. The Steyr vehicles were returned to the depot and replaced shortly afterwards by APCs arriving to each company individually.[11] Hectic driver training began on the APC at once. Fuel was so short that trips to collect it were combined with training.[12] Because the APC was the principal armament of Peiper's battalion, I think it appropriate at this stage to review the vehicle from its earliest origins.

We can see the historical predecessor of the APC atop the Brandenburg Gate in Berlin – the Quadriga. The chariot is drawn by four horses and driven by Eirene, Greek goddess of peace and daughter of Zeus. In her hand she holds a baton with the Iron Cross and eagle. The chariot may be seen as the most ancient predecessor of the APC and panzer, and was the first armoured vehicle in the history of warfare. With its disc wheels it proved its military value 5,000 years ago and was used in battle by the Sumerians long before the Christian era. The Persians used chariots with spoked wheels and bells on the axles. The value of speed was recognised and archers and spearmen engaged the enemy

21

from the chariot. If their endeavours failed, they would jump down to take on the foe in close combat, fighting with swords and daggers. The Persian king Kyros (reigned c.559–529 BC) recognised that although the chariot might break through the enemy lines, it could not always hold the territory gained. He had chariot variants designed and built able to carry twenty men who dismounted after breaking through and fought a surprised enemy on foot with sword and bow. The idea of the APC evolved from this. The Greeks used chariots, and Caesar reported that the Germans manoeuvred their barricade-wagons very skilfully. In the Middle Ages wagons were manned by archers and handgunners. By the fourteenth century carts were already being equipped with cannon. The forerunner of the tank had been born.

The common historical predecessors of the German armoured infantry were the cuirassiers of the heavy cavalry. More than 200 years ago they rode into battle wearing armour from head to foot. From 1481 they had been the oldest branch of service and fought with sword and carbine on horseback. The dragoons would follow them as the second wave, and the tactic was even continued in the Thirty Years War. Only after did the cavalry wear fewer items of body armour to improve their mobility in battle. Until well into the nineteenth century, the infantry was queen of battle but cavalry the decisive arm. In the Second World War cavalry gave way to the panzers.

In order to give the infantry mobility in the role of panzer grenadiers, and to allow them some protection, they were provided with armoured troop carriers usually known in English as APCs. In the panzer divisions, APCs had a major tactical significance. After the panzers had penetrated the enemy frontline, they were often unable to hold out in the enemy hinterland for long because infantry protection was required to consolidate territorial gains. The panzer grenadiers represented a new type of soldier. It was they who made modern battlefield planning of massed panzers possible. Only the panzer grenadiers could follow attacking panzers quickly cross-country and, even on their own, storm enemy positions and defend a captured position against counter-attack.

As previously mentioned, Guderian's tactical planning was decisive in developing the right vehicle. The panzers required the grenadiers to use the speed and armour protection of their carriers when alighting on the field of battle. This called for a half- or full-track with light armour, able to follow the panzers over any terrain and equipped with enough armour plate to afford its occupants protection against infantry fire and shell splinters.

In the years before the Second World War, the German armaments industry was so overwhelmed with orders for new developments and the production of vehicles that the manufacture of half-tracks, with the exception of artillery prime movers, took a back seat as against full-tracked vehicles. This led to a design based on the existing chassis of a half-track towing vehicle already in production, and which came as a one-tonne or three-tonne variant. In order to meet Guderian's requirement, these were given a superstructure of thin armour, 1.2cm at the front and 0.8cm laterally. They were first known as MTWs (*Mannschaftstransportwagen*) and then SPWs (*Schützenpanzerwagen*), or APCs in English.

Both before and during the war various designs evolved from the light APC (Sd Kfz 250) and the medium APC (Sd Kfz 251) for various battlefield purposes, not only for panzer grenadiers but also for the other branches of service. The chassis (HKl 6p) of the three-tonne medium APC was developed by Hanomag, the armoured super-structure manufactured by Büssing-NAG of Berlin-Oberschönweide in cooperation with Deutsche Werke of Kiel. Design work began in 1937 and the first deliveries made in 1938. The superstructure consisted of armoured front (or bow), centre, floor and stern sections. The main parts were joined by welding or riveting bulletproof armour plates. To deprive shells of penetrative momentum, the armour plates were fitted sloping. Those set horizontally were resistant to small arms. The crew compartment was at the centre and rear of the vehicle and separated from the engine space by a bulkhead. Ammunition and packs were stored below the lateral seating. The vehicle had a double-flap rear door. Seating for the driver and radio-operator was adjustable. Driver and co-driver had adjustable flaps for the viewing slits, protected by replaceable glass. The armour plating was 1.45cm thick ahead and 0.8cm at sides and rear. A demountable and rotatable MG 42 with armour shield was set on the armoured roof above the driver. Some APCs had the MG but not the shield. At the rear of the crew compart-ment, designed to accommodate a section, was the swivelling arm for another MG. This was the usual armament of the section-sized three-tonne APC. The APC battalion of the Leibstandarte was equipped with the APC Sd Kfz 251 model C in November 1942. There were numerous variations, mainly differing from each other by the armament, 7.5cm cannon, anti-tank gun, flamethrower and so on.

Besides this three-tonner there was the one-tonne chassis Sd Kfz 250 for a half-section. The basis was the Demag prime mover with shortened bogie and different cooling system, steering column, fuel tank and exhaust. Armour replaced the original steel hull. Büssing-NAG of Berlin made the armoured superstructure. The front armour with shield was bolted to the rear armour. The welded armour sheets forward were installed sloping, and the horizontal protection was proof against small arms fire. Hull and superstructure were bolted together. From 1940 the Sd Kfz 250 had the Maybach HL 42 TUKRR engine with semi-automatic Maybach VG 102 128H transmission with seven forward and three reverse gears. The layout was much the same as the bigger version with the crew compartment situated to the rear of the motor room bulkhead. The entry door was in the rear panel. Up to seven men could be carried besides the crew. The armour was 1.45cm thick on the front, 0.8cm at sides and rear, total weight 5.8 tonnes. This light APC appeared in numerous variants.[13]

In the APC battalion of the LAH, the vehicles with the companies, of the heavy units and some HQs were initially the one-tonners while elsewhere exclusively three-tonners were delivered. Peiper considered the APC training for the companies to be very inadequate because exercises involving the APC at platoon or company level were ruled out by the shortage of fuel.[14] One manoeuvre carried out at battalion level was marching for miles with full pack, Peiper constantly appearing alongside the platoon to look over the men and their commanders. My No 12 Company was given the task of attacking the 'enemy' from the rear.[15] The platoons practised getting into the APCs, disembarking and jumping clear through the rear door, and also leaping out over the sides.[16]

The men had their doubts about the armour, and some men of No 13 Company fired at it with small arms to see if the plating was truly bullet-proof, which turned out not to be the case.[17] One NCO from each platoon was sent to an APC training course with the Army at Weimar,[18] and between 14 October and 6 November 1942 intensive training was carried out including at night. During the preparatory phase in France some of the companies began to make changes to their APCs which others would copy on the Eastern Front. Many APC crews secured tree branches the thickness of an arm along the top of the lateral plating to reduce the splinter effect in the open crew compartment.[19] No 11 Company made a striking innovation by fitting an additional armour plate on the front for better protection against direct hits.

APC driver Johannes Bräuer said:

I remember well when we got the new APCs in France that shortly afterwards Guhl and Wolff carried out a firing test with small arms and carbine ammunition on the front section and between the two visor flaps, the results of which were not made known for a few days. In every case the rounds had penetrated and because of that they got a large smithy or something similar to make two 1cm thick fluted steel plates, these being secured with strong iron brackets one over the other at the front 5cm ahead of the front armour.[20]

Other companies partially reinforced the front of the vehicle with spare track links.

Every company in Peiper's battalion received eighteen APCs. Four platoons made up a company. The first three squads had four APCs of which one was allotted to the platoon commander with his troop – many fitted with a 3.7cm anti-tank gun – while the three sections per platoon were carried in the three remaining APCs. Fourth (Heavy) Platoon had one heavy MG and one mortar squad. Initially one-tonne APCs were available to the commanders of the fourth platoon.[21]

Nos 11, 12 and 13 Companies were equipped in this way: the company commander and troop leader each had their own APC, the latter being a one-tonner. No 14 (Heavy) Company consisted of the anti-tank platoon with three 3.7cm guns. SS-2/Lt Gührs, the platoon commander, had served as an SS-Private with the anti-tank platoon of No 20 (Heavy) Company in 1941 and returned to No 14 Company direct from officer training at Bad Tölz. Later, SS-2/Lt David Margait took over the platoon.

Also attached to No 14 Company was the anti-tank section with three one-tonne APCs armed with the Panzerbüchse 41: the infantry gun (IG) platoon with four 7.5cm guns drawn by APCs (SS-2/Lt Erhard Noth) and the tank-gun platoon with short-barrelled 7.5cm guns fitted aboard. This platoon was formed by Gührs in January 1943. Finally came the pioneer platoon (SS-Sgt Wilhelm Haferstroh) with four APCs. The company commander was SS-Captain Rolf Kolitz, who had been in charge since 1941. All weapons, MGs, heavy MGs, mortars, tank guns and 3.7cm anti-tank guns could fire from aboard the APC, all of which were also fitted with wireless. Three-axle Krupp and Opel-Allrad vehicles were available for refuelling purposes. Besides shooting, cross-country and driver training, the NCOs had tactical training at the sand tables, often in the evenings. It was always to be expected that Peiper would turn up without warning. He was very hot on training and the tactical further education of his officers and NCOs and insisted on it constantly.

I was attached to 4th Heavy Platoon, No 12 Company (SS-2/Lt Bölk) made up of the mortar and heavy MG half-platoons. Each half-platoon consisted of two groups on four APCs. The heavy MG APC had an MG 42 on a mount forward and one on a swivelling arm at the rear. The mortar half-platoon was equipped with an 8cm mortar on reinforced floor plates inside the crew compartment: an additional plate was available for use outside the vehicle.[22] I was a member of the heavy MG section (SS-Sgt Egmont Eichler). The other crewmen of my APC were SS-Sgt Herbert Hesse, driver Broska and radio operator Klinger. Rudi Rayer and Gerhard Kendzia from No 19 Company were also in my half-platoon. In the autumn of 1942 about twenty German community leaders from the Siebenbürgen in Hungary and the Romanian Banat, including Willi Depner, a German Youth leader in Romania, came to the Battalion as volunteers and joined No 12 Company. No 11 Company was led by SS-Lt Paul Guhl. One of his platoon leaders was 19-year-old SS-2/Lt Werner Wolff who had returned from officer training at Tolz as the youngest officer in the LAH Division. No 13 Company was commanded by SS-Lt Otto Pinter (Iron Cross First Class), platoon leader under Peiper in 1941. His own platoon leaders now were SS-2/Lt Heinz Tomhardt, Kurt Thumeyer, Joachim Kaden, Wolfgang Pfitzner and later Georg Preuss. Battalion surgeon was SS-Lt Dr Robert Brüstle assisted by SS-2/Lt Dr Friedrich Breme.

All companies had experienced NCOs and men, some of whom had already received the Iron Cross First and Second Class for their bravery on the Eastern Front, examples being my heavy MG section leader Egmont Eichler, SS-Sgt Karl Kaspari, SS-Grenadier Karl Übler and SS-Grenadier Hans Seiffert of No 14 Company's pioneer platoon. These men, the experienced campaigners of the Eastern Front, the fresh panzer grenadiers and the young platoon leaders recently turned out by officer training, formed an ideal community which by virtue of its lust for action seemed well qualified for great military achievements. Because an APC afforded too little space for a complete section of twelve men, Guhl ordered that on operations only six should be carried.[23] At the sand table he took the opportunity to discuss tactical operational ideas. For him, APCs in an attack should proceed on a broad front hanging well back. His adage was: 'The attack is nourished from depth'.[24]

Jochen Peiper dedicated himself with energy and much thought to the training of his Battalion, and soon impregnated it with the hallmark of his striking personality. He had also cultivated a very good rapport with the townspeople of Verneuil, making contact with the local clergy and representatives of the French nobility,[25] even going so far as to invite the latter to the officers' mess at Battalion. He mostly limited contact with the men to the calls of duty although he did appear at the companies' social evenings. On his visits to the company quarters he was always 'the Commanding Officer', but could be boyish and once at Verneuil challenged a leading grenadier to a game of table tennis.[26]

On 30 November 1942 SS-Major Hugo Kraas, deputising for Wisch as regimental commander, noted about Peiper:

> His mental capacity is well above average. He has a very good general education. Physically he is well developed and athletic. He is tough and has endurance. Peiper is totally reliable, of decent character and a cooperative colleague. He is a keen observer and critical in his judgements. In the tactical area and in battle training, his knowledge of the service and his achievements must be designated as very good.[27]

Before Christmas I went on home leave to West Prussia. In the first week of December 1942 tests for tropical suitability were carried out which led to speculation that we might be going to North Africa. Also in that month, Peiper was sent on an officers' gunnery course at the Army panzer school, Putlos. On 24 December 1942 the divisional commander SS-General Sepp Dietrich made a Christmas visit to all units. While the men were still hoping for Africa, on 30 December orders came for the Leibstandarte to be fully armed and equipped by 7 January 1943 and to be provided with winter clothing. Now it was obvious to everyone: a new campaign in Russia was imminent. On 31 December we celebrated New Year in and around Verneuil in high spirits, circulating amateur humorous verses and remarks directed at officers, NCOs and men. Training went on: platoon commanders held classes on winter warfare, and the men had make-and-mend sessions, putting things in good order in preparation for the coming campaign. New gas masks were distributed and on the evening of 4 January 1943 No 14 Company received additional APCs. On 7 January a tank-gun platoon was formed, initially of three, later of six, APCs under SS-2/Lt Gührs. Peiper addressed all company and platoon leaders about the new campaign.[28]

The advance party of two officers, five NCOs and one man led by SS-Captain Bormann was first to leave, from Argentan station.[29] On 11 January the battalion was equipped with the FmW 41 one-man flamethrower, and with effect from 13 January the motorcycle platoon was disbanded. On 16 January we received winter clothing, service activities being limited to instruction and sport. On 30 January, his birthday, Peiper was promoted to SS-Major, and we listened to speeches by Hermann Göring and Adolf Hitler. On 11 January the Division had begun to entrain for the East. Leave-taking from the French was mostly warm, for the relationship between the men of the Leibstandarte and the local inhabitants over the previous months had been untroubled and accompanied by mutual respect. Many French mothers even stood with tears in their eyes as the tall young soldiers left their homes.

'The departure from my billet was distressing. I shall visit them after the war with Gisi [his wife – author's note]' wrote SS-2/Lt Gührs.[30] No 14 Company loaded its fifty-nine vehicles on the low-loaders at Verneuil on 31 January in heavy rain, the men thinking of the imminent campaign in the East which – everybody knew – would demand much of them. 'I am looking forward to the campaign and believe that we shall have the fortunes of war on our side again. We are all very optimistic,' wrote Gührs in his diary, his words reflecting the morale of the men of Peiper's APC Battalion and the Leibstandarte in general.[31]

In the official *Training Instructions for the Panzer Arm – Leadership and Deployment of the Panzer Grenadiers* it states:

Panzer grenadiers (armoured) are the steel assault troops of the panzer division. Their characteristic, very mobile activity is the precondition for operations. They are part of a very close fighting community with the panzers. They perform their individual tasks with bold, rapid thrusts. Their great mobility, their ability cross-country, armour, high firepower and fine officers make them capable of mastering the most difficult situations quickly and successfully. Panzer grenadier groups fight from the APC. Enemy action and terrain can bring about the sudden change from being transported to fighting on foot. Yet even to this fighting on foot, the manoeuvrable heavy weapons aboard the APC give their own individuality. The zest for attack and boldness, linked to lightning-fast decision-making and great flexibility, distinguish the panzer grenadier.[32]

Now, as a panzer grenadier, I was about to embark upon my second campaign in Russia. I had the feeling of being well-trained amongst a proven fighting community of young soldiers whom I had fought alongside on various occasions since June 1941. What would the New Year bring me?

Chapter Four

The Battle for Kharkov,
27 January–29 March 1943

Tank gun Platoon: SS-2/Lt Erhard Gührs
3 x APCs with 7.5cm gun, gun commanders: SS-Corporals Willi Mewes, Fritz
    Jacobi, Emil Knappe.
SS-Corporal Karl Johann Neumann (fell 15 February 1943 Novaya Vodolaga)
Pioneer platoon: SS-Sgt Wilhelm Haferstroh
4 APCs, SS-Corporal Albert Krüger
Infantry Gun-platoon
4 x 7.5cm IG guns on APCs.

The 3rd Battalion, 2nd SS-Panzer Grenadier Regiment LSSAH loaded
up in sections at Argentan railway station, No 13 Company on 27
January 1943, while the fifty-nine vehicles of No 14 Company (SS-2/Lt
Erhard Gührs) entrained on 31 January 1943 at Verneuil. The trains
followed the route Rouen–Amiens–Arras–Osnabrück–Hannover–
Lehrte–Ludwigslust–Königsberg–Elbing–Eitkau–Wirballen–Vilna–
Minsk–Gomel.[1]

SS-2/Lt Gührs confided to his diary:

We are at Vilna and curving round to the south. We are in Russia. An
almost home-like feeling seizes us. Why should that be? From the
eternal yearning for the East? Or because the snow lies deeper here?
Or because life itself here is a battle? That must be it. The West was
too bourgeois. We were too well fed. Here one must return to being
a man. We reach Minsk. Kursk must be in Russian hands. Increased
danger of partisans. The railway people tell us of trains dynamited,
burnt-out wagons and so on. We should evacuate the leading wagon
because of the danger of mines. Naturally nobody takes any notice.
But just in case, I nurse my MPi [submachine gun]. . . 6 February
1943. In Gomel we found out that the train ahead of us actually had
been mined. Nearby was an LAH train with Tiger panzers.
Everything is rolling. We are going to detrain east of Kharkov. We all
expect the war in Russia to be decided this year . . . I hope that winter
is soon over, so that the struggle can begin . . .[2]

The first task for the LAH was to detrain south-east of Kharkov and
secure that stretch of the Donetz between Smiyev and Chotomlya. The
first elements of the division arrived at Chuguyev on 28 January 1943
and were taken immediately to field fortifications previously
reconnoitred. The Leibstandarte was part of the SS-Panzer Corps

General Command under SS-General Hausser. The planned attack by the whole corps was pre-empted by the brisk Soviet advance. Great gaps appeared along the front east of Kharkov, and the corps itself was endangered. The affected sections of the Leibstandarte began digging in with the assistance of Russian civilians. On 31 January 1943 the German Sixth Army capitulated at Stalingrad.

The first elements of Peiper's APC battalion reached the Eastern Front on 2 February 1943, though not together. My No 12 Company reached the front line on 7 February. Five days before, the advanced units of 1st and 3rd Battalions, 2nd SS-Panzer Grenadier Regiment were ordered to dig in. It was 31°C below. The situation was estimated thus in regimental orders of 3 February 1943:

> Superior enemy has broken through the defensive front on the Don with massed tanks and artillery and is pushing westwards. The actual direction of the thrust is not yet clear. Enemy advanced units reached Pechenegi at 1330 hrs on 3 February 1943. A further advance to the Kubyansk–Chuguyev highway is to be expected on the night of 3 February 1943.[3]

In the order 2nd, 3rd and 1st Battalions, 2nd SS-Panzer Grenadier Regiment (SS-Colonel Theodor Wisch) set up the defence. On the evening of 4 February 1943, the forward elements of Peiper's APC battalion and the pioneer platoon on the eastern edge of Skripai were included in the main frontline.[4]

Regimental orders of 3 February 1943 recorded:

> 3rd Battalion with no companies but an attached 3.7cm flak platoon, is defending the section ordered and from 5 February 1943 will reconnoitre towards Blagodatnoye. No 11 Company, strengthened by a 7.5cm anti-tank platoon will, in the case of an enemy advance, move over the Isyum–Kunie line to the eastern side of Balakleya and so place itself that the enemy advance will be slowed by delaying tactics from our own positions.[5]

After midnight on 6 February 1943 a Soviet attack in company strength against Peiper's APC battalion was beaten off at Skripai. No 11 Company in concert with 3rd SS-SP Gun Battalion LAH attacked Andreyevka at 2115 hrs and reported the location clear of enemy forces for the loss of six men dead and four missing; SS-2/Lt Kurt Thumeyer of No 13 Company and forty-seven non-NCOs were wounded. Two light MGs, one mortar and an anti-tank gun were captured.[6] Other Leibstandarte units fended off the enemy's constant attacks. The Das Reich Division neighbouring the Leibstandarte was outflanked to the north, the LAH to the south, but the immediate priority was to assist the 320th Infantry Division to break back across the Isyum–Smiyev highway and place it on the right flank so as to extend the German frontline further south.

On 7 February 1943 orders came from division to hold Andreyevka. The 320th Infantry Division was in the process of assembling thirty kilometres away and would attempt to break through to the Leibstandarte at Balakleya. The 2nd SS-Panzer Grenadier Regiment war diary recorded:

> 1230 hrs. Guhl's unit (No 11 Company) reports substantial enemy infantry seven kilometres east of Andreyevka . . .
> 1500 hrs. Two large enemy columns approaching Andreyevka from the north-east and south-east. No 12.Company having detrained sent to reinforce at Liman.
> 2230 hrs. Guhl's unit reports destroying an enemy squadron.
> 2300 hrs. Guhl's unit requesting reinforcements.[7]

Guhl had radioed: '2200 hrs. Send up reinforcements at once. Bring ammunition, rations and fuel. Care needed on Smiyev-Andreyevka highway. Enemy probably in the south.'[8]

On 7 February 1943 my No 12 Company, strengthened by the SP-guns of SS-Captain Rettlinger's 3rd Battery, retook Andreyevka which we had evacuated a short while before. This skirmish was the first confirmed Close-combat Day for Nos 11 and 12 Companies, also my 11th Close-combat Day. That night the Battle Group destroyed a T-34 while No 11 Company reported the capture of one T-34, one field gun, one anti-tank gun, two mortars and one hundred horses. On the morning of 8 February the Russians attacked the entire frontline held by the Division. The 2nd SS-Panzer Grenadier Regiment war diary recorded:

> 1235 hrs. Battle Group Guhl reports that Andreyevka is only being held at the western end. The highway towards Georg is being kept free. The Battle Group is receiving heavy artillery fire and is under attack from tanks on three sides. The Battle Group has been ordered

to withdraw to Liman and reinforce the right flank of II Battalion as far as the Donetz.

SS-Grenadier Heinz Glenewinkel, No 13 Company, noted in his diary just two words to cover this day: 'Close combat.'[9]

Together with the HQ and Nos 11, 12 and 13 Companies, I received my 12th confirmed Close-combat Day at Skripai on 8 February 1943. We lived and fought in temperatures of 28° below zero.[10] The 320th Infantry Division was fighting, east of Balakleya and completely cut off, protecting the right flank of the Leibstandarte. From there to the southern flank of the Leibstandarte was forty kilometres. At Merefa a Battle Group from 2nd Battalion, 1st SS-Panzer Regiment and the SS-Motorcycle Infantry Battalion of Das Reich was formed on 9 February to attack the Soviet flank. The Soviet intention to encircle Kharkov had been clearly recognised meanwhile. The Soviets were planning to push through to the Donetz Basin to cut off supplies to the German front at the river Mius, and then wipe it out. If they succeeded, Manstein's Army Group South would lose contact with its rear, causing a major threat to the entire Eastern Front.

The war diary states:

9 February 1943. Guhl's unit will remain at Liman to assist 320th Inf.Div.
1245 hrs. Guhl's unit ordered to evacuate Liman and proceed to Smiyev.[11]

The vehicles of No 14 Company of the APC battalion unloaded from the transporter train on the evening of 8 February and set out at once, rolling through the retreating German and allied Axis troops via Kharkov to Smiyev, reaching Battalion at 1600 hrs on 9 February, where they were immediately declared operational.[12] SS-2/Lt Gührs described the critical situation in his dairy: 'It is crazy. A Luftwaffe lieutenant shook my hand and told me how happy they were to see us . . . the Russians are attacking along the whole front in great numbers. Our Battalion has a stretch of it nine kilometres long.'[13]

In the recommendation of the German Cross in Gold to Jochen Peiper it was said of the initial operations of his APC battalion:

3rd Battalion, 2nd SS-Panzer Grenadier Regiment LSSAH led by SS-Major Peiper went directly from the railway unloading yard at

Kharkov into action, first with the aim of setting up a strongpoint ahead of the division's right flank at Andreyevka and at the same time creating a prepared position to receive 320.Inf.Div. Peiper achieved these objectives but was encircled on 7 February 1943 by strong Russian forces (two infantry regiments and a tank brigade). After holding the strongpoint for two days, Peiper's battalion penetrated the ring and regained our front line. In the execution of his orders he inflicted upon the enemy very high casualties and destroyed two T-34s. Peiper distinguished himself in all this by skilful leadership and great personal bravery.[14]

On the night of 10 February 1943 the entire 2nd SS-Panzer Grenadier Regiment LSSAH set up a new front line. Peiper's battalion became the reserve at Podolchov. The panzer grenadiers suffered in the icy cold: bread and butter were frozen hard as stone. The APCs received a coat of whitewash as camouflage.[15]

10 February 1943, 1430 hrs. 13 Company was ordered to close the gap between the left flank of I Battalion and the right flank of II/1 Regiment. One platoon of 12 Company was brought up to assist and attack. 1700 hrs. The enemy attacked Lisogubovka in company strength and was repelled by the counter-attack of 12 Company. Assignment for Battalion-Peiper: During the night of 10 February, Battalion-Peiper including two platoons SP-guns is to attempt to break through to Smiyev with the column of ambulances sixty vehicles strong, establish contact with 320 Inf Div and escort out the transport of 320.Inf.Div.wounded.

SS-2/Lt Gührs, the commander of the three 7.5cm gun APCs of No 14 Company, wrote:

The provisional orders for Operation Peiper: we have the task of crossing the river Donetz by night, fighting our way through the main Russian front line and proceeding for twenty-five kilometres into enemy territory in order to extract German division Herz. They have 10,000 men and 1,500 wounded. A crazy plan, but a task close to the heart of the panzer grenadiers. Our battalion will have seven SP-guns along. My own gun will head the rearguard. – It is 1600 hrs. I am getting ready and putting my affairs in order. Should I give Rosin my diary so that it arrives home safely? Jacobi has told me that he has to take his SP back to Poltava 140 kilometres away for repair. Now I only have one besides my own. I also have no information about the ammunition-panzer. In the evening we will be getting the limpet mines, hand grenades etc.[16]

The APC battalion was at Podolchov. Peiper prepared very conscientiously for the difficult operation of extracting the 320th Infantry Division from Russian-held territory.

12 February 1943. 0430 hrs. Operation Peiper set off, overwhelmed the enemy on the Krassnaya Polyana highway and cleared it for the ambulance convoy. Parts of the column arriving late were fired on by the enemy, six of our vehicles being destroyed.
0640 hrs. Operation Peiper reached Smiyev without enemy contact.
0800 hrs. Battalion-Peiper was ordered to reconnoitre towards Liman and establish contact with 320 Inf.Div.
1400 hrs. Contact established. Operation Peiper provided protective cover for the billets of 320 Inf.Div. at Cheremushnaya–Sidki–Samostye–Butovka overnight.

Once contact with the division had been established, Peiper sent Gührs to General Postel, commanding officer of the 320th Infantry Division, as liaison officer. 'The Division looked awful, everything defied belief,' Gührs recalled.

13 February. Snow flurries. Battalion Peiper left Sidki in the early hours and reached Vodyanoye at 1150 hrs. Enemy had blown up the bridge on his side to cut off the retreat of Battalion Peiper. III Battalion mopped up Krassnaya Polyana and forced the enemy eastwards, thus freeing the west flank for the transfer out of the wounded. We are repairing the bridge.
1630 hrs. All ambulances have made it to our lines. Battalion Peiper has received orders to set up as divisional reserve at Merefa.

In his diary that day Gührs added a few words to the sober description from the war diary above: 'The wounded transports assembled. We were to struggle through escorting them. At Vodyanoye we had a hard fight with a Russian ski battalion. By evening we were celebrating. Crossed over. My gun had fired forty-two rounds. We had six dead. By 1900 all elements were back.'[17]

Jochen Peiper himself wrote a long account of the operation to bring out the badly-battered 320th Infantry Division with its numerous casualties:

. . . III/2.SS-Panzer Grenadier Regiment LA, halted at a river there (Donetz) for its part had orders to advance forward of our lines to Smiyev, round up the remnants of 320 Inf.Div. and smuggle back its 1,500 wounded. For this purpose the Battalion was given all available ambulances and a large number of empty lorries. Our own lines ran along a stream (Udy) over which was a long wooden bridge. On the other side was a weakly defended village (Krassnaya Polyana). Contrary to our expectations, we reached Smiyev without serious enemy contact, halted at a river there (Donetz) and waited for Postel's [commanding officer, 320 Inf.Div] vanguard to come in sight.

A little later General Postel arrived with a great bevy of vehicles and officers. His first question was why we had not crossed the river. He waved aside my reply that the ice would not bear us, but then at the same moment an adjutant reported, 'Herr General, the ice is not thick enough, the first SP gun has already cracked it.' General Postel was very relieved and said that he would halt here and we had to take over the protection. He was irate that our lines were so far back. Then he went off.

After a long wait, which we spent sitting in our APCs with a nasty feeling, the Army division turned up. We all thought the same thing: Beresina! Napoleon's retreat must have looked just like this. Those capable of walking led, followed by the lightly wounded. The seriously wounded brought up the rear. A picture of despair on horse-drawn carts and sledges. As there was not enough room for everybody on these, the unlucky ones were hooked up and towed along on their stomachs. Our surgeons and medics had meanwhile arranged a system in which the wounded got something to eat, a hot drink and then first aid. I remember clearly the complaints of our battalion surgeon Dr Brüstle next morning. He and his colleague had operated all night (mostly frostbite) and nobody came from 320 Division to help. We secured the area and, hollow-cheeked, stared into the ghostly night convinced that this would not keep going satisfactorily for long.

Next day [13 February] we set off with the enormous long convoy. The Division and the wounded on the highway, ourselves with the fighting elements fanned out either side as flank protection. When we finally got to the stream with the long wooden bridge, we saw that the latter had been reduced to smouldering struts. A Russian ski battalion was occupying the village, where they had mutilated and massacred numerous German medics and drivers (stragglers from the day before), and now opened up on our convoy from all sides. My Battalion captured the village after bitter house-to-house fighting, set up a bridgehead, ushered our returning comrades over the ice and secured the makeshift bridge. Once the last vehicle had reached the far bank, my APC battalion returned to Smiyev in order to reach our own lines, hugging the horizon behind the Russian front.

According to General Postel's account they 'had not had to fight their way out continuously' but had marched out fairly unmolested, always behind the Russians. What made the situation critical had been the quickly decreasing mobility, the growing ballast of those unable to walk and the crisis of morale after the German front lines stopped coming nearer, and started receding.[18]

Fifty years later, SS-Captain Guhl, commander No 11 Company, remembered how appalled he had been at General Postel's appearance and arrogance, adorned in a white cape in contrast to the ragged, exhausted infantry of his division.[19]

SS-2/Lt Rudolf von Ribbentrop of the Leibstandarte panzer regiment stated:

I have never forgotten the imperturbable – often bordering on blasé – manner in which Peiper made his report. He depicted making contact with the commanding officer, 320 Inf.Div. in February 1943 as follows. The Division crossed the Donetz after Peiper, having driven a long stretch through the Russians, offered the 320th his hand. When General Postel was informed that contact to his rearguard had been lost, he established calmly and cold-bloodedly that it was already the problem of 'Aunt Frieda' (an expression for the HDV Nr 300, military command) and said the rearguard should sacrifice itself should the opportunity present itself! Peiper's opinion of what this general should do was similar![20]

This successful operation by Peiper was mentioned in the recommendation for the award of the German Cross in Gold as follows: 'After recovering the defensive sector along the general line Rogan-Lisogubovka-Mirgorod, Peiper received orders to proceed with his

Battalion to Smiyev to establish contact with 320 Inf.Div. Peiper completed the assignment and brought back 750 wounded of 320 Inf.Div. While doing so his Battalion came across an enemy ski battalion blocking his retreat and he wiped it out to the last man.'[21]

I experienced these first days of winter warfare in the rank of SS-Leading Grenadier with the heavy-MG half-platoon of SS-Sergeant Adolf Sellmeier in No 12 Company. I was No 1 gunner on the forward MG of SS-Corporal Eichler's APC. The attacks were swift, the APC companies fanning out across a broad front, motors speeding them over snowy terrain towards the enemy. The attacks were loud, the air filled with the drone of the Maybach engines, the bursts of fire from the forward MGs, the dry bark of the 7.5cm cannon. The assault tactics of the APC battalion closely resembled the cavalry attacks of earlier centuries. The task of the cuirassiers of that time was now the province of the APC. Therefore Peiper compared the assaults of his APC battalion to cavalry cavalcades.

In its initial operations, the APC battalion proved itself by its outstanding aggressive spirit. Under the resourceful leadership of its commander, speed and the skilful use of firepower made it into an effective and powerful weapon. Peiper accompanied all battalion attacks in an APC together with his adjutant Otto Dinse. He imbued the APC battalion with spirit and SS-Captain Guhl's assertion 'The unity of the Battalion was the guarantee of success' was universally valid.[22]

The tactically very demanding command of an APC battalion could only be undertaken from the front and not from a command post in the rear.[23] During operations Peiper had constantly to assess the situation and make quick decisions regarding where an attack would be most favourable as the battle unfolded and to identify where the enemy's weak points offered the most promising chances of success. A constantly changing battle scenario was an everyday occurrence for him. His APC crews were young panzer grenadiers who matured under fire on the Eastern Front to become highly valuable, flexible warriors, led by expert NCOs and officers keen to fight.

Basically the attacks were made from the vehicles, providing the advantage of speed and flexible fire direction. Should a problem arise on the right-hand side, the APC crews would make smoke that side and give it a wide berth on the left. Rapidity, surprise and the enormous impression the APCs made were the principal elements for their successful deployment with the Leibstandarte. Jochen Peiper wrote:

'The APC battalion used to attack the Russian positions like a cavalry unit: we came up at full speed from several sides, firing from all barrels.'[24]

What we see here is APC tactics for the modern panzer grenadier as the men themselves experienced it. Former SS-Corporal Günther Wagner, No 13 Company, described it:

The companies proceeded platoon-wise on a broad front against the enemy positions. If a valuable target was identified: Stop and shoot – after destroying it, roll on.

When taking anti-tank fire the order would come by radio 'Ausbooten!' for infantry engagement. This meant that each APC followed a curve across the terrain with the rear doors open allowing the men to leap clear, spreading the section in a long, staggered line facing the enemy. The APC would complete the circle and come up behind the section, the wireless operator at the forward MG providing covering fire.

The heavy platoon had two APCs with heavy built-in MGs, and two APCs with an 8cm mortar, these being secured to a baseplate fixed aboard the APC; for use outside the vehicle a second baseplate was used. This heavy platoon provided supporting fire from the rear – the mortars from concealment, a haystack, a hut, etc. At this time I had charge of two mortar APCs.[25]

On 14 February 1943 3rd Battalion set out through the still partially burning city of Kharkov for Merfa. The convoy had all its APCs and the supply/baggage train. '15 February 1943. 0710 hrs. Battalion Peiper received orders to attack Ossnova from the north via Kharkov.'[26]

This attack had been requested by SS-Division Das Reich. On the advance to Ossnova an APC was put out of action by a Molotov cocktail. SS-2/Lt Gührs, tank gun platoon leader of No 14 Company, wrote:

At midday we attacked five companies of theirs south of Kharkov. Another panzer out of action, Neumann dead . . . several wounded. In the evening I halted with No 13 Company at the same spot. We had to abandon Kharkov. We were to leave at first light. It was another sleepless night. The Battalion had a strip forty kilometres long to protect. Battle Group Witt has surrounded a Russian army which will be destroyed. If we keep firing with Nebelwerfer rockets the Russians will reply with gas. 'We'll be waiting,' we replied.[27]

SS-Corporal Günther Wagner, No 13 Company, wrote of that day:

> The APC battalion came up to cover Army units on the outskirts of
> Kharkov so as to facilitate the most orderly withdrawal possible. We
> stopped in a street below a raised highway, the APCs behind it,
> infantry on it. Suddenly about 400–500m away an ambulance with
> motorcycle sidecar escort – both marked with Red Cross insignia –
> came at high speed towards the passage under the bridge. At that
> moment the two vehicles drew fire from the surrounding houses.
> About 200m before the safety of the embankment they came to a
> standstill. I do not think any order was necessary for the crews to
> enter this district of the city at full speed and destroy the enemy
> there.[28]

This was just one of numerous incidents experienced by the panzer
grenadiers of the LAH in which the Soviets committed serious breaches
of the Geneva and Hague Conventions as regards land warfare. The
war against the Soviets surpassed previously set standards because the
Russians often failed to comply with those agreements in force res-
pecting the treatment of enemy soldiers, prisoners and the wounded.
Frequently German infantry would find the mutilated bodies of
comrades massacred by the Russians. As a result of these experiences
the determination grew amongst German soldiers to fight to the bitter
end and never be taken prisoner by the Soviets.

The Soviets entered the north-west of Kharkov on 15 February 1943,
and at 1240 hrs Corps Raus radioed that the city could no longer be
held. The German units remaining in Kharkov would not survive
unless they pulled out at once. It was in this critical situation that the
Commanding General, SS-Panzer Corps, Paul Hausser, took his lonely
decision to evacuate Kharkov against the Führer's orders to prevent
the annihilation of the survivors there. He pulled the front back behind
the Udy river, and thus Kharkov was abandoned by German troops.

At midday on 16 February 1943, Peiper radioed that his battalion was
at Komarovka. The following day the APC battalion counter-attacked
against a Soviet thrust south of the Udy at Merefa. On 17 February he
received instructions that the enemy advancing through the Msha
Valley was to be stopped at Kolessnikov, and he was to take Ziglerovka
on the morning of the 18th. My company together with elements of
Battalion HQ fought at Babei on 17 February where I was credited with
my 13th Close-combat Day.

That night there was a thaw. Peiper's APC battalion drove sixty kilometres. On 19 February it was ready to operate from Krassnograd. The infantry gun platoon of No 14 Company had been to some extent routed, and at this point No 11 Company had fifteen dead.[29] SS-2/Lt Erhard Gührs, tank gun platoon leader in No 14 Company, accompanied a night attack with my No 12 Company:

> A motorcycle messenger suddenly turned up with the orders. It was 1400 hrs. On the instructions of the Führer the Battalion was to make an attack with the aim of pushing our lines forward. I was to go along in the leading tank-gun vehicle of 12 Company. At 1800 hrs we reached our readiness area. The thrust through the enemy lines went off surprisingly well. There was bright moonlight. We felt our way forward cautiously. This was my first night attack. At 2330 hrs we reached out first objective, a defended village. The Battalion deployed. My platoon was on the right flank. A magnificent scene in the moonlight. Our first shells crashed into the village from 800m. Two Russian guns offered a weak reply. Panzer after panzer pushed through the village unstoppably. In an hour we were all through. I noticed it was 0030 hrs. The village was burning like a torch behind us.

In the APC battalion of the Leibstandarte the encounter had been fought using the APCs not as personnel carriers, but as valuable fighting machines in themselves. My comrades and I had mastered the quick change between fighting aboard, and rapid disembarking in order to break down the last enemy resistance before remounting to proceed with the attack. This tactic was practised in Peiper's Battalion with great success and élan. Peiper's night attacks were his special tactical refinement. SS-Captain Guhl remembered: 'Night attacks were always successful because the enemy did not expect to be attacked at night. This factor and speed were the guarantees of success.'[30]

Guhl, from Stuttgart, became a night-attack specialist, and always led his company from the front.

20 February 1943. Battalion Peiper prepared for another attack, this time against Yeremeyevka, where the enemy was present in strength with armour. The tempo of the attack was prejudiced by deep snow drifts.

0630 hrs: Yeremeyevka and the Lenin Factory taken. Enemy totally routed. Battalion Peiper mopping up to the south and south-east. 1000 hrs. 3rd Battalion ordered to occupy Rossovachotnoye as a base for the reconnaissance section.

At 0902 hrs Peiper had a message sent to 2nd Regiment: '0630 hrs Yeremeyevka and Lenin Factory taken. We have gone on another five kilometres east. Am occupying and securing the areas captured. Enemy totally broken, fleeing east-south-east.'[31]

SS-2/Lt Gührs continued with No 12 Company's APCs:

We re-formed behind the village of Kasachiy Maidan. As it was getting light in the east, so we continued our attack in that direction. Hardly anybody mentioned the biting cold. We stopped for a short while to make preparations before the next village. A Russian regiment had been reported there with heavy weapons. We made another attack which left nothing to be desired in determination. 'Where the Leibstandarte flits, all enemies collapse' we sang in France. Here it became fact. Our panzers ground through the snow. Russian positions were overrun, and they took to their heels. We pursued and caught them up. The Leibstandarte took their regiment apart.

We had far exceeded the second objective of our attack when the APC right ahead of me was knocked out by an anti-tank gun. Hesse was killed. The order came to stop. The purpose had been achieved, two villages taken. We had advanced twenty kilometres and destroyed a regiment together with its weapons. The village was cleared of the enemy.

The APC which had been hit immediately ahead of Gührs' vehicle was a total wreck. I had been aboard it. Just before the anti-tank shell hit I had changed places with wireless operator Klinger at the forward MG and gone to the gun at the rear. My APC commander SS-Corporal Herbert Hesse and Klinger were killed. Our APC belonged to the heavy-MG group of SS-Corporal Egmont Eichler No 12 Company heavy platoon. Eichler and his driver Broska were wounded. I was hit in the face by a shell splinter but after treatment by SS-Lt Dr Breme at the APC battalion dressing station I returned to duty the same day. For Yeremeyevka and Kasachiy Maidan on 19 February 1943 as part of Staff, Nos 11 and 12 Companies I was credited with my 14th Close-combat Day. On 1 March 1943 I received the Black Wound Badge. The leadership of the attack represented another stage in the recommendation for the award of the German Cross in Gold to Peiper:

. . . In waiting at Staroverovka, the Battalion received the order to capture Ziglerovka. The mission was carried out by night against fierce resistance. An enemy battalion was hit hard. Four 7.62cm field guns, an infantry gun, ten mortars, MGs and numerous small arms were destroyed or captured.

Peiper pushed ahead from there at once to Kasachiy Maidan and on the way met another enemy battalion which he engaged with determination, inflicting heavy casualties here too, after which he occupied the town. Now he prepared the attack with his Battalion on Yeremeyvka, and despite a substantial enemy presence took this town too at daybreak.

Exploiting the enemy's confusion, the Battalion advanced to Leninskiy and broke the last resistance of the Russians there. The enemy fled eastwards across open country, was overtaken and suffered heavy casualties. The Battalion destroyed a T-34 and a light tank; one T-34, six 7.62cm field guns and 300 horses were captured. Three sledge columns were wiped out. Enemy losses amounted to between 800 and 900 dead. SS-Major Peiper distinguished himself during all these engagements by the prudent command of his Battalion and personal bravery in the face of the enemy, and has proved himself worthy of high recognition with the German Cross in Gold.[32]

SS-Corporal Günther Wagner, No 13 Company, described the combat experiences of APC men as follows:

The rear door of the APC was completely blocked by ammunition and packs. If we were fired upon we had to leave over the sides. After the first few days in action there ensued practical completion of fitting out. Spare track parts were hung over the front section or sometimes an additional armour plate would be fixed with long bolts. Because we had many wounded in the elbow and upper arm from ricochets and splinters, we very quickly fitted beams or tree-trunks along the upper edge of the slanting side armour. This had the additional advantage of making it more comfortable for sitting during the long drives.[33]

SS-Grenadier Kuno Balz, No 13 Company, remembered another innovation: 'The protective shields for the MG 42 were very poor in our opinion, for if you were firing off-centre, the shield turned with the MG and rifle or MG fire hitting it would then ricochet into the wagon. Therefore in action we would site sandbags near the shields to prevent this.'[34]

On the night of 22 February 1943 the APC battalion headed for Krassnograd after a 70-kilometre drive southwards. On 23 February Peiper reported Dar Nadeshdy and Kulikovka free of enemy troops. At 2300 hrs the battalion was ordered to maintain constant contact with SS-Totenkopf Division at Volny and in the Vshivaya sector. Elements of the Battalion HQ and my No 12 Company encountered the enemy at Ssachnovchina.[35] For 24 February 1943 at Ssachnovchina with the HQ and No 12 Company I received credit for my 15th Close-combat Day.

The APC companies maintained constant reconnaissance. Russian partisans attacked a German column of ambulances, and my No 12 Company responded by attacking an occupied village. During this fighting near Krassnograd on 24 February, our company commander SS-Lt Lux Westrup dismounted from his APC and knelt to the left of the armour link protection, firing at the enemy with a rifle. He was hit and fell dead. The commander of the heavy platoon, SS-2/Lt Otto Bölk, was wounded by a bullet which penetrated his steel helmet. On 1 July 1943 he received the Iron Cross First Class. At midday on 26 February 1943 the much-liked Westrup was interred near Krassnograd. The ceremony was attended by off-duty officers and men. Peiper spoke a few words at the graveside in Westrup's honour. SS-Captain Georg Bormann took command of No 12 Company.

Peiper would spend much time contemplating his plans of attack and often led the operation in his APC with adjutant SS-Lt 'Pan' Dinse. They had an excellent relationship with mutual give and take and unqualified trust in each other. Peiper was always an example for me. Highly intelligent, his conduct was exemplary and particularly in action he did not spare himself. He was head and shoulders above his superiors.[36] Included in his sometimes unconventional style of leadership was his tendency to ignore signals from Regiment which interfered with his intentions. This was recognised at Regiment.

On 28 February Peiper's battalion was on the defensive at Kegitshevka, under Russian attack from the north-west and north-east. Three Soviet tanks were destroyed. At 1315 hrs, No 11 Company launched a flanking attack from Petrovka against the enemy force at

Kegitshevka and overwhelmed a Soviet battalion. At 1605 hrs the APC battalion was so hard-pressed that the Chief of Operations at Division discussed with Peiper whether the battalion should not pull back during the night to the west bank of the Vshivaya and attack to the south-east next morning. SS-2/Lt Gührs noted:

> In the morning, waves of Stukas. Today is Sunday. At midday went with the radio panzer and my Kwk to 13 Company. We launched an attack. The Russians were caught on the hop. Fought against anti-tank guns. We veered right about and attacked Rassochovatoye. Enemy very strong. After an hour we made smoke and cleared out. One APC fell by the wayside burning. In the dark we drove back following 11 Company. Subsequently I joined Peiper in 12 Company. It was raining and snowing at the same time, and pitch black. There was no pleasure in this. Even here we found fresh traces of battle. At 2000hr we got to Losovaya. The place was crammed. Elements of the reconnaissance section, two panzer companies. 12 Company on guard here. I instructed my gun crew. Jacobi's gun claimed three anti-tank guns.
>
> At midnight a messenger came. I went to see Peiper. At least I got three hours' sleep. At the command post there was a mad rush. The commander was on the telephone. The place was a beehive. The new situation was announced. We were told we were to make an attack at six in the morning with the panzer and reconnaissance sections. The Battalion assembled immediately at Petrovka. The drivers' lot was not to be envied. Snow, slush and no lights. I had the column make ready. Then we set off. First there was a bottleneck. After much shouting and cursing we found the way out. On a bridge we collided with a Nebelwerfer rocket unit. They wanted to get the artillery preparations done early and be ready to open fire at 0430hr. One of the panzers went into a ditch. Everything was a shambles again. Behind us was a panzer company wanting to get to Ziglerovka. At 0300 hrs we were still in Petrovka.

On 1 March 1943 Peiper attacked Yeremeyevka via Ziglerovka and wiped out an enemy column. The attack originally planned on Kegitshevka via the Vshivaya sector was called off because a thaw had turned the terrain into rugged and heavily rutted mud. SS-2/Lt Gührs recorded:

At 0600 hrs the assembly at Ziglerovka was terminated, we had a piece of bread and a noggin of 'offensive spirit' for breakfast. Our companies had been attached to the panzer companies. The weather was terribly unfavourable. Thick fog, visibility hardly 100m. A target for every anti-tank. Despite everything the attack had to go ahead. I did not like the look of it. I drove in our radio panzer. At Kashachiy Maidan the Russians were taken by surprise and the attack was too massive. Five kilometres further on things turned nasty. They were shooting from everywhere. We simply could not see anything. The enemy anti-tank let us come up close and then let our panzers have it. Two were burning. The crews got out. We were being hit everywhere. The Russians were firing from cover of the mist and we could see nothing. After an hour of this useless wrestling the attack was called off. We rolled back to Ziglerovka. It was enough to make you weep. I was very depressed.

I experienced the attack of 2 March 1943 with the leading company. SS-2/Lt Gührs was with No 12 Company.

Today we attacked in three Battle Groups. Attack and pursue. We got a full tank and re-ammunitioned. We assembled north of Kofanovka at 0700 hrs. The Luftwaffe was very active today. The attack began – first objective Logviny. I accompanied 12 Company. We took Logviny. Anti-tank fire from the right left us cold. The Russians bolted. We set off in hot pursuit. Obviously we rolled quicker than they could run. The Battalion rolled forward in open order. We came under fire. To my left an APC was hit. Next moment an SP gun fell victim, smoke rising up. The crew baled out. There was nothing for it but to make smoke and observe. Three tanks and two anti-tank guns were shooting from over there with all barrels. After ten minutes the road was clear. All wiped out. To the left, on high ground, more positions. We headed for them and attacked. We overcame these new trenches, nothing more blocked our path and now we could resume the pursuit. Darkness brought a bloody day to a close. The Russians would probably have something like 800 dead . . . we had one man fallen. He did not die in vain. We captured about ten field guns, destroyed two enemy tanks and advanced forty kilometres!

When the battle had run its course, Peiper remarked in his humorous way that we had been to the 'wrong funeral'. In the evening we got to Melechovka, ejected the Russians and settled in. I was with No 12 Company. A successful day was at its close. It was just a pity that two panzers were land-mined on reconnaissance.

Together with the HQ and Nos 11 to 14 Companies inclusive, I was given credit for my 16th Close-combat Day at Logivy on 2 March. All elements of Peiper's battalion were involved in the battle for Logviny.[37] No 13 Company lost seven APCs in the fight for Melechovka. On 2 March No 11 Company under SS-Captain Guhl hit the retreating enemy on the flank, wiped out two companies and captured two batteries of artillery and a large number of anti-tank guns, supply vehicles and horses. Next day while in pursuit Guhl took the well-defended village of Pecheivka. The terrain being difficult, Guhl made a wide detour to attack the surprised enemy from the rear and, at the head of his men, led them into the houses. He also rammed an anti-tank gun with his damaged APC. I was given credit for my 17th Close-combat Day at Pecheivka on 3 March.

On 4 March 1943 the battalion attacked Stanitshnoye, which was defended by an anti-tank front. Guhl's company on the right wing became embroiled and in the midst of heavy defensive fire raced at full speed beyond the village, negotiated three minefields and, led by Guhl in the first APC, rolled back into Stanitshnoye where five 7.62cm field guns and four anti-tank guns were destroyed, and a battalion staff taken prisoner.[38] At Stanitshnoye I was with No 12 Company alongside our Nos 11 and 13 Companies and Battalion HQ. 'The men have enormous faith in the commander's luck. Jochen Peiper is becoming an idol!' Gührs wrote. This observation is representative of the way the whole battalion felt about its commander.

At 2000 hrs on 4 March 1943 the following signal was sent: 'Battle Group Peiper took Stanitshnoye at 0815 hrs and pursued the fleeing enemy to Jevdokimovka and Lichova. Three APCs were lost.'[39] An APC driver stated:

Peiper was our model. Everybody said, he just sat in the panzer and in that way the new fighting tactics developed. Drivers who had always been denigrated as two-a-penny were now at a premium. Without then you couldn't use your APCs. We pulled no punches in driver training; we practised changing track links, track padding and retaining pins. Now whenever we were in action everyone knew his way around with a screwdriver and when ordered could monitor and adjust.

After the first direct hits three or four track parts were fixed at the front to deflect incoming shells. At the workshop we would have two armour plates welded to the front plating in such a way that the reserve track parts could be stowed there. From this the idea developed that they would deflect shellfire from ahead and avert damage. Luckily no driver was at liberty to pick and choose his section or superiors, otherwise each one would have promoted himself to commander-driver. There were no good and bad drivers, for the rivalry was intense and in his own way each man was the best.[40]

For 4 March 1943 at Stanitshnoye I was credited with my 18th Close-combat Day with HQ and Nos 11, 12 and 13 Companies.

'5 March 1943. 3rd Battalion reconnaissance reports heavy enemy presence at Gavrilovka, flowing eastwards.'[41] Now the whole SS-Panzer Corps and the Leibstandarte was on the offensive. Everyone was fired up. SS-2/Lt Gührs wrote:

In thirty days the fortunes of battle have turned again . . . I have not described how it was looking here on the whole. Now perhaps I can say. I might have found solace in confiding to my diary 'We are losing the war'? Perhaps a thousand other diarists did so. One despaired. People were flooding back westwards. We asked ourselves if words of encouragement and bravery were just empty talk. Then we received the Führer's Order of the Day and appeal. The fate of our Volk was balanced on a knife-edge here. Then we fought . . .

Our panzergrenadier-battalion has ploughed a bloody furrow in the soil of Russia. Perhaps we have taken the lead over all of them. Wherever there was something going on, there we were. When SS-Lt-Col Meyer was with the Führer to receive the Oak Leaves, the Führer told him that the intervention of the Leibstandarte in this theatre of war had been decisive on the southern front.

On 6 March 1943 at 1000 hrs the entire APC battalion arrived at Bridok via Hills 193.8 and 188.9. For his achievement in this attack, next day a telex was sent recommending Peiper for the award of the Knight's Cross:

SS-Major Peiper, commanding officer 3rd Battalion 2nd SS-Panzer Grenadier Regiment Leibstandarte SS Adolf Hitler, was ordered on 6

March 1943 to advance to Peressel (objective for the day) after breaking down enemy resistance along the line southern edge Prossyanoye–Lyashova–Gavrilovka and advancing. Setting out at 1145 hrs, by 1345 hrs he had reached the southern edge of Peressel and at 1400 hrs broke through an enemy assembly area in the process of development and on his own initiative, far exceeding the objective for the day.

He drove through enemy columns and at 1530 hrs ejected strong enemy forces from prepared field positions at Federovka-Bridok, setting up a bridgehead. He held this bridgehead despite being cut off from all contact to the rear and was under attack by strong enemy forces from all sides. Three T-34s were destroyed. In this way, SS-Major Peiper created the preconditions for the successful attack on Valki on 7 March 1943.[42]

For Federovka on 6 March I was credited my 19th Close-combat Day.

On 7 March the APC battalion made possible the advance of 1st SS-Panzer Grenadier Regiment by an attack on Valki from the east.

7 March 1943. Battalion Peiper (with 1st SS-Panzerjägerabteilung) pushed on to Cheremushnaya as far as the Rollbahn to Lyubotin and met up with the reconnaissance section on the north-east edge of Valki.
2000 hrs: Battalion Peiper received orders to advance to Komuna passing Karavan.[43]

The 2nd SS-Panzer Grenadier Regiment (SS-Colonel Theodor Wisch) reached Federovka and Bridok at midday, where 1st and 2nd Battalion relieved the 3rd Battalion force. Wisch later pointed to Jochen Peiper, Hugo Kraas and Kurt Meyer as the Leibstandarte commanders as the motivators who set the standards. The reconnaissance group of Oak Leaves holder SS-Lt-Col Kurt Meyer and 1st Battalion 1st SS-Panzer Regiment (SS-Major Max Wünsche) were ordered to attack Valki. After breaking through an anti-tank front north of Sneshkoff Kut towards 1315 hrs the battle group headed into Valki from the south-west, leaving Meyer and Peiper to discuss the next move.

8 March 1943 0630 hrs. Commanders' conference. Set out 0700 hrs. Battalion Peiper reported many enemy at Ogulzy. Because of difficult road conditions and the most severe country the advance proceeded

only slowly. The battalions secured for the night on the line 198.3-north edge Ogulzy. After breaking very determined enemy resistance at Karavan, Battle Group Peiper set up a bridgehead.[44]

Peiper wrote of the No 11 Company operation as follows:

On 8 March 1943 the Battalion, advancing from the south, stormed towards Lyubotin, set up a bridgehead in a surprise night operation and took the town the following day. Guhl proved once again his cool-headedness and prudence. Despite heavy defensive fire and a sudden bombardment by Russian heavy mortars, he was one of the first to the bridge, put himself in the blind spot of the close-combat troops and took out numerous anti-tank and tank guns on the flanks.[45]

Elements of the Staff and Peiper's Nos 11, 12 and 13 Companies were involved in close combat near Revchik. For Revchik on 8 March I was credited my 20th confirmed Close-combat Day.

On 9 March 1943, Peiper was decorated with the Knight's Cross. The news went round the battalion in a flash. The men were not only proud of the award to their commander, but saw in it also a confirmation and recognition of their own endeavours. Peiper himself had no time for celebration. March 9th was just another fighting day.

9 March 1943, 0730 hrs. Battle Group Peiper passed forward from Lyubotin and at Komuna regained contact with 1st Regiment.
1100 hrs, 3rd Battalion attacked Bogatiy and destroyed a strong Russian battalion.

For Lyubotin on 9 March I was credited my 21st confirmed Close-combat Day.[46]
At 1855 hrs Peiper signalled to 2nd SS-Panzer Grenadier Regiment:

(1) Battle Group Peiper from 0600 hrs proceeded from reference point 628 in north-easterly direction to point 612 Komuna, where restored contact with 1st Panzer Grenadier Regiment.
(2) 1100 hrs, attacked Bogatiy, destroyed a Russian battalion.
(3) My battalion occupied eastern end of Bogatiy.
(4) Enemy losses: one heavy mortar battery with 23 mortars, two 12.2cm guns, four 4.7cm guns, six tank guns, five heavy MGs,

seven light mortars, 25 lorries, 250 dead Russians.
(5) Own losses: Fallen – one NCO. Wounded: Two men (one retained
with main body).[47]

Also on 9 March, SS-Captain Paul Guhl and SS-2/Lt Werner Wolff, both
of No 11 Company, were awarded the Iron Cross First Class.

Peiper's complete battalion, with elements of Nos 6, 10 and 16
Companies of 2nd Regiment were involved in close combat at
Lyubotin. At 1000 hrs, Battle Group Meyer and 1st SS-Panzer Regiment
reported having made contact with SS-Totenkopf Division at Olshany.
The Leibstandarte was to attack Kharkov from the north, Das Reich
from the west, while Totenkopf was to cover the flanks and rear of the
Leibstandarte. For the attack on Kharkov, No 1 Company 1st SS Anti-
Tank Battalion (SS-Captain Prinz) with 7.5cm anti-tank Marders was
attached to Peiper's Battalion at the outset. At midday on 10 March
1943, 1st SS-Panzer Grenadier Regiment led by SS-Colonel Fritz Witt
captured Dergachi in the face of bitter Soviet resistance. The reinforced
reconnaissance section set out from Dergachi-East for Cherkasskoye
and Zirkuny, which they reached by evening. During the evening and
night 1st Regiment arrived at a position on the approach road
Cherkasskoye-Kharkov as far as the airfield on the northern outskirts
of Kharkov. Divisional orders stated:

(1) Enemy completely surprised and overwhelmed by the rapid
advance of the Leibstandarte.
(2) SS-Panzer Corps is to take Kharkov on 11 March 1943, protected
on the eastern flank at Merefa by elements of SS-Division Das
Reich, and on the north and north-west flank along the line
Russkoye–Dergachi–Festki–Olshany by SS-Totenkopf Division . . .[48]

The fresh assault on the city of Kharkov began on the morning of 11
March 1943. Next day the APC battalion moved up with the attached
7.5cm anti-tank Marders and 3rd SP gun battery (SS-Captain
Rettlinger). The war diary records:

12 March 1943.
1030 hrs: 3rd Battalion set off and proceeded along the main highway
towards 'Red Square' after previously establishing contact with 1
Regiment, turned east and regained contact with the reconnaissance
section on the Staro–Moscovska road.

The author received the Close-combat Clasp in gold, the German Cross in Gold, the Wound Badge in gold and other decorations. He survived at least 84 days of close-combat, was wounded on six occasions and as a panzer grenadier destroyed four enemy tanks on the Western and Eastern Fronts.

(TOP) The author on a visit to the house of Hitler's parents at Leonding near Linz, winter 1940.

(BOTTOM) Units of 4th SS-Totenkopf Standarte parade through a Dutch town, autumn 1940.

(TOP) The author's No 19 (MG) Company, LAH in the East in 1941. Originally entitled 'After the panzer attack, Gibermanovk'. From the left (top) platoon commander SS-2/Lt Hans Scharna (d.22 November 1941), a section leader (fell 2 August 1941), gunner 2 Müller, Schlumbaum, Corporal Rohrberg: (left) Section leaders Scheppmann, Warnitzke, Michael Britzlmayr, Lindner. Lying down, Seelig and Müller 2.

(BOTTOM) SS-Captain Heinz Kling, commander No 18 Company LAH, 1941. In 1943 he commanded the Tiger Company of the Panzer Regiment, was awarded the Knight's Cross and in the rank of SS-Major led the 501st Heavy SS-Panzer Battalion as his final command.

(TOP) Peiper issuing his final instructions from an APC to the author's company commander, SS-Captain Georg Bormann before an attack. Behind Bormann is Paul Guhl.

(BOTTOM) SS-Captain Paul Guhl, commander of No 11 Company; Georg Bormann, commander No 12 Company and battalion adjutant Otto Dinse (with bottle).

(TOP) The APC battalion in winter with the new MG 42.

(BOTTOM) The APC battalion often launched night attacks in Russia.

(TOP) Panzer grenadiers of the Battalion preparing for a counter-attack.

(BOTTOM) Karl Menne of No 12 Company. The front of the APC has been reinforced with track links.

(TOP) Kharkov, March 1943. At the centre Karl Reutlinger, 3rd Sturmgeschütz (SP) Section, LAH, to the right is Fritz Witt, commander 1st SS-Panzer Grenadier Regiment.

(BOTTOM) 12 March 1943. APCs of No 11 Company in Kharkov. SS-Corporal 'Pieke' Bliesener nicknamed his APC 'Strolch' (scallywag): behind him comes the APC of SS-Corporal Karl Kempfe. This vehicle came under fire shortly after the photo was taken and Kempfe was killed. The additional armour plates at the front are clearly visible.

(TOP) Panzer grenadiers in an APC near Mk IV panzers of the LAH.

(BOTTOM) SS-Corporal Hannes Duffert on a tank-gun APC of No 14 Company.

1600 hrs: Between Lopany river and the main highway two Russian battalions were wiped out.

The APCs of No 11 Company on the outskirts of Kharkov rolled through the streets one behind the other. Behind SS-Corporal Bliesener's APC 'Strolch' came the panzer of SS-Corporal Karl Kempfe who would be killed shortly after a photograph was taken of them. The Russians put up a very determined defence, and now Peiper's panzer grenadiers were forced to fight their way into the city in indescribably fierce street-to-street and house-to-house combat. The APC battalion sustained considerable losses. After Peiper linked up with SS-Major Max Hansen, commander of 2nd Battalion 1st SS-Panzer Grenadier Regiment at Red Square, he established a bridgehead in Staro-Moskovska Street and then employed two APCs to restore contact to Panzermeyer's reconnaissance unit at the fork in the road to Chuguyev.

After heavy fighting, 2nd Battalion 2nd SS-Panzer Grenadier Regiment took the main railway station and then moved up to Katerinoslavska Street to contact Peiper's battalion.[49] The bridge over the Kharkov river was renamed after Jochen Peiper. SS-Corporal Martin Säuberlich's APC of No 12 Company was hit by a tank round on the Peiper bridge and lost one man killed.[50] My own heavy-MG half-platoon leaders, SS-Sergeants Adolf Sellmeier and Bruno Wessels, were both awarded the Iron Cross First Class on this day. Fifty-three Iron Crosses Second Class were also handed out. SS-Grenadier Glenewinkel of No 13 Company noted in his diary. 'Broke through to Red Square. Attack over the blown Peiper-bridge. Heavy street fighting. Our Company losses 30 men.'[51] For Kharkov on 12 March 1943 I was credited my 22nd confirmed Close-combat Day.

Peiper's orders for the following day were: 'Reinforced 3rd Battalion/2nd Regiment to regain firm contact to Battle Group Witt at the Chuguyev/Voltshansk fork in the road.'[52] That same day Peiper's Battalion was involved once again in fierce street fighting in the Ukrainian capital.

13 March 1943. 3rd Battalion in heavy house-to-house fighting at the bridge over Kharkov river on Moskovska Street. In stubborn, bitter fighting a bridgehead was set up and constantly expanded.
1300 hrs. 3rd Battalion reached the Korsykivska-Konyushevo fork and met up with the reconnaissance unit. 1st and 2nd Battalions cleared the individual neighbourhoods systematically in close

cooperation with 3rd Battalion and by nightfall had reached
Saikivska Street where they secured to the south-east, east and north-
east.[53]

The APC battalion attack set out from the Peiper bridge, my No 12
Company leading. My company colleague SS-Corporal Martin
Säuberlich wrote: 'In recapturing Kharkov, 1st Platoon with SS-Lt
Schmidt on the far side of the so-called Peiper bridge cleared out the
blocks of housing which were then occupied by a group to the left
under Schmidt, the other to the right. We crossed the bridge in the
APCs, got out and then the house-to-house fighting continued'.[54]

SS-Lt Hans Schmidt was wounded on 13 March during the taking of
the bridge and the subsequent street fighting.[55] His 1st Platoon suffered
heavy losses crossing the bridge and was reduced to only section
strength. After the platoon in the APC had crossed the bridge, they
dismounted and advanced to the tractor works where, with SS-
Corporal Säuberlich, the last section leader, dropped out wounded.[56]
SS-Corporal Jacobi, commander of a 7.5cm tank gun APC of No 4
Company received a direct hit and was killed.

Jochen Peiper remained an example and hero to his men in the street
fighting. SS-Leading Grenadier Heinz Freyer, No 11 Company, remembers him at Kharkov: 'When we were dismounted and fighting in the
houses, the theatre, the tractor works, he was always at the front.'

Gührs took over the pioneer platoon after its leader Haferstroh was
wounded. This platoon was not on the authorised strength for the
Battalion, but had been present in the old No 20 (Heavy) Company and
was re-equipped with APCs and remained until the war's end. Its
existence shows the difference in the Leibstandarte between what was
officially 'surplus to requirements' and what was absorbed into it. That
an APC battalion in its operations, in which speed was of the essence,
needed its own pioneers for the clearance of landmines in order to
prevent an advance from stalling, goes without saying. Even the
Leibstandarte panzer regiment had pioneer platoons, and later a
panzer-pioneer company.

At 2035 hrs 2nd Regiment signalled to Division: 'Battle Group Peiper
has been extending bridgehead over river Leharki around Staro-
Moskovska Street since early hours. Enemy resistance extremely fierce.
Each individual housing block has to be cleared systematically.
Russians sit in them with MGs, anti-tank and tank guns and fight to
the end.'[57] SS-Leading Grenadier Oswald Siegmund of No 13 Company

wrote: 'On 13 March 1943, a Sunday, there occurred the fiercest, most dreadful fighting on the so-called Peiper bridge. No 12 Company lost half its men in the street behind the bridge. Fighting around the GPU building. Our Company leader Tomhardt was wounded again and cut off with elements of a platoon. 7 Section fell closed up.'[58]

SS-2/Lts Dieter Kohler, No 12 Company, and Joachim Kladen, No 13 Company were also wounded. The fighting in the maze of streets was hard, the enemy being cleared out block by block in close combat. For this purpose even the 8.8cm Flak guns and artillery were brought up. The Soviets defended with MGs, MPi's, tank guns, tanks and anti-tank. Their tanks lurked in the entrances to housing blocks and courtyards. By the evening the Leibstandarte had two-thirds of the city in its hands. This 13 March 1943 counted for me as my 23rd Close-combat Day.

For 14 March Peiper was ordered: '3rd Battalion, 2nd SS-Panzer Grenadier Regiment, attached to reconnaissance unit, is to advance along Petinska Street to the railway bridge and there secure the area. The housing block south of the street up to and including Uralska Street is to be cleared. If necessary take the Experimental Farming Institute.'[59] The War Diary records:

14 March 1943 0800 hrs, the battalions resumed the attack heading south east into sectors ordered and against heavy resistance reached Voksal railway station. In dogged street fighting under determined leadership one by one the housing blocks were seized from the enemy and by 1645 hrs the entire city centre was in the firm grasp of the Leibstandarte.

Kharkov on 14 March was my 24th confirmed Close-combat Day.
In the afternoon all German radio stations broadcast:

Special Announcement! From the Führer's Headquarters, 14 March 1943. The Wehrmacht High Command announces: Army Group South, which in fighting of weeks' duration repelled the enemy back over the Donetz in a counter-attack, has recaptured the city of Kharkov. Units of the Waffen-SS, with powerful Luftwaffe support, engaged for several days in a hard struggle to encircle the city from the north and east. The enemy losses in men and material have not yet been assessed.[60]

SS-General Sepp Dietrich, commanding the Leibstandarte, received the

Swords to his Knight's Cross with Oak Leaves. On 15 March 1942 the clearing of the remaining districts of the city proceeded according to plan and were brought to a conclusion. In this way the 300-kilometre long gap in the front between Army Group Centre and Army Group South caused by the loss of Stalingrad and its consequences was closed and thus one of the most difficult crises on the Eastern Front resolved.

The Leibstandarte brought the Soviet attack along a 100-kilometre stretch east of Kharkov to a standstill, knocked out significant enemy troop units and after that covered the advance of Das Reich and Totenkopf from the south and south-west of Kharkov. Then the entire SS-Panzer Corps had attacked to the north, turned back south and in a determined circling operation recaptured Kharkov on 14 March 1943.

Chapter Five

The Seizure of Byelgorod, 18 March 1943

In order to force the weakening enemy back across the river Donetz, the Leibstandarte was ordered to occupy Byelgorod, north of Kharkov. If this succeeded, it would enable a front to be established along the Donetz.

On 17 March 1943, south of Nechoteyevka, Peiper's battle group (including 7th Company 1st SS-Panzer Regiment, SS-2/Lt von Ribbentrop) came upon an anti-tank front which was penetrated at dusk. The entire APC battalion based itself around Hill 215.3.[1] March 17th 1943 at this location counted as my 25th confirmed Close-combat Day.

Byelgorod was the objective for the LAH and the Army's Gross-deutschland Division which was to come up from Borissovka with an armoured group to the east to shut down the Kharkov–Byelgorod Rollbahn (one-way highway) and railway line. On 18 March 1943, a day of bright sunshine, the reinforced 2nd SS-Panzer Grenadier Regiment arrived after previous reconnaissance by the APC battalion. Two Tigers were delivered to Peiper in the evening. The Stuka attack on the Russian line Krestovo–Kaumovka was carried out at 0700 hrs and ten minutes later Peiper reported that he had breached the line and was heading for Otradnyi.

18 March 1943
0415 hrs 3rd Battalion making reconnaissance as ordered.
0830 hrs Battalions set out for attack. The enemy, taken totally by surprise, fled in droves.
1000 hrs 3rd Battalion reached Krasnaya Niva.
1100 hrs Battalion Peiper eight kilometres east of Byelgorod, and on his own initiative pushed on for Byelgorod far beyond his set objective.

1130 hrs In a coup de main Peiper took the town, and was given instructions to defend it in strength to the north and west.[2]

Peiper's astounding success was initially received with disbelief at Division and Corps. SS-2/Lt Gührs, No 14 Company, wrote:

18 March 1943. Sunshine, snow. Peiper summoned the company commanders and myself as tank gun platoon commander early to inform us that several Waffen-SS divisions and the Panzer Grenadier Division Grossdeutschland had been assigned for Byelgorod. Then he said that he had been to the Stuka command post and they had promised to bomb the Russian blockade on the highway at 0700 hrs. The Battalion was to stand by and – taking advantage of surprise – drive through the Russian lines on the highway. We had two or three Tigers. Our aim was to reach Byelgorod. With my tank gun platoon I was to put a stop to any resistance. It went as planned and we broke through.

Over the radio Peiper urged the fastest pace. The Russians rubbed their eyes. Their tanks were still under tarpaulins, they were laying cables and performing their morning routine as we roared through the villages heading for Byelgorod. How they were faring ahead I had no idea for our column was rather long. But we kept on rolling. Gradually the Russians realised what was afoot and far behind I saw the first of their tanks giving chase, but our speed was remarkable. Through a valley, over a bridge and to our surprise we were in Byelgorod. Later I heard that our first signal was received . . . with disbelief at Division: 'Heavy house-to-house fighting in Byelgorod'. Second message: 'We hold Byelgorod'.

I knew nothing of the visit by the divisional commander with the Storch because I had to protect the bridge to the rear with my platoon.[3]

Peiper's signal at 1135 hrs – 'Byelgorod taken in coup de main. Eight tanks destroyed' – encountered difficulties in transmission. Immediately after capturing the town he ordered his adjutant Dinse to send the message but he was unable to establish contact. Eventually Dinse got it sent from the radio of a war correspondent in one of the accompanying vehicles.[4]

Otto Dinse, SS-Hauptsturmführer

Decorations: Gold Close-combat Clasp, 1 September 1944 as commander, No 12 Company 2nd SS-Panzer Grenadier Regiment, 1st SS-Panzer Division LSSAH: German Cross in Gold, 3 May 1945, Operations officer 1st SS-Panzer Division LSSAH.

24 October 1912 Born Hamburg-Altona

November 1929 Joined 31st SA-Standarte

1 July 1931 Altona 4th SS-Standarte: 1/1932 adjutant, 3rd Sturmbann

12 March 1934 SS-Untersturmführer (2/Lt)

18 February 1935 Joined 28th SS-Standarte *Hans Cyranka* at Hamburg

20 April 1935 Promoted to SS-Obersturmführer (Lt)

30 April 1937 Promoted to SS-Hauptsturmführer (Captain)

15 May 1937 At Staff/XIV Section, adjutant to Police President, Bremen

3 October 1939 Joined Leibstandarte

31 July 1940 Completed officers' course (3.Kriegs-Junkerlehrgang) at Tölz and took command of platoon, 2nd Ersatz-Battalion, Leibstandarte.

9 November 1940 Commissioned as SS-Untersturmführer (2/Lt)

21 July 1941 Platoon leader No 17 Company LAH

3 August 1941 Wounded: then Staff officer and later adjutant, 4th Battalion LAH

12 November 1941 Awarded Iron Cross Second Class

20 April 1942 Promoted to SS-Obersturmführer (Lt) and became Peiper's adjutant.

20 April 1943 Received Infantry Assault Badge in Bronze

June 1943 On leave until 18 July 1943 when took over 14.Company.

1 September 1943 Received bronze Close-combat Clasp

16 September 1943 Received Iron Cross First Class

From November 1943 led his APC Company on Easter Front.

6 December 1943 After Guhl was wounded, took command of APC Battalion.

22 December 1943 Wounded Eastern Front

2 January 1944 Wounded Eastern Front

2 June 1944 Recommended for award of Close-combat Clasp in Gold.

20 August 1944 Wounded for fifth time, Falaise pocket. At military hospital, Osnabrück, received the gold Wound Badge.

1 September 1944 Notified of the award of the Close-combat Clasp in Gold.

12 December 1944 Received Close-combat Clasp in Gold at Ulm from Reichsführer-SS Heinrich Himmler based on 56 confirmed Close-combat Days. Returned to Ersatz-Battalion.

1 March 1945 Operations officer/Leibstandarte. Finally he served as adjutant of 1st SS-Panzer Grenadier Regiment.

19 December 2000 Died at Hamburg.

Once the APC battalion had entered Byelgorod, SS-Captain Guhl, commander of No 11 Company, went at once to the banks of the Donetz to seal off the bridges. Soviet tanks attacked him there but his company beat them off with anti-tank guns and panzers, six enemy tanks and numerous guns being destroyed. No 11 Company took the hard-pressed eastern end of Byelgorod in fierce house-to-house fighting.[5] Guhl was wounded, and SS-Corporal Reint-Stomberg of his company was killed.

An SS-Corporal in one of the aforementioned Tigers wrote:

On our further approach two T-34s challenged us, these we des-troyed without difficulty. To the left of the highway was an enormous expanse of terrain over which hundreds of Red soldiers were fleeing to the rear, driven by the fear of being overrun by our major thrust. They ran, coats flapping, as if their very souls depended on it. We were not interested in what was happening either side of us, however, but concentrated solely on reaching our goal at full speed, the town of Byelgorod.

At about 1130 hrs Byelgorod loomed before us. We could not read the name on the street sign since it was in Cyrillic script, but it could only be Byelgorod, which we were bent on capturing. Coming up from the south-west, we drove cautiously over a wooden bridge, which however bore the weight of our panzer well, and went north into Byelgorod. Two APCs protected our rear. Almost at the town entrance came the shout, 'Tanks behind!' The APC crews jumped out and found cover in a ditch. 'Turret to six o'clock!' our commander ordered, and we swivelled the turret round fast, for the Soviet tanks were only 200m away. We scored a direct hit with our first round, the victim being a General Grant type of American manufacture, difficult to miss at that range. After this success came a signal warning us that enemy tanks lower down on this road would bring our ammunition-panzer and support vehicles under fire: we should attempt to keep the road open at all costs. We turned back at once, our tracks stirring up the softened sand.

When we reached the wooden bridge again, we saw a T-34 completely blocking the approach road 300m distant. We opened fire at once, obtaining a hit in his motor room, from which smoke began to issue but despite this the T-34 returned fire until our next round silenced the gun and ended the affair. The road was free again. Meanwhile a second Tiger from our company had rolled up after clearing the Rollbahn and now all our vehicles could enter Byelgorod with impunity. The town fell to us and we had achieved our objective.[6]

I watched this encounter between the Tiger and T-34 from the wooden bridge. Apart from this T-34, I saw a KvI and KvII [Soviet heavy tanks] on the edge of town, both of which escaped. Our APC had engine damage and was stuck between the wooden bridge and the Tiger. During the exchange of fire our vehicle was hit, Corporal Bussacker and I being wounded by shell splinters. My wound was in the back. After medical attention at the Battalion casualty clearing station I returned to my company and APC the same day. For my part in the taking of Byelgorod on 18 March 1943 I was awarded my 26th Close-combat Day.

At 1935 hrs Peiper signalled to Regiment: 'Enemy losses, ten T-34s, one T-40, one T-60, two General Lees, ten 7.62cm guns, six 4.7cm anti-tank, 14 small anti-tank, 19 heavy and 34 light MGs, 38 lorries, several sledge columns destroyed, various flame-throwers. Own losses: one dead, six wounded.'[7] Once more, Peiper's lightning-fast assessment of the situation outside Byelgorod and his resulting manoeuvres brought the Division a success which might not have been achieved so easily a little later.

Next day Peiper was relieved at Byelgorod:

19 March 1943: In the morning 2nd Battalion took over security from 3rd Battalion.
1200 hrs: Battalion Peiper ordered to head west to link up with Grossdeutschland Division.
1315 hrs: 3rd Battalion left and reached Strelezkoye at 1355 hrs, destroying seven enemy tanks in a fierce exchange. The enemy has destroyed the bridge: the Battalion is spending the night at Strelezkoye.[8]

For my part in the above action outside Strelezkoye on 19 March 1943 I was awarded my 27th Close-combat Day.

Peiper's battalion was reinforced by the two Tigers and No 7 Company 1st SS-Panzer Regiment commanded by SS-2/Lt Rudolf von Ribbentrop, who remembered:

That day the armoured group had to reconnoitre to the north. In front of my Company were one or two Tigers with some APCs. Leaving the cover of woodland the leading vehicles came under artillery fire. One of the APCs received a direct hit and burst into flames. Because the armoured group apparently had no orders to accept battle, it drew back into the woods. Jochen Peiper graced this decision with the observation, 'There is no bouquet to be won here!' Then suddenly he asked the panzer crews who was prepared to go back out and check to see if anyone was still alive in the burning APC, and if so bring him back. I understood that the APC commander was a sergeant with whom Peiper had served for several years. At that I volunteered with my Panzer Mk IV and rolled out towards the APC. I was certain that as soon as my panzer was visible to them the enemy artillerists would fire at it and so I jumped out and searched the burning APC for signs of life. I collected a few personal documents and identity tags and upon my return assured Peiper that there were no survivors. I observed how important it was for Peiper to be sure, for he thanked me most warmly.[9]

'20 March 1943. 0600 hrs: 3rd Battalion feinted to the north. 0845 hrs: 3rd Battalion reached bridge at Shopino, wiped out an extremely tenacious defence and after repairing the bridge headed for Kloh Ssmelok Trudu. 1200 hrs: Battle Group Peiper left as ordered. 1400 hrs: Arrived Oskotshnoye and Satchnevkolodes, remained there on security duty towards the north, the left flank maintaining contact to II Battalion.' For my part in the battle at Shopino on 20 March 1943 I was awarded my 28th Close-combat Day.

Here the APC battalion came under attack from Soviet bombers, whose gunners fired into the open APCs. I was hit in the face and chin, and my company commander, No 12 Company, SS-Captain Georg Bormann, was also wounded. This was the third time I had been wounded in the winter fighting and now had four wounds. Death had long been stalking me but still found me elusive. After treatment at the battalion dressing station I returned to my company and APC the same day. Thus ended the Kharkov operations. The Liebstandarte had won a great victory in the offensive following hard defensive fighting. Many of its brave soldiers had made the greatest sacrifice for this success: their lives.

Chapter Six

Interlude and Preparations for Kursk, 29 March–4 July 1943

The actual strength of 2nd SS-Panzer Grenadier Regiment on 1 April 1943 was 66 officers, 358 NCOs and 2,095 men.[1] At Easter, 3rd Battalion, initially at Kharkov, moved out to Klenovoye. After heavy losses in the battle for Kharkov, the Leibstandarte had to provide personnel for the setting-up of its sister Hitlerjugend Division and headquarters of I SS-Panzer Corps Leibstandarte, it being planned to merge Leibstandarte and Hitlerjugend into the I SS-Panzer Corps. Changes in personnel were also made in Peiper's Battalion. SS-2/Lt Gerhard Babick led my No 12 Company from the beginning of April 1943 until relieved by SS-Lt Georg Preuss, previously platoon commander with No 13 Company. On 26 April Peiper nominated SS-2/Lt Erhard Gührs to head No 14 Company, replacing SS-Captain Kolitz, now with Hitlerjugend.

On 20 April the companies of the APC battalion paraded to receive decorations earned at Kharkov. Amongst others to whom Peiper handed the Iron Cross First Class was the medical orderly in my company, SS-Sgt Rudi Kuhfuss. Thirty-seven NCOs and men received the Iron Cross Second Class and 361 Panzer Combat Badges in bronze were awarded amongst men of the APC battalion. On 22 April I was given the silver Wound Badge.

At Klenovoye the APC battalion received an influx of new men from the Leibstandarte reserve battalion, while further reinforcements came in the shape of former Luftwaffe servicemen transferred into the Waffen-SS. These ranged from trained recruits to senior sergeants. One of the men we received in No 12 Company was a former Stuka pilot with the Iron Cross First Class and Luftwaffe front clasp. This NCO had flown his Ju 87 under a bridge during an attack on England, and had been given a disciplinary transfer.[2] I was ordered on an NCO's course at Olshany where the instructor was my new company commander, SS-Lt Preuss. I did not like it much and was quickly returned to unit which I had long felt to be my home.

The Leibstandarte received new camouflage uniforms. Corresponding to the season of year they were lightweight and bore various green patterns. My colleagues and I were issued trousers, slip-on jackets, uniform jackets and field caps made of this camouflage drillcloth. Outwardly in all this one recognised the new type of tightly-knit warrior community who wore no insignia of rank nor decorations. The Leibstandarte would fight the coming Battle of Kursk with new weapons and this revolutionary battledress.

The entire 2nd SS-Panzer Grenadier Regiment was spread across villages near Kharkov, an area of low uplands broken by woods and lakes which offered welcome opportunities for bathing. My No 12 Company was at Klenovoye. Peiper was lodging with a Russian married couple in their hut, the practice of many company commanders in the battalion.[3] Division ordered several weeks of training programmes to get the new intake up to scratch. Exercises at battalion level were carried out with panzers and artillery. At the beginning of May 1943 the Reichsführer-SS visited the Leibstandarte, including our APC battalion.[4] As from 5 May, night exercises and gunnery practice on the terrain increased. On 6 May Peiper was decorated with the German Cross in Gold for his achievements in February. On 16 May, SS-Lt.Col Hugo Kraas assumed command of 2nd SS-Panzer Grenadier Regiment and Albert Frey took over 1st Regiment: both were promoted to full colonel on 21 June.

On 15 June 1943 the former commander of the light infantry gun platoon, No 14 Company, SS-2/Lt Noth, took over No 16 (Infantry Gun) Company, 2nd SS-Panzer Grenadier Regiment and took with him all the 7.5cm guns, vehicles and equipment. To replace this equipment, No 14 Company had a new infantry gun platoon equipped with six Grille ('Crickets'), 15cm infantry guns on a Panzer 38t chassis.

The organisational arrangement was unique. No 14 Company, 2nd SS-Panzer Grenadier Regiment LAH was then the only known example of its kind throughout the entire German Wehrmacht. Officially the APC battalion had no Grille platoon on its authorised strength. In all other panzer and panzer grenadier divisions of the Army and Waffen-SS, Grille were distributed amongst the regimental infantry gun companies of the panzer grenadier regiments to replace towed artillery. The deployment of Grille in the APC battalion resulted from a suggestion by Peiper which had been accepted internally at Division. No order for this special arrangement came down from SS-FHA or

OKH/Army General Staff/Org.Abt, the competent offices.

The regimental infantry gun companies of the two SS-Panzer Grenadier Regimens remained equipped with towed light and heavy weapons until just before the Normandy invasion in 1944. Peiper transferred the newly convalesced SS-2/Lt Otto Bölk from No 12 to No 14 Company, and Bölk picked as his Grille gun captains SS-Ldg.Grenadiers Rudi Rayer, Gerhard Kendzia and myself from the heavy-MG half-platoon of No 12 Company. SS-Sgt Bernd von Bergmann, recently passed out from officer training, became Bölk's deputy.[5] The Grille platoon was trained by Bölk, von Bergmann, SS-Senior Sgt Otto Woelky and SS-Corporal Pierzig from No 16 (Infantry Gun) Company.

The Grille was an imposingly large, heavy 15cm (5.9in) infantry gun (Sfl) 33/1 No L/12 on the Panzer 38(t) chassis. It stood 2.4m high, was 4.61m long, weighed 11.5 tonnes and had a top speed of 35 km/hrs. The Leibstandarte received the Model H (Sd Kfz 138/1). They required a crew of five, the gunlayer had a panoramic telescopic sight 36 at his disposal. The first batch delivered to the APC battalion had radio but the feature was then discontinued. In 1943/44 the sole manufacturer of the Grille was BMM, Prague. Apart from a dark yellow basic colour the guns were delivered without camouflage livery. Later versions delivered elsewhere had a coat of camouflage. In our company they were given a dark yellow and brownish coat with black crosses on the sides but no serial numbers.

The platoon of six Grille represented significant firepower. Peiper had recognised that the heavy 15cm guns on the panzer chassis could follow panzers into battle and provide the APC panzer grenadiers with valuable fire support. In this way Peiper significantly increased the combat power of his APC battalion within the division's armoured group and thus made Guderian's tactics even more effective. Within a short time the Grille commanders were familiarised with the new vehicle and concluded their artillery and driver training. Surprisingly, SS-Corporal Pierzig was retained as a Grille captain after the training finished and so I became gunlayer in Gerhard Kendzia's Grille. Pierzig went later to Hitlerjugend. Another batch of six Grille were received by the heavy company, SS-Panzer Reconnaissance Battalion, LSSAH. No 14 Company also had three tank gun APCs armed with the 7.5cm short-barrelled gun, each commanded by SS-Corporals Duffert, Mewes and Jacobi. These had radio fitted. The platoon leader had only a solo motor-cycle at his disposal initially. The heavy anti-tank group led by

SS-Senior Sgt Jochen Thiele had three APCs with the 2.8cm Panzerbüchse 41 anti-tank gun. The carrier vehicle for this heavy gun was the rare Sd Kfz 250/11. It had a crew of six, weighed 5.53 tonnes, carried 168 rounds for the gun and 1,100 rounds for the MG. The vehicle was 2.135m high, including the gun's protective shield. The anti-tank platoon had three anti-tank guns on APCs. The pioneer platoon was led by SS-Senior Sgt Hafrestroh. Our company commander was SS-2/Lt Erhard Gührs.

I was reunited with a number of my former colleagues from No 12 Company. My new No 14 Company would usually be split up into platoons across the APC companies on operations. We had forty-nine vehicles, with another ten expected. Peiper's adjutant SS-Lt Otto Dinse went on leave at the end of June, his post being taken by SS-2/Lt Werner Wolff from No 11 Company.

In a conference at Fourth Panzer Army, Peiper displayed his grasp of tactics and strategy and his ability to develop a plan at lightning speed, as Gührs recalled:

I was with him at talks on strategy, particularly the situation conference with the Army before the Battle of Kursk. A meeting of about 60 officers. Peiper and I were the only Waffen-SS. When the Army 1a [Chief Operations Staff Officer] had finished giving out his orders and enquired if anybody had anything to add, Peiper asked for the staff, went to the map and designed a new plan which found unanimous approval. It was simply brilliant.[6]

Between 21 and 27 June 1943 exercises were held at company and battalion level. In the APC battalion reveille was at sunrise, so as to allow the men to rest during the midday sun. No extra fuel was made available by Division for exercises and so fuel had to be diverted from authorised purposes. Heavy weapons training suffered most from these shortages. Peiper's APC battalion was to form the division's armoured group in combination with the panzer regiment and 2nd Battalion 1st SS Artillery Regiment equipped with the Wespe and Hummel self-propelled guns. This would therefore be an armoured group in a position tactically to breach the enemy line and defend against attack. It was Guderian's grand idea of the modern panzer army.

In mid-June, the panzer grenadiers of the Leibstandarte were informed of the demands made by the enemies of the German Reich.

Should they win, the Allies would occupy the whole country, organise the mass murder of officers, the deportation of soldiers, the mass sterilisation of men and women, impose US and Soviet government and then divide up the territory. The British merely wanted to put 250,000 officers into concentration camps in the British Empire colonies. These brutal threats were by no means hinted at secretly but were published openly, particularly in the United States, in numerous books and newspaper articles, and were known to millions. Even in Germany, these hate-filled demands of the Americans were assessed and published in German newspapers. In 1941 in the United States Theodore Kaufman wrote *Germany Must Perish!* and in 1943 a book by Louis Nizer and Henry Morgenthau entitled *What to Do with Germany* demanded the dismantling of German industry and the transformation of the country into a soulless agrarian state.[7] The Allies rejected the idea of an armistice or partial capitulation and demanded nothing but total capitulation to them all simultaneously.[8] Day by day and night by night their aircraft bombed German cities, eradicating residential areas, destroying factories, roads and railways. The toll of civilian casualties inflicted in this new form of terrorist warfare mounted steadily. Thus the Germans had long known that their only chance of survival lay in the fanatical fight to the finish and the concentrating of all their forces.

During our carefree interlude at Klenovoye the Battalion held a sports festival which all enjoyed. In these activities Peiper's men often got wet unexpectedly, for example in obstacle races in which the watery regions had to be crossed with amphibious vehicles. There was a football tournament in which the players had to wear disguise. The referee took a strict line from the outset and wore a steel helmet: I was behind our goal and lobbed a smoke candle into the penalty area when our opponents looked likely to score.

The relationship with the inhabitants in and around Klenovoye was excellent. The local women did the men's laundry in exchange for food. Battalion surgeon Dr Brüstle accepted Ukrainians as well as our own men as patients. Meanwhile the coming operation loomed ever nearer and the men suspected that our peaceful sojourn in Klenovoye was not going to last much longer.

On 29 June 1943 my company commander Gührs wrote in his diary:

1030 hrs commanders' conference. It is beginning. X-Day is secret. The organisation of my Company is very difficult. As a Company it is far too big. I have 49 vehicles and need another ten, plus three Sfl anti-tank vehicles also said to be on the way. A giant fighting force. I left the conference at midday fairly satisfied. With every reason. I shall be leading the Company in the operation. This operational order will unleash a fearful lot . . . the Grille will exercise their guns tomorrow . . . the commanding officer will arrive in the evening . . . Jochen Thiele [senior sergeant and anti-tank commander] is back from leave. He speaks of high morale in the Homeland.

30 June 1943. Gunnery with Grille satisfactory . . . then commanders' conference. We move out tonight. At 1400 hrs I addressed the Company on the operation. Platoon leaders' conference. At 1800 hrs I dined with the platoon leaders and Company troop leaders . . . The Commander rang me. Departure is put back until tomorrow morning early. Our hosts are pleased we are not leaving yet. It is touching.

On 30 June 1943 all Battalion and Regimental commanders assembled in Sepp Dietrich's divisional headquarters to receive their orders for the coming offensive. Even here he did not forget to remind his officers 'to bring his men back safe and sound'.[9] The divisional commander in the coming operation was SS-Brigadier Theodor Wisch. On 1 July 1943 SS-Lt Georg Preuss was awarded the Iron Cross First Class for his past service as platoon leader in No 13 Company.

Chapter Seven

Operation Citadel – the Kursk Offensive

On 1 July 1943 Peiper's APC battalion was attached to the armoured group as a tactical measure. This marked the first appearance of the tactical concept of the 'armoured group'. According to Guderian's principles of panzer tactics, the panzers in the panzer divisions, panzer grenadiers in APCs, self-propelled panzer artillery, panzer reconnaissance forces and panzer pioneers should be grouped together under the leadership of an experienced commander in every division so as to achieve the greatest possible firepower, mobility and fighting ability. These armoured groups were pure panzer formations in which panzer grenadiers could excel within operational principles. Wherever these armoured battle groups were deployed, they had success to the last day of the war. The Leibstandarte armoured group fought in various sizes to the end.

At the beginning of the Kursk offensive, the Leibstandarte armoured group consisted of the APC battalion, 2nd Battalion 1st SS-Panzer Regiment, one company of the anti-tank battalion, 2nd Battalion SS Artillery Regiment and No 6 Company SS Flak Battalion. The commander of No 14 Company observed: 'We moved out at 0500 hrs. My fighting force is large, eighteen panzers. The torrential rain last night has ceased, the Rollbahn is still fairly soft. Two panzers stayed behind. Otherwise, luck accompanied us to Korusha where we have been since nightfall. During the night we shall make our next leap forward.'

The APC battalion reached the new area in the early hours of 2 July 1943. At midday Peiper held a situation conference in which he revealed the final details of the impending attack. The men slept in tents. On 3 July in glorious weather the battalion had a rapidly-organised feast, a sign of the good morale in Peiper's unit that the men could eat so heartily just before a major offensive.[1]

Attacking on the Eastern Front called for forces greater than Germany

69

had available in the spring of 1943, compelling Hitler to go on the defensive. After the capture of Byelgorod, Army Group Centre could no longer extend as far as the left flank of Army Group South west of Byelgorod. This opened a rent in the front 200kms long and 120kms deep to the west. It was the purpose of Operation Citadel to close the gap. Strong forces of Army group Centre would head south and meet up with parts of Army Group South heading north. II SS-Panzer Corps of Fourth Panzer Army with Army Group South stood ready to advance to the north. Considering the options open to him in his defensive policy, Hitler concluded that a limited offensive aimed at destroying strong enemy forces, thereby shortening our lines and strengthening them with reserves, was the best answer. This would immediately deprive the enemy of the opportunity for a decisive offensive in 1943. It was planned originally to launch the operations against the Kursk salient by mid-May 1943 at the latest, but the date was repeatedly postponed because of delays in the delivery of armaments, among other reasons.

The Leibstandarte was part of Hausser's II SS-Panzer Corps in Lt-General Hoth's Fourth Panzer Army. Because the new 1st Battalion of the Panzer Regiment was still in the process of conversion to a Panther battalion in Germany, the Leibstandarte Panzer Regiment during the Kursk offensive consisted of only the three companies of 2nd Battalion plus No 13 Tiger Company and No 14 (Pioneer) Company. The SP-gun battalion, the three batteries of which had just received one platoon each of 10.5cm assault howitzers, and the anti-tank battalion were also available. On 2 July 1943 the Division had eleven Tigers, seventy-two Mk IVs, sixteen Mk II and IIIs and thirty-one SP-guns operational. Many of their units had already moved up on 1 July while the armoured group (APC battalion, Panzer Regiment, 2nd (Armoured) SS Artillery Regiment and No 6 Company Flak Battalion) reached the readiness area on the night of 4 July 1943.

Over the preceding weeks the Soviets had not been idle, knew what the Germans proposed to do and had taken defensive measures accordingly. Here alone they had dug 9,240km of trenches. Eight defensive strips and lines lay over a depth of 300km. Never before had a territory been militarised in such a manner, and so built up with trenches, bunkers, field positions, anti-tank nests, whole anti-tank-fronts and observation posts. The Soviets had paid special attention to an effective anti-tank defence. Every Red rifle company had its teams lurking with petrol bombs, hand grenades and limpet mines ready for the Tigers in particular. Besides the new anti-tank guns they had the 5.7cm anti-tank gun, anti-aircraft guns, Stalin Organs [multiple rocket-launchers], tanks and SP-guns built especially for anti-panzer work, some of which would be buried up to the turret. About 1,500 anti-tank mines lay around the Kursk salient to a breadth of 1km. The 81st Rifle Division alone had buried 2,133 anti-tank mines and 2,126 anti-personnel mines in its sector.[2] Strong reserves of tanks and artillery stood ready. German reconnaissance had reported 212 enemy tanks facing the Leibstandarte's line of advance on 3 July 1943.

Enemy advanced sentries were to be wiped out at 2300 hrs on 4 July 1943. The divisional order read:

. . . The depth of the enemy defensive zone and the narrow corridor for our advance dictate fighting from depth. The incursion itself will be made by assault troops immediately after artillery and Stuka preparation. Fire protection by Tigers and SP-guns. Artillery preparation from Y+15 to Y+65 (0315-0405 hrs). Increased artillery bombardment from Y+60 to Y+65 (0400 to 0405 hrs). Stuka attack on point 220.5 from Y+50. Last bomb to fall Y+65 . . .

(e) Armoured group LAH (planned structure: Panzer Regiment – without Tiger Company and without No 1 Company, 3rd Battalion, 2nd SS-Panzer Grenadier Regiment, one company anti-tank battalion, 2nd Battalion Artillery Regiment, No 6 (Light) Company Flak Battalion) will hold itself in readiness, after the anti-tank strong-holds east of Bykovka have been removed, to break through east of Jakovlevo to the north-east to establish a bridgehead over the Psell.[3]

It had been agreed with VIII Air Corps that they would support the attack operating from the strongpoint at II.SS-Panzer Corps. Regarding the mood prevailing at Leibstandarte immediately before the attack Gührs wrote on 4 July:

This morning at 0900 hrs operational conference with Lt-Col Schönberger. Then conference with commander [i.e. Peiper] . . . I have updated my maps and informed the platoon leaders of the order to Company for readiness and about the attack. The fever of the hunt is slowly gripping me. Will we pull it off as planned? We must brace ourselves. May fortune accompany us . . . When one gives his thoughts free rein on the eve of battle, one uncovers a variety of emotions. I have personally a very sure feeling. All around the general enthusiasm is growing. The tank-gun platoon is singing military songs. The infantry-gun platoon is calibrating its MGs. We are scheduled to set off at 2100 hrs . . . the Homeland will soon learn that we remain strong. We are all happy to be present for it. And I am glad!

All knew the significance of the great offensive beginning on the morrow. Tension gripped every panzer grenadier. All knew that in the way of things, tomorrow would be the last day in the lives of many of them.

The Russian advanced sentries were taken out around midnight on 4 July in hard close-quarters combat. Peiper stood by impatiently. His adjutant SS-2/Lt Werner Wolff wrote a letter to his girlfriend Helga in their home town of Memel in East Prussia:

At this point I have the last chance to write to you before the attack. My thoughts are constantly with you. The Russian artillery is firing at us but it does not worry me much. I must shut off my thoughts of you now. This is not a letter in parting, only a dear, dear greeting. In an hour we shall set off. I know it is going to be a hard and difficult battle, but we are confident. The enemy will be defeated. Today I understand much more about the purpose of the battle. I see a runner near me holding the picture of his girl in his hands; it is not difficult to guess that very many must be thinking of their loved ones at home. That binds us all the more firmly together. Even I cannot think coldly and soberly yet. I think of and believe in Germany – and you. I would like to kiss you again – I shall do so mentally. I cannot see my star, the skies are too cloudy. Even so our thoughts will meet. Mine should not upset you, you have nice dreams of me and the passion of my thoughts would shock you. Please forgive my poor handwriting; it is still very dark and I can hardly read it myself. When shall I hear from you, have something to read next I do not know. Probably not for some weeks. Farewell, Helga. Your Wolf.[4]

On 5 July 1943 at 0405 hrs the two SS-Panzer Grenadier Regiments of the Leibstandarte set out. Before them lay 25kms of mined terrain strewn with barbed wire entanglements, subterranean bunkers and trenches. 2nd Regiment under SS-Lt.Colonel Hugo Kraas reached the anti-tank ditch below Hill 220.5, as did 1st Battalion of 1st Regiment. After having dug in because of the heavy shelling from the west bank of the Worskla, 2nd Regiment moved out once pioneers had laid bridges across the anti-tank ditch and, supported by Tigers and SP-guns, took Hill 220.5 after a five-hour battle. At midday 2nd Regiment took Hill 217.1 about 800m north-east of it, from where they gave support to 1st SS-Panzer Grenadier Regiment and, half an hour later, occupied Hill 215.4, 2.5kms south of Bykovka. After 1st SS-Panzer Grenadier Regiment (Frey) attacking to the north right of where 2nd Regiment had crossed the tank ditch, it drew up alongside 2nd Regiment and they entered Bykovka together.[5]

Peiper meanwhile was still kicking his heels awaiting orders for his battalion. Not until 1430 hrs did the order come for the armoured group to advance through the enemy positions east of Jakovlevo and set up a bridgehead over the Psell. At 1800 hrs the panzers and APCs rolled over the forward line at point 234.8, but at daybreak near Jakovlevo came across an anti-tank front, at which point Division ordered a halt. Gührs, my company commander, wrote of this first day:

It was eleven o'clock and hot. We were still in the readiness area awaiting our moment. I had camouflaged my company relatively satisfactorily in a small wood. I was happy with it. I had never previously known such a major effort by the Russian air force. The battle had been raging since 0300 hrs. Then it all died down. The infantry seemed to have made inroads. The shelling of our readiness area ceased.

We have seven wounded in the Battalion, Captain Wandt has a light head wound . . . we hoped our airmen would soon have superiority. The Führer issued a call to his soldiers regarding this offensive. At 1400 hrs our time arrived. The armoured group moved out. We crossed our own frontline. The infantry had thrown down the first barriers in the bitter battle. The Russians defended with flame-throwers. An anti-tank front has often bogged down a whole battalion. Our panzers suffered some losses to mines. SS-Captain Kling's three Tigers broke through the Russian forward lines. As we followed up, the first sector had already been crushed. Our first casualties fell to shelling on the approach route. At 1800 hrs we set off with the panzers through fields of corn, valleys and over uplands. It was almost dark when we ran up against the Russian second line. The forward panzers received heavy anti-tank fire and our scattered vehicles came under much shelling. We stopped. Russian tanks ahead. Dig in for the night, came the order.

I lined up the company behind me. Buhr shared my trench. Peiper told us the situation. Possibly we may have to reckon with a Russian tank counter-attack. Not so nice. I had just stretched out in my trench when the first aircraft arrived. Machine-gunning and bombing. The same old stuff. Difficult to get used to it again though. Then they came again. The skies were full of parachute flares.

The division rolled. Panzer Mk IVs, Tigers, SP-guns, APCs, Grilles, self-propelled artillery, anti-tank vehicles, amphibious vehicles and Kübelwagen made up our steel fist spewing steel. In my Grille I received a wound to my right hand from a splinter but did not seek medical attention. This mobile warfare demands lightning-fast decisions and the equally rapid reaction to a thousand dangers arising. If an APC were hit, those who were able baled out and sought cover. After that the attack continued. The blood of many men flowed that day. Night fell. My crew and I slept in our Grille. During the night it rained for two hours. In the darkness the anti-tank guns, flak, the reconnaissance battalion and panzer grenadiers formed an all-round defence ('hedgehog') ahead. At 0500 hrs on 6 July 'the Russians fired with artillery and tanks on our advance. Finally the Stukas came to help us,' Gührs said.

Frey's 1st SS-Panzer Grenadier Regiment attacked Hill 243.2 east of Jakovlevo and captured the mined and wired position at 0945 hrs. By 1330 hrs 1st Regiment had taken Hill 230.5 in close combat and created the basis for the operations of the armoured group. SS-Brigadier Wisch led the attack of the armoured group personally through Lutshki North, Teterevino on the Psell sector. At 1315 hrs and 1400 hrs Russian tanks attacked 1st SS-Panzer Grenadier Regiment and 1st Battalion, 2nd Regiment respectively east of Jakovlevo. The first of these two attacks came up against the LAH armoured group: after losing eight tanks the Russians backed off. SS-Captain Heinz Kling, commanding the Tiger company, saw his chance at once and '. . . set off in immediate pursuit of the enemy, and without regard to his personal safety as leader of the armoured group captured the high ground west of Prochorovka. This brought our spearheads 60 to 70kms deep into enemy territory. In these two days, his Company destroyed fifty T-34s, a KvI and KvII, also forty-three anti-tank guns of medium and heavy calibre.'[6]

The APC battalion reached the hill 2km south-west of Teterevino, from where we advanced to the high ground north of it. For my participation in this attack on Teterevino on 6 July 1943 I was awarded my 29th Close-combat Day. Gührs described it thus:

We were confronted by a strongpoint high up. Over midday the infantry attacked and captured it. Hats off to the infantry! We suffered casualties to artillery and tanks. Schellhorn fell. Good old Mewes was wounded, six wounded in all. A great pity. We have not even had what you might call a proper attack yet. In the afternoon the Russians tried to take back what they had lost. A tank brigade attacked us on the flank. Our panzers took up the challenge. The first tank battle for the Leibstandarte. I watched it from the ridge. It was really something!

We came around the ridge with the battalion and prepared for a fresh attack to the north-east. Elements of the panzer and recon-naissance units were already on their way there. Then we set off at full speed for the north. We were flanked left and right. Could we still reach the Psell? Keep going, keep on going. Alongside panzers and reconnaissance panzers we made a broad front. Then suddenly we hit trouble. Mines scattered on the road and in the terrain anti-tank and tanks behind a tank ditch higher up. Four panzers hit mines. The APC of the Stuka liaison officer went up in flames. No, we could not do it. It was too dark anyway. Teterevino at least was still in our hands. Would we be able to stay here? They would have to be strong on our flanks. We secured for the night. I spent the late evening at the Battalion command post. I went to sleep at midnight.

At 0130 hrs a telephone call from No 12 Company. Lt Preuss was looking at six Russian tanks. More in front of No 13 Company. Will the Russians force us out? Funny, hardly anybody was excited. We took to our weapons. The battle lasted into the early morning. The Russians got a pasting. They lost five of their sixteen T-34s. Six Russians defected. They reported being members of an armoured corps which came down from Moscow on 5 July. The last reserves already? . . .

In the night there was a crazy incident. Three Russian tanks drove through our position, infantry sitting on the hulls. Hussar bravado. One of Kling's Tigers was protecting the road in the dark. He reported destroying three tanks at a range of ten metres.

The Leibstandarte occupied the line Teterevino North (APC battalion)–Lutchki North–Pokrovka East–2kms west of Ulyanoff. On 7 July 1943 1st SS-Panzer Grenadier Regiment took Pokrovka and Jakovlevo and also prevailed in fierce defensive fighting against Soviet tanks coming from Oboyan. The Luftwaffe provided Stuka and bomber support. At

Lutchki too, several Soviet tank attacks were repulsed. At 0600 hrs, after Stuka attacks on the Rollbahn at Teterevino, the APC battalion, the Leibstandarte armoured group and the armoured group of Das Reich Division headed for Prochorovka. At 0710 hrs Soviet tanks came up from the north and north-east, and an engagement ensued until midday. Then the Russians made off from whence they came.

Gührs wrote:

It is impossible to describe all what went on. We shot down a reconnaissance aircraft. This happened at least ten times a day. It became routine. The Russians had cut us off. Nobody got excited about it. We felt very superior to them. On the ridge to the right of us Major Tychsen [commanding officer 2nd Battalion SS-Panzer Grenadier Regiment Das Reich] became embroiled in a scrap with Russian tanks and destroyed thirty-five of them.

Today I washed myself for the first time in five days. I explained the situation to the section leaders. We would remain here today. I hid the company in a nearby fruit plantation. It was awfully hot. No 11 Company had seventeen casualties from a bombing raid. At about 1600 hrs one of our reconnaissance aircraft reported thirty-five tanks behind the ridge preparing to attack. We were sitting with Peiper and SS-Major Gross. Gross attacked at once with his panzers and destroyed sixteen tanks without loss to ourselves. At 2200 hrs commanders' conference. We are to attack again early tomorrow, towards the west. Large tank units are on the flank, which we have to destroy.[7]

The LSSAH occupied the line Lutchki North–Jablotshki–Bol Majatshki–Pokrovka. It had destroyed seventy-five tanks, twenty-three guns and twelve aircraft. Over the previous three days the Leibstandarte had destroyed a total of 123 tanks, thirty-seven guns and twelve aircraft. Massed Russian tanks were threatening the flanks of II SS-Panzer Corps. Accordingly Fourth Panzer Army had decided to launch an attack with all its forces against the enemy to the north.

On 8 July 1943 the Leibstandarte armoured group set off to the north-west at 0800 hrs. Before Wessely at 0920 hrs the group came across at least forty enemy tanks. The battle lasted an hour. After regrouping the armoured group headed west at 1100 hrs to recommence the battle for Wessely at 1205 hrs. Gührs wrote of it:

Preparation and attack. It was midday before it really started. War correspondent King was with me. We were the second wave behind the panzers. We took the first village but it got difficult around Rylskiy and Wessely. Dug-in tanks, anti-tank guns, infantry etc. This is a charming war. I will describe the situation. I could not make progress ahead. To the left there were Russians. To the right was the original direction of attack, now blocked by Russians. Five kilometres behind us, that is to say the village from where we had set out, the Russians had arrived with 35 tanks. Poor infantry. Peiper was behind the ridge the other side of the panzers . . . To our rear the situation resolved itself. Two Tigers had remained behind at Teterevino with damaged tracks. They annihilated all enemy tanks which broke into the town. This is easy to write but was an incredible achievement.

Peiper took command of the battle group and ordered an immediate attack on Rylskiy with a mixed formation of panzers and panzer grenadiers. Now the panzers would see how panzer grenadiers are accustomed to attack! We rattled off ahead of the panzers at an unheard of rate. Peiper's voice in the headphones: 'Go, Gührs, go! Wandt [commander, No 13 Company], Go! Keep up!' and so on. It was a crazy ride. I urged my men to hurtle forward. Our strength lay in speed. We had to use it to the full. My Company kept going magnificently. The anti-tank gun APCs were now close behind me. Wandt was at my left.

Another 800m to the village. The enemy fire was becoming ever fiercer, explosions to the left and right of us, ahead and behind. I was wearing the headphones and giving orders through the microphone. Thus I could hear nothing. Left of me smoke was being laid. The swathes drifted over us. Only another 500m. Surely we should make it now. Then two Russian tanks came through the smoke firing wildly. I made smoke myself and gave the order to pull back. 300m to the rear was a small depression. This gave us some cover. The lieutenant commanding the smoke battery received a direct hit in his APC. All dead. I moved up attempting to give cover to the right. No 11 Company (Guhl) did the same to the left. Our panzers were still well back. They could not match our speed.

My Grilles drove up to form a firing front as I roared over the ridge. Suddenly I saw 17 tanks ahead at 1,500m. One opened fire but missed. I ordered my artillery to engage them. Six Grille guns are murderous. As it got dark I disengaged and tried to speak to the commander by radio. I turned left for better reception but could not maintain any type of conversation. Finally Preuss [No 12 Company] cut in. I had him indicate his position by starshell.

The prisoners told us there had been 80 tanks in the nest. These had bolted when faced by a few grenadiers. A Tiger destroyed 14 which had appeared before a village during the course of the battle. God, it was hot when I reported to Peiper at 2000 hrs. It was raining again. We were all pleased with our success. At 2100 hrs we rolled back. I led. We spent the night at Lutshki North.

In the battle against the anti-tank front reinforced by tanks, the Tiger company had distinguished itself again. Kling on the flank with four Tigers destroyed several dug-in enemy tanks. With elements of the APC battalion he came up on the enemy from the rear, forcing their withdrawal. The Tigers destroyed forty-five tanks that day.[8] That 8 July 1943 my untreated hand wound of the 5th got worse, and at the dressing station they kept me in until the 10th.

SS-Captain Guhl captured thirty-one enemy tanks. A total of eighty-two tanks was destroyed by the Leibstandarte. Because supply to the armoured group was being constantly interrupted by enemy tanks, it received orders to withdraw to the security region of Division. On 9 July the armoured group was to remain behind our main front line. That day the APC battalion rested at Lutchki.[9] The 1st SS-Panzer Grenadier Regiment reached Rylskiy without a fight. The commanding officer of 2nd SS-Panzer Grenadier Regiment, SS-Lt-Colonel Hugo Kraas, wrote: 'The enemy knows what he is up against and is gambling all on one card; he is hurling himself at us with diabolical intensity! A large-scale tank battle is in the offing; it seems as if each new phase of our operation brings an escalation. With the amassing of all our forces we shall achieve the sheer impossible!'[10]

The previous days had shown that panzer grenadiers aboard the APCs in combination with the tanks of the panzer regiment could bring successes. The officers of all weapons branches had been won over to this new tactic of the division's armoured group. Furthermore the possibility of tight control of the formations by radio had been quickly recognised. The Panzer Arm now had the vehicles at last it needed to complete the set, so to speak, and recognised in the panzer grenadiers the worthy colleagues to follow them at the same rate of speed in the most difficult terrain. The very close cooperation strengthened their mutual trust. The necessary rapid liaison on the battlefield could be maintained by radio and runner. The precondition for the direction of large formations of panzer grenadiers was wide-ranging, forward-looking thinking, decisiveness and the ability to convey a decision in a short, rapidly-transmitted radio order. Peiper was master of this. In encounters with enemy armour, the superiority of panzers and grenadiers conveyed in APCs was obvious.

On 10 July 1943, despite not having full use of two fingers on my wounded right hand, I got into Kendzia's Grille again as gunlayer. At 1045 hrs the Leibstandarte set off with 2nd SS-Panzer Grenadier Regiment. The men of the APC battalion had been sat at Teterevino waiting to head north after the breakthrough was achieved. Objective was the eastern side of Prochorovka. After a tough fight the attack gained ground although 1st and 2nd Battalions 2nd SS-Panzer Grenadier Regiment were held up by artillery fire from the heights north of the Psell. 2nd Battalion took Hill 241.6 with Tiger and SP-gun support. The Russians had reinforced it with dug-in tanks. Peiper's adjutant Werner Wolff destroyed a T-34 in close combat: his staff officer SS-2/Lt Günther Hülsen was killed. At his own request the administrative officer, SS-Captain Herbert Molt, replaced Hülsen.

The six Grilles proved their worth in these encounters. They rolled immediately behind the APC battalion. Their 15cm guns took out many Russian field and artillery positions, anti-tank guns and bunkers. It was originally planned that the fire direction post for the Grille platoon would be aboard the platoon officer's APC, but in practice the platoon officer, SS-2/Lt Otto Bölk, rode aboard one of the Grilles.[11] Because the gun captains came from the heavy MG platoon of No 12 Company, they were expert at indirect shooting. They had no rangefinder of the type available to heavy MG and mortar teams. We gunners had to use thumb and forefinger to lay the gun and fire. Therefore the chances of hitting were not so good unless one had a fairly good eye for distance. Even so, a man with poor ability in this regard could still get quite close. I always took pains to carry as much ammunition as possible on my Grille so as to have the best chance of surviving any prolonged battle which might arise. To my right, near the loader, were the shell racks; facing ahead to the right near the radio unit were shells and more shells on the floor plates under a tarpaulin. The Panzer 38(t) carried AP and anti-tank shells. Every Grille also had a 30cm shell for penetrating thick bunker walls. These large-calibre shells were produced from July 1942 to increase hitting power. The head contained 54 kilos of explosive. With a muzzle velocity of 105m/sec they had a maximum range of 1050m. The later HL-shell 39 weighing 24.6kg could penetrate 16cms of steel. They looked like an oversize stick grenade with stabilising fins. I fired one at a Russian position once. I declined to carry other types, also known as 'anti-concrete shells' because it was strenuous work and also dangerous having to get out of the Grille during a battle to load one into the barrel from the outside.

On 11 July 1943, 1st and 2nd Battalions 2nd SS-Panzer Grenadier Regiment set out over difficult terrain to attack Prochorovka. After softening up by Stukas, at 0905 hrs 2nd SS-Panzer Grenadier Regiment and the Reconnaissance Battalion attacked, enabling 2nd Battalion to capture the northern side of Hill 252.2 in close combat with Tigers and SP-guns supporting. A section of the anti-tank ditch was captured by SS-Captain Becker's 1st Battalion: pioneers put up bridges. At 1015 hrs Peiper's battalion with the armoured group received orders to move out, crossed the ditch at 1230 hrs and attacked the southern part of Hill 252.2. After heavy fighting the armoured group captured 252.2 close to Swch.Oktyabrsky. Peiper's entire battalion was involved in close combat there.[12] For my participation on 11 July 1943 on Hill 252.2 I was awarded my 30th Close-combat Day.

The Stuka direction officer accompanied the attack in Peiper's APC, as during the Stuka attack on Swch.Oktyabrsky a bomb hit his own APC, destroying it and killing the crew. Three Tigers assisted the attack on the height west of Prochorovka by destroying twenty-eight anti-tank and six field guns.[13] Restricted by the lack of protection on the flanks, the armoured group stopped before the enemy at 1450 hrs. The Leibstandarte, whose neighbouring divisions had not come up, was left alone along the line Storoshevoye West – eastern end of the wood to the north of the village – north-west of 252.2 – the height west of Swch.Oktyabrsky – east side of Hill 252.2.

SS-Grenadier Erich Schöbel of Guhl's No 11 Company described his own experience of the battle thus:

Towards midday on 11 July 1943 there was torrential rain. We attacked but were brought to a standstill because the enemy was too strong. The pioneers had to clear mines the Russians had laid. Then our APC commanded by Corporal Willi Bott was hit by an anti-tank round which came through the hatch. Bott was fatally wounded in the lungs. We baled out. I – co-driver/radio operator – was hit in the chest with serious blood loss. I reported the fact to my officer Guhl. He radioed back: 'If Schöbel can still drive, APC back to supply with Corporal Bott and the wounded.' I did as ordered and then reported to the main dressing station.[14]

SS-Captain Guhl himself was wounded in the thigh by a shell splinter. After Dr Breme at the APC battalion's temporary dressing station had drawn out the splinter and let the wound cool, he was back at Company next day. SS-Lt Preuss, commander No 12 Company, was shot through the neck and was taken to the corps military hospital at Kharkov.

I had been with my Grille near the anti-tank ditch. Some rocket launchers fired their fiery-tailed missiles towards the Russians who reacted with heavy artillery fire on the Grilles' sector. SS-Sgt Bernd von Bergmann, deputy commander of the Grille platoon, and company runner SS-Ldg Grenadier Schwanke were wounded, while Grille gun captain SS-Corporal Bachmann was killed. SS-Captain Dr Brüstle, battalion surgeon, was also wounded but remained with the men. SS-Captain Herbert Molt, a replacement staff officer, was killed on a motorcycle journey. On the evening of 11 July 1943, war correspondent Dr Herbert Schgramm wrote the following draft for a magazine article about Peiper's battalion:

Seven days attacking. Seven days close combat for every field position, every trench, every tank ditch, for the whole deeply staggered system of fortification that the Soviets had laid around the threatening armoured fist of Kursk. Seven days of broiling heat and downpours, of howling, whistling iron, ceaselessly interspersed by endless diving waves of Stukas and the whistling passage of predatory fighters, the steady rumbling of panzer motors and tracks, angrily humming and clanking, the hammering of machine-guns, the bark of all calibres of flak, the roar of orders and the cries of the wounded and dying.

Seven nights, summer soft or streaming with rain, aflame in the artillery barrages of the Soviets and the bombing by their 'flying sewing machines', diligently searching for our supply units and reserves in the crammed woods. In those seven days and nights there were minutes longer than hours and yet it seemed as though the attack had begun only yesterday. The assault on 'Red Height', the battle for the second tank ditch, the advance to the Rollbahn, close combat with the T-34, the great tank cemetery at Rutshny Wood and the four hours yesterday afternoon when our APCs were under heavy shellfire and the panzers near us did not receive the order to return fire – all these experiences compact themselves in the memory as if they were not spread across seven days but were lived in just one. Only the key phrases in my calendar, the names of villages and battles, commanders, officers and men bring chronological order once more to the events.

It is now the evening of 11 July. Between the Soviet field positions captured today the APCs of the fast battalion stand regularly spaced and the men are pleased that tonight there are no trenches to be dug, that they can sleep the night in Russian-dug trenches and bunkers. None of them is really happy, however. Least of all the battalion commander, wandering in irritation between the trenches and holes. The day was a disappointment for him. Precisely now, when the defensive system had been broken and the way ahead lay free, his hour had come, the hour for the roaring pursuit of the enemy, through the enemy. And then the Halt from above! The hours under artillery barrage, the ordered silence of the accompanying panzers, which are not allowed to fire even at recognised targets. 'Short steps!' they said. 'You are too far forward, wait for the neighbouring divisions!'

Even we had been looking forward to driving out with Battalion Peiper on one of his famous attacks and we understood his disappointment, the disappointment of his battalion. For it is utterly and completely his battalion, proud of its special weapon and proud of the tasks it has been set. But this war in the East is not one in which officers and men are offered few opportunities to prove themselves. Who knows what tomorrow will bring?

Meanwhile the panzer grenadiers search the trenches, here and there hauling out a Bolshevist, who has stayed behind deliberately and now raises his hands with a sheepish grin. In a trench they find a fallen Commissar whom we lay on the slope so as not to have to keep stepping over him. Between the specks of blood on his battle blouse the red enamel of the Order of Lenin shines. Captured submachine guns and automatic rifles are thrown on the heap. We have a long Russian anti-tank gun for each of our crew transport lorries. In the darkness the rugged field kitchen comes up and after all the recent rain a spoonful of soup makes one feel good. The sentries have been posted – we shall be sleeping with the men of the Company troop in a small, primitive bunker, but it is too early yet to turn in. The earth has absorbed the day's downpours and the herbs of the wild fallow land waft exuberantly the aroma of thyme, peppermint and camomile. The lungs open greedily after all the evil vapours and smoke of the day. Slowly the sounds of battle fade and we settle down to sleep. My pistol to the left. Submachine gun to the right and my steel helmet as a pillow. In vain a bed-bug, enjoying my wrist, tries to disturb me and fails. Through my dreams the day's events traipse silently.[15]

In the evening of 11 July 1943 I discovered that the gunsight of my Grille was defective. It was too dark to repair the damage.

Chapter Eight

12 July 1943 – The Death Ride of the Soviet Tanks at Prochorovka

On 12 July 1943 it was planned that the armoured group of 2nd SS-Panzer Grenadier Regiment and the Reconnaissance Battalion would occupy Prochorovka and Hill 252.4 after taking out the threat on the flanks at the Psell river together with Totenkopf Division. July 12th 1943 was to go down in history as the day of the tank battle of Prochorovka. It was the greatest tank battle in history. Early that morning, 150 Soviet tanks broke through our front line and headed at speed for Peiper's APC battalion on Hill 252.2 south of Prochorovka, and for 1st SS-Panzer Grenadier Regiment at Swch Stalinsk.

Near Prochorovka I was one of those surprised by the waltz of the T-34s. My company commander SS-2/Lt Erhard Gührs wrote of it:

The previous night we had taken a hill [252.2] and ejected the Russians from their defensive positions. We occupied their holes and trench system. Sentries were posted. They attacked at 0700 hrs. The Russians had 148 tanks spread out over a kilometre in front of our sector. Nearly all of us were asleep when suddenly here were aircraft and a huge mass of tanks with infantry sitting on the hulls. It was hell. They were around us, over us and between us. We fought man to man. Jumping out of our holes we fetched the limpet charges from our APCs, jumped back in and waited for the moment to attack every enemy we could. The battle lasted only two hours. By 0900 hrs we had the battlefield firmly under control. My company alone had destroyed fifteen Russian tanks.[1]

The six Grilles were near the anti-tank ditch that morning. The pack of Soviet tanks roared towards us, tank and artillery shells exploding in the earth all around. I noticed two T-34s, stationary and firing from a farmyard. And my gunsight not working! But there was no time, we all wanted to survive. The two T-34s would not stay long after spotting the Grille. I had to fire two straddling rounds, one long, one short and the third might hit. I tried it, was lucky in my estimation of distance and destroyed both tanks at a range between 1,100 and 1,200m. SS-2/Lt Otto Bölk, Grille platoon commander, was hit below the collar bone by a chunk of shrapnel the size of a fist. I drove him to the main dressing station but in vain, for Bölk, who had been my platoon leader since the autumn of 1941, died three days later in the Corps military hospital at Kharkov. After leaving the dressing station I went to the workshops.

During the Soviet offensive, SS-Sgt Rudi Vieten took command of the Grille platoon. My company colleagues SS-Leading Grenadiers Erich Jost and Günther Vogel of the anti-tank group each destroyed an enemy tank in close combat. My company destroyed fifteen in all. SS-2/Lt Gührs tried to describe the inferno of the battle: 'The mental pressure threatened to tear me apart. One can tolerate the most terrible things . . . no Russian tank survived. 148 of them lay mangled and crushed on the battlefield. We were superior . . . but it was a victory bought at a price. I found little Polanski dead in the trench, 2/Lt Bölk mortally wounded. I do not want to list them all.'[2]

The commander of the last tank-gun APC, SS-Corporal Hannes Duffert of No 14 Company and SS-2/Lt Rudi Wetzel of No 11 Company both fell, and many others. SS-Ldg Grenadier Johannes Bräuer, driver of SS-Corporal Fröbel's mortar APC in No 11 Company remembered:

I had been around since the beginning of the war in Soviet Russia, from Zhitomir to Rostov, but never had I experienced anything like the hell of Prochorovka. It all happened within such a short space of time that one hardly knew what to make of it. In a flash we were wedged in by T-34s, firing in all directions, ramming each other because so many of them were exploding and burning. We had limpet mines but no Panzerfäuste [shoulder-fired rocket launchers], and T-34s kept coming over the ridge, racing down the slope through our readiness position and then tumbling over and over in the anti-tank ditch. It must have been 0900 when I was hit by splinters in my left eye and lung and given a dressing by Captain Brüstle. I was unable to see and how I got out of that inferno remains a mystery to me to this day.[3]

Peiper was equally surprised by the mass incursion of Soviet tanks. In the midst of the deafening detonations of anti-tank and high explosive shells, the hell of exploding tanks, burning APCs and shouting Germans and Soviets, Peiper showed himself to be the champion of the battalion: he was a panzer grenadier just like his men. As a Russian tank clanked and rattled past nearby, Peiper ran ducked down towards it, jumped aboard at a favourable moment, clambered on the turret, pulled open the hatch and threw a bundle of hand-grenades inside. No sooner had he jumped off than a dull explosion shook the T-34.[4]

His adjutant Werner Wolff lay with an MG in the foremost line, firing at the advancing Red infantry. He took over command of No 13 Company when Wandt was wounded, and led it against the waves of onrushing Soviet tanks with such steadfastness that Peiper recommended him at once for the Knight's Cross for his bravery:

On 12 July 1943 our battalion lay in reserve on the slope south of Prochorovka on Hill 252.2 The Russians surprised us by coming through our lines with about 150 tanks, carrying infantry on the hulls and with infantry following behind, firing with all barrels between the APCs, whose panzer grenadiers were in trenches and foxholes. The hour of his greatest trial had arrived for Wolff. With great energy and on his own initiative he took command of a Company whose men were leaderless due to its commander having become a casualty, organised immediately a defensive front, placed anti-tank teams in position and retrieved from burning and exploding APCs, at the greatest risk to his person, weapons and ammunition. This fulfilled the preconditions for holding out to the end. Wolff destroyed a T-34 in close combat and in hand-to-hand combat with the enemy commanding general killed the man with the latter's own dagger. When in the evening of that hot day an entire enemy armoured corps had been totally wiped out and the old front line restored in a counter-attack, the success was most closely linked to the person of SS-2/Lt Wolff. Through his responsible action, he proved himself a shining example and to have crisis-proof leadership skills.[5]

SS-Lt-Colonel Frey, commander of 1st SS-Panzer Grenadier Regiment, said: 'I watched as individual APC drivers with their lightly armoured vehicles attempted to ram Russian tanks with their heavy armour broadside-on . . . it seemed to me to be a form of expression of the unshakeable will of our men to survive and win'.[6] SS-Corporal Erhard Knöfel of Guhl's No 11 Company remembered the part played by the Grilles:

The limpet charges of that time were given work, but some failed in the tumult. That was how 2/Lt Wolff cracked his tanks, however. We were in close touch with him. There was a lot of vexation about the Russian infantry being on the hulls because they prevented our limpet-mine teams from getting aboard. Then our Grille and the SP-guns began to 'reap their harvest' firing directly from the anti-tank ditch. The Russian attack began to stall.

Now all hell was let loose: stabs of flame – and armoured cupolas flew through the air. We had casualties too. While applying a dressing, kneeling, I got shot through the thigh. Belt with pistol off – emergency dressing – seek cover. I found a hole nearby and was just about to jump in – and what did I see? Two pairs of eyes staring anxiously at me, men of a Russian tank crew, also without weapons.[7]

Jochen Peiper described the battle and one of the numerous men who excelled himself that day; SS-Captain Paul Guhl:

On 12 July 1943 the Russians came down from Hill 252.2 just south of Prochorovka with about 150 tanks, rolled over our infantry and, firing from all barrels, were amidst the battalion held in reserve on the reverse slope. Paying no heed to the enormous tank and infantry fire, Guhl jumped from hole to hole organising the defence and close-combat teams, and fetched ammunition and weapons from burning and exploding APCs . . . even wounded, lying between two exploding panzers, without prospect of early medical attention, Guhl was a shining example of fulfilment of duty and steadfastness in crisis. A little later he decided upon a counter-attack with quickly rallied elements and won back the old front line.[8]

Among the many men of the APC battalion who destroyed a Soviet tank was SS-Senior Sgt Adolf Sellmeier, who took out two T-34s with limpet mines. 19-year-old pioneer Hellmuth Kohler of No 1 Company of the Pioneer Battalion LAH jumped aboard two T-34s and destroyed them with bundled charges. SS-Grenadier Rudi Nadler of No 10 Company 2nd SS-Panzer Grenadier Regiment destroyed a T-34 in close combat, his third during Operation Citadel. Even No 7 Company's medical orderly took one out.

War correspondent Dr Herbert Schramm set down his impressions:

In the vagueness of morning sleep a violent artillery barrage must have been thundering down on our positions for some while, but we were not yet awake enough to distinguish between dreams and reality . . . then we realised and were ready. The Silesian, a leading grenadier, wanted to go back to the APC to fetch more limpet mines and hand-grenades, but his company commander called him back: 'They're coming!'

Through the explosions dancing up in front of our panzers we heard the drone and then the roar of several T-34s approaching at high speed and passing overhead. The thin roof of the bunker trembled and the earth trickled down between the wooden beams, but it held. Those were the first. Perhaps three or four rolled over our trench, difficult to be sure. Now we began to emerge from the trench, so narrow that two men could hardly stand abreast.

Outside all hell was let loose. An APC – not ours – was in flames. We were still receiving fairly heavy artillery fire. Here and there was a wrecked T-34, we had no idea why or by whom, and the exploding munitions added to the fireworks raging over the sector in suffocating clouds and in crashing, smashing detonations. Thank God our vehicle was still untouched. The leading grenadier sprang to it through smoke and explosions and emerged soon after with limpet mines, rifles and hand-grenades. The others of the company fetched what they needed. Some struggled with a captured anti-tank gun, but the beast would not work. More thunder. It sounded like a mad galloping herd of wild horses or buffalo, and the earth trembled under the rolling stamping. Smoke and steam meanwhile were so thick that the eyes watered and the lungs hurt to breathe. Vile and insidious this poisonous yellow cloud, this steaming, stinking breath of the modern god of war. From within him appeared in grey uncertain shapes the powerful forms of the forward rolling tanks, coming ever closer at high speed.

A loud shout, challenging as if in jubilation, drew our eyes to the right. There stood the commander, slightly stooped, the butt of the carbine against his shoulder and the barrel, from which the plump grenade protruded, following the giant outline of a T-34 heading for us in its raging, rattling progress. The battalion commander, perhaps thirty years of age, who in photographs looks like a thoughtful, well-dressed actor and likes ironic repartee, this young, battle-hardened leader, was like the tense trigger of the carbine, waiting for the releasing pressure of his forefinger. The glittering Knight's Cross on the camouflage shirt shook a little as if lightly stirred by his nerves.

The Soviet tank thundered up, grew gigantic out of the swathes of mist and droned over the trench three metres away. At the same instant – the eardrums quivering painfully – the commander's rifle-grenade hit him in the sensitive rump. He rolled on twenty or thirty metres, then stopped, trembling. Our shrill cries of joy were heard by the SS-Major, who laughed, happy and proud as a boy, his teeth bright in the sun-tanned face. 'This day counts towards the Close-combat Clasp, men!' he called, but they were distracted and enraged that the T-34s were going too fast for them to get aboard and attach their limpet mines.

Meanwhile the thin line of infantry protecting the front had come down to us to be shared out between holes and trenches. 'They are coming!' Did somebody shout it or did we all know instinctively? In the whitish-yellow fumes hanging over our trench between the tall grasses, shadowy human forms began to appear. Perhaps they thought that their tanks had crushed everyone, or that we were crouching, petrified, in the holes. Nearby an MG began to chatter. The commander's adjutant, a young SS-2/Lt [Wolff], who the day before yesterday personally destroyed a tank, manned the MG. To his right was a corporal. He looked for a target with his submachine gun and spotted a Bolshevist approaching, stooped and hesitant, no more than thirty metres away. Now he had him in his sights, but when he squeezed the trigger he was answered by a soft, mocking click. Damn, what's wrong? In feverish haste he fitted one magazine after another – always the same result. The gun had jammed and could not be made good in seconds.

A shadow ahead had come closer. Suddenly the corporal was struck across the legs as if by a giant stick, and he collapsed forward. He does not remember until later the resounding crack of the hand grenade and the soft groaning of the senior sergeant, who sank down at his left. The corporal tried to stand but failed. There must be something wrong with his feet. So as not to be an obstacle in the narrow trench, he crawled to the senior sergeant, his company commander, and the two wounded men were dragged gasping into the bunker.

The mood was not at all as one would expect from a unit with at least two dozen T-34s at its back and hordes of advancing infantry ahead . . . in the bunker they listened out and tried to guess what was going on from the sounds of battle. Then the company troop leader appeared, a quiet Austrian, and sat beside his commander, whose every order he read yesterday from his eyes. Now the commander has only one eye, and the other is thickly bandaged. The 08 he held was red all over, as though lacquered with blood. [This was the Viennese SS-Corporal Erich Pinczker, who fought as an SS-Corporal with 2nd Führer Escort Company at the end of 1944.] And now the commander appeared: 'Up you get boys, a panzer will take you back!' Four men dragged the senior sergeant to the panzer which stood halted near the trench, returning to Division with shell-damage. Therefore reinforcements were on the way and the men no longer alone.[9]

SS-Lt Rudolf von Ribbentrop destroyed fourteen Soviet tanks that day. He was awarded the Knight's Cross on 15 July 1943.[10] His platoon leader SS-Lt Walter Malchow destroyed seven tanks.[11] SS-Lt-Colonel Kraas, commanding officer of 2nd SS-Panzer Grenadier Regiment, was wounded under the right eye by a shell splinter. Numerous enemy tanks were destroyed by the panzer grenadiers of the Leibstandarte in close combat, 143 of them by 2nd Regiment alone. On 12 July 1943 the Leibstandarte destroyed a total of 192 Russian tanks. During the offensive, No 14 Company's supply unit had remained behind at Klenovoye. The daughter of the village mayor laid flowers on the graves of the fallen of No 14 Company interred there. She visited the small cemetery daily to read the names of the fallen, some of whom she had known.[12]

By 17 July 1943 the Leibstandarte had transferred out, the armoured group occupying the area west of Teterevino. Gührs wrote:

When we were relieved there four days later, I had fifteen dead and more than thirty-five wounded. Hannes Duffert fell on the last morning, Corporal Kamprad [company troop leader] seriously wounded. As for me, I had my guardian angel. On 13 July I was temporarily deaf. My left ear-drum was ruptured. I had some minor cuts in the neck from earlier. Corporal Lorenz was dead, I heard. I had seen him stretched out afterwards. They were grim days, but full of proud victories. We cut ourselves off from the enemy and nobody knew to where. We had two days of peace and quiet. How our men have grown old!

In the major fighting none of the six Grilles had been lost to enemy action although hit by countless shells and splinters. They had been proved successful. On 17 July 1943 Gührs wrote: 'I got the Iron Cross First Class from Peiper and command of No 13 Company. Captain Dinse was to take over my old Company once he got back from leave. On the night of 18 July 1943 we set off again for the area west of Byelgorod. It was hinted that we were bound for Stalino.'

The twelve-day tank battle came to its end. I painted two thick white rings and the silhouette of a T-34 on the barrel of our Grille to mark our two kills. For the 12 July 1943 at Prochorovka, and 13 July in defence of hill 252.2, I was awarded my 31st and 32nd Close-combat Days. I was now 21 years of age. As a result of the wound to my hand I now had blood poisoning in the right arm. As this was worsening acutely, I had to be hospitalised. On 17 July 1943 I was flown by Ju 52 to Kharkov. Soon after taking off the aircraft was harassed by Russian anti-aircraft fire. Being walking wounded I sat at a window and watched the tracer coming up. In the military hospital at Kharkov I met SS-Lt Georg Preuss, still recovering from the submachine gun bullet through his neck.

I had now been fighting for two years with the Leibstandarte on the Eastern Front, in 1941 on the MG, in 1943 around Kharkov at an MG fixed to an APC and recently as the gunlayer on a Grille in the great offensive at Kursk in July 1943. I had proven myself as steadfast and reliable in every battle. I had experienced four Close-combat Days in the hail of shells, bombs and splinters during Operation Citadel, had been wounded five times and despite having no gunsight or range-finder had destroyed two Soviet tanks. Aboard a Grille I had been present at the attacks by the APC battalion and had contributed to the successes of the armoured group. Yet for all this there was no Iron Cross First Class for me, nor promotion in the Leibstandarte.

At Kharkov military hospital I experienced an example of the especially strong bond existing between SS-officers and their men. One day 2/Lt Konrad Nickerl appeared in the wards and had a number of patients line up. He called their names from a list. He told us that we had to go absent before midnight because there was a transport train going to the Division in Italy. Whoever missed this train would never return to the 'old heap'. Discharging ourselves without papers and written orders, we had to make for a certain place in the city where an SS-Lieutenant would take us to the train. And all went as planned. On 24 July 1943 I went to the Field-Convalescence Company/Field Reserve Battalion and boarded the train on 30 July. During the journey the train passed through Upper Silesia where SS-Captain Robert Arthecker obtained a leave pass for me. On 4 August I went home on leave.

My battalion had loaded at Byelgorod on the 'Lightning Arrow'. On 29 July Gührs wrote: 'At 0300 hrs we began loading and left the station at 0838 hrs. A strange feeling. This time I had left so many good men behind. Corporals Kamprad and Bachmann had died of their wounds I heard. Where Duffert and Dreyer were buried was now back in the Russian hands. I asked myself why I had survived.'

Chapter Nine

The Leibstandarte in Italy, 5 August–24 October 1943

During the Kursk offensive the Americans landed in Sicily on 10 July 1943 and the situation for our Italian allies worsened dramatically. The Italian Army was demoralised and the collapse in Italy was expected soon. This would plunge the beleaguered German southern front into great danger. In order to keep the situation in northern Italy in check, the Leibstandarte was given the task of going overland from Innsbruck through South Tyrol to Upper Italy, protecting the Brenner–Verona highway and standing ready to disarm the Italian units stationed on the plain of Po as soon as Italy defected from the Axis.

On 2 August 1943 the first Leibstandarte transport trains arrived at Innsbruck. Destination for the elements arriving on 2 and 3 August was Trento. On the night of 4 August No 13 Company of the APC battalion unloaded at Innsbruck. Gührs noted in his diary:

Wonderful journey. Five days in the most glorious weather without incident. Yesterday, however, another wagon almost burnt out . . . according to what all the bombed-out Hamburg people say our beautiful city is a heap of rubble. Weighed down with these cares we go forward towards the next operation. Perhaps that is the right mood in which to fight against the British and Americans . . . This is wonderful scenery here. We are in the valley between two mountains. A glorious landscape.[1]

It was a masterpiece of organisation to load a fully-equipped panzer division aboard transporter trains in such a way that they could unload all together at the destination. From 5 August Peiper headed the wheeled elements of his battalion by road from Innsbruck over the Brenner via Brixen and Bozen to Trento and handed in the transport papers for the numerous parts of the chain. The men received an enthusiastic welcome from the population on their drive through South Tyrol and were given wine and fruit in abundance.

On 7 August Peiper's battalion adjutant SS-2/Lt Werner Wolff was awarded the Knight's Cross, the highest award for bravery, won on 12 July 1943 at Prochorovka. At age twenty he was the youngest officer in the battalion and could be certain of the sympathies of Peiper, whom he idolised in his youthful enthusiasm.[2] Peiper himself had received the Tank Destruction Badge on 21 July: this decoration was made to Wolff and those other men in the battalion who had taken out an enemy tank in close combat during Operation Citadel, amongst those in my company SS-Leading Grenadiers Günther Vogel and Erich Jost.

The APC battalion arrived at Trento on 13 August and received orders to move next day to the west side of Verona. In case of need, the Leibstandarte was to support 44th Infantry Division in the Brenner sector from the south. On 19 August 2nd SS-Panzer Grenadier Regiment transferred to the Reggio-Emilia/South Polodenza/Scandiano area. For the exhausted troops of the Leibstandarte, the move to Italy was pleasant and interesting after the harsh months of privation in Russia. In Mondovi, Peiper organised joyrides in an Italian aircraft for men of the battalion. Contact with local dignitaries and clergy of the Italian town was quickly established, and the mayor of Mondovi invited the commander of No 11 Company, SS-Lt Hans Schmidt, and a number of his men to dinner.[3] On 28 August the APC battalion held a festival and on 30 August challenged German Army units to a sports day. Werner Wolff was successful for the Battalion in boxing and sabre-fencing.[4]

That same month the battalion marched singing through the town of Reggio-Emilia led by Peiper, Wolff and Paul Guhl three abreast. This impressive march was filmed for the weekly cinema newsreel and recorded for a radio broadcast. My Grille platoon was led by SS-Sgt Rudi Vieten, recently a recipient of the Iron Cross First Class, transferred to No 14 Company from No 12 Company. On 1 September 1943 the first Close-combat Clasps were awarded in the Leibstandarte. When I returned from leave on 17 September I picked up my bronze clasp at the company office. Besides myself in the company SS-Leading Grenadiers Erich Jost and SS-Grenadiers Tony Motzheim, and Willi Pluschke of the pioneer-platoon, also received the award.

Although the units had been urged to distribute the clasps on 12 April 1943, nothing had come of it until September. Only during the quiet period in Italy had the unit leaders had time to make the necessary entries in the pay/service books. The following APC battalion officers received the bronze clasp: Wolff, Preuss, Gührs and Guhl. For their close-combat days at Kharkov, Otto Dinse, then battalion adjutant, and the former commanders of Nos 12, 13 and 14 Companies respectively, Bormann, Pinter and Kolitz received the bronze clasp. In all 178 officers and men in the APC battalion were awarded the bronze Close-combat Clasp.[5] Only the bronze clasp was awarded on 1 September 1943 although it is certain that a number of battalion members had amassed considerably more close-combat days than the fifteen required for the bronze clasp. I had personally survived 32 confirmed days as had SS-Leading Grenadier Paul Zwigart of No 11 Company. Division awarded Peiper the silver clasp.

On 16 September 1943 my new company commander, SS-Lt Otto Dinse, was awarded the Iron Cross First Class for his services as adjutant during the Kharkov operation: similarly distinguished were pioneer-platoon leader SS-Sgt Wilhelm Haferstroh and 'tank crackers' Erich Jost and Günther Vogel. Wounded tank-gun leader SS-Corporal Willi Mewes was sent on leave, never returned to the company and received the Iron Cross First Class ten months later. Seventy-eight NCOs and men received the Iron Cross Second Class. SS-Captain Paul Guhl was seconded between 13 September and 9 October 1943 to a battalion officers' course at the Panzer School, Versailles, leaving SS-Lt Hans Schmidt to take temporary charge of No 11 Company.

The attitude of the Italian Axis partner was no longer certain. On the morning of 8 September 1943 the Italian king had assured German envoy Dr Rudolf Rahn that he would remain loyal to Germany and his treaty obligations. A few hours later Rahn was informed by the Italian Foreign Ministry that Marshal Badoglio had surrendered uncon-ditionally to the Allies. Prior to this the Italians had been negotiating secretly with the Allies for several weeks without advising their German allies of the fact. That night the royal family, Badoglio and many government ministers fled Rome and were conveyed by an Italian warship to the Allies in southern Italy. This was the Italian betrayal anticipated by Hitler. German units now had to defend Italy on their own. It was made known to the Leibstandarte divisional staff towards 1800 hrs on 8 September 1943 that Italy had capitulated. II Panzer Corps was ordered to the highest state of alert.

Units of the Leibstandarte reached the Italian barracks at 0100 on 9 September and ordered the men to surrender their weapons. At 0105 hrs, Peiper's APC battalion received orders from Division to reinforce the Panther group at Reggio. From 0155 hrs the Battalion occupied post offices, railway stations and disarmed barracks. At 0500 hrs the artillery barracks at Reggio yielded up its weapons and shortly thereafter Peiper reported the fulfilment of his mission and returned to the former stand-by area. In Verona 1st SS-Panzer Grenadier Regiment and the SP-group disarmed the Italian garrisons, and the 650 officers and 16,599 other ranks at Cremona were made prisoners-of-war by the 1st and 3rd Battalions. Once the disarmament process was almost complete, it was announced that after handing over their weapons the Italians would be allowed to return to civilian life or could enlist in the Wehrmacht as auxiliaries. Martial law came into force throughout the corps area.

Peiper's battalion moved from Reggio to Alessandria and Asti where it disarmed the Italians without resistance. The 2nd Battalion, 2nd SS-Panzer Grenadier Regiment occupied Turin while 1st Regiment reached the outskirts of Milan. It became known that day that Italians in the south were now openly fighting against Germany, causing all Italians to be treated as prisoners-of-war. The APC battalion was responsible for setting up the prisoner transports. After applying for authorisation from the Transport Commander at Turin station, the trains headed for Germany. Men of the Battalion accompanied the prisoners as far as Innsbruck. The assembly camp for 2nd Regiment was the cavalry barracks at Corso Stupinigo, Turin. On 11 September 1943 the APC battalion proceeded from Asti to Alba and Bra, where disarming was continued. At Alba the Italians surrendered their weapons voluntarily. The men of the Leibstandarte profited much by equipment and vehicles from Italian stocks. Peiper's battalion wore Germany Army tropical kit, sand-coloured short trousers and shirts.

Under SS-Sgt Vieten our six Grilles took prisoner a whole regiment with its staff, a colonel and 4,500 men. The commander of No 12 Company, SS-Lt Georg Preuss, captured an Italian officers' training school with all its personnel. Eight men of No 13 Company received the surrender of a fully-occupied barracks. Despite provocations from the civilian population the disarming of Turin went off according to plan. Milan was occupied, but the troops there were allowed to retain their weapons. The removal of prisoners to Mantua began.

At 1130 hrs on 12 September Peiper's battalion arrived at Cuneo, elements of No 11 Company discovering that the Italian soldiery had decamped from the barracks leaving the local population to loot it. Up to 11 September in the disarming process the LAH had taken 106,046 Italians prisoner plus numerous vehicles, 428 MGs, 38,591 rifles, 391 aircraft, 27 tanks, 49 AA guns and much more. The Division advised II

SS-Panzer Corps that large parts of the Italian Army had fled into the mountains south-west of Turin.

On 14 September at Cuneo the APC battalion captured an Italian general of Forty-Fourth Army. Peiper's new orders were to continue the disarmament process south of Cuneo. On 15 September his men disarmed Limone and Tenda; on 16 September the battalion met resistance south of Cuneo and was obliged to use its heavy infantry weapons to quell it. Disarming went on until 1700 hrs, being continued that night in the Boves-Chiusa region. Peiper set up his command post at Cuneo and SS-Lt Dinse was appointed second-in-command. Around 18 September together with three other leading-grenadiers I was appointed head of transport for a train carrying 900 Italian prisoners of war which we accompanied to the Brenner. For this reason I was not present when partisans kidnapped Harness-Master SS-Sgt Karl Wiezorek and technical NCO SS-Corporal Kurt Butenhoff at Boves. In the operation to free them a number of APCs came under fire, and only when the Grilles appeared did the enemy pull back, enabling the hostages to escape. The heavy guns caused damage and fires in houses at Boves in which twenty-three inhabitants lost their lives. SS-2/Lt Gührs reported: 'Before the fighting around Boves, Peiper had ordered me to urge the inhabitants of the surrounding villages to prevail upon the Italian soldiers and vagabond partisans to surrender their weapons. No form of pressure was exerted on them. To the contrary, for the restoration of law and order I received in my district the Order of the Heart of Jesus from an Italian delegation.'[6] On 23 September Field-Marshal Rommel issued the following Special Order: 'Any sentiments held by German soldiers towards pro-Badoglio forces wearing the uniform of their former comrades-in-arms are totally misplaced. Whichever of those men elects to fight against German soldiers loses any right to quarter and is to be treated with that harshness appropriate to the scum who suddenly turns his weapons against his friends . . .'[7] On 21 September Benito Mussolini came to Forli after his liberation by Otto Skorzeny. I was amongst his escort for a few days before he moved to his seat of government on Lake Garda. On 4 October Peiper moved his Battalion back to Cunmeo and on 16th of the month to Felizzano-Nozzia with the Battalion command post at Felizzano.

I was given the job of driving the ammunition lorry for the Grille platoon. My former gun-commander Kendzia went to the pioneer platoon as driver. The remaining Marders were transferred out and the tank-gun platoon disbanded. The next few days passed without incident. On 20 October Army Group B gave notice that the Leibstandarte would soon return to the Eastern Front. We were issued winter equipment for the vehicles and winter clothing for ourselves. On 22 October the LAH was redesignated as a panzer division, and all SS divisions and regiments were given numbers. The APC battalion was now 3rd Battalion (Armoured), 2nd SS-Panzer Grenadier Regiment LSSAH.

Chapter Ten

Back to the Eastern Front, 15–30 November 1943

Leaving for the transports on 24 October 1943, Peiper's battalion came under the orders of the Panzer Regiment, and on the afternoon of the 26th the first elements of the battalion loaded at Alessandria. We had been issued winter kit: thick fur-lined anoraks with large hoods, grey outside, white inside, thick padded trousers, leather boots with felt lining, fur-lined gloves and head protectors.

The situation on the Eastern Front had changed for the worse since we had left it. By mid-October 1943, General Koniev's 2nd Ukrainian Front had established three bridgeheads east of Kremenchug over the river Dnieper. Dnyepropetrovsk had been lost on 25 October 1943, and another enemy push was aimed at the industrial region around Krivoi Rog. Von Manstein's First Panzer Army with Army Group South had successfully counter-attacked this threat from Koniev. Also at this time the Soviets had retaken Melitopol from Army Group A in the south. This endangered the Crimean Narrows at Perekop.

On 3 November 1st Ukrainian Front under General Vatutin assembled either side of Kiev with thirty infantry divisions, twenty-four tank brigades and ten motorised infantry brigades for a major offensive to recapture Kiev, which was achieved on 6 November. The railway marshalling yards at Fastov, 60kms west of Kiev, important to the LSSAH for unloading its transport trains, fell to the enemy on 7 November: on the 11th the Russians reached Radomyshl on the Teterev and on 13 November regained Zhitomir.

In order to prevent the threatened northern flank of Army Group South from being cut off and destroyed, the Army Group had been forced to act promptly. 1st SS-Panzer Division LSSAH and 1st Panzer Division of the Army were given the job of supporting the northern flank. Even while unloading, units of the LAH had to beat off major attacks by the Soviet vanguard.

Grille platoon commander Vieten requested me as a gun-captain for

99

the platoon. As I knew they were a loader short, I took over as temporary loader on one Grille until I could move up. By 14 November the HQ, No 11 and No 12 Companies of Peiper's battalion had still not arrived in the East while No 13 Company had had to start fighting as soon as it rolled off the unloading ramp.[1]

On 15th the Leibstandarte headed north for the Kiev–Zhitomir highway with 1st Panzer Division on the left, and 25th Panzer Division and 2nd SS-Panzer Division Das Reich protecting the right. That day other elements of the APC battalion arrived, No 14 Company being reinforced from units of Panzer Group Dinse.

No 14 (Heavy Armoured) Company, 2nd SS-Panzer Grenadier Regiment LSSAH

The principal posts in No 14 Company between 15 November 1943 and 1 March 1944 for the fighting in Russia were occupied as follows:

Company commanders: SS-Lt Otto Dinse, SS-Sgt Jochen Thiele
Acting CSM: SS-Corporal Eduard Funk
Harness-master: SS-Sgt Karl Wiezoreck
SPW Instructor: SS-Corporal Kurt Butenhoff
Paymaster: SS-Corporal Roog
Quartermaster: SS-Corporal Springmann

Grille platoon:
SS-2/Lt Bernd von Bergmann
SS-Sgt Rudi Vieten (wounded December 1943)
Section leader SS-Leading Grenadier Otto Brockmann (fell 21 November 1943)
Commanders of the six Grilles:
SS-Leading Grenadiers Otto Brockmann (fell 21 November 1943), Werner Kindler, Rudi Rayer: SS-Corporals Emil Knappe, Heinz Klose, Helmut Feldvoss

Pioneer-platoon:
SS-Senior Sgt Wilhelm Haferstroh: four APCs

Flamethrower half-platoon:
Commanders of the three flame-thrower APCs: SS-Corporals Schuster and Richter, SS-Leading Grenadier Rudi Schwambach

Marder half-platoon:
Gun-captains of the three Marder IIIs: SS-Leading Grenadiers Karl-Heinz Rodenstein, Siegfried Seberra, Werner Kindler, Kurt Wiemann, Karl-Heinz Fetzer: Leading Rifleman Ludwig Clement

On 16 November the 1st SS-Panzer reconnaissance section took Turbovka and Divin, and 1st SS-Panzer Grenadier Regiment took Wilnya. Panzer Group Dinse repelled enemy forces attacking Lissovka and Moshorino.[2] On 17 November after a reconnaissance by the APC battalion from Turbovka to Lutchin, Dinse's No 14 Company, supported by ten Tigers of No 13 Panzer Company under SS-Captain Kling and a platoon of pioneer armour took Lutchin at 1540 hrs after a 90-minute battle against five T-34s. On the night of 18 November the Panzer Group at Lutchin fought off a battalion-sized attack coming from Federovka. On 19 November a powerful enemy force forced Battle Group Dinse into the western part of Lutchin. When this was followed by an attack of regiment size at Lutchin, 2nd Battalion, 2nd SS-Panzer Grenadier Regiment was sent to Lisovka as reserve, the more so because the enemy was attempting to detour around Lutchin to the north to threaten the flank of the division.

Over the two days at Lutchin, Panzer Group Dinse/Kling destroyed thirteen T-34s, twenty-five anti-tank guns, a 12.7cm field gun, several light anti-tank guns, lorries and tow-tractors.[3] For my service with No 14 Company at Lutchin on 17 and 18 November 1943 I had my 33rd and 34th Close-combat Days confirmed. On 19 November elements of Dinse's No 14 Company were engaged in close combat on ridge 176.9. For this engagement I had my 35th Close-combat Day confirmed.

On the night of 20 November after relief of their units at Lutchin, Kornin and Divin, the Leibstandarte advanced along the line Morosovka–Wodoty Brusilov. At 1530 hrs on 19 November Peiper reported the arrival of the remainder of his battalion at Biala Zerkov.[4] At 0100 hrs the following morning, the reinforced 2nd SS-Panzer Grenadier Regiment and 2nd Battalion 1st SS-Panzer Grenadier Regiment advanced left and right of the Wodoty Brusilov road. The Panther group reached Piliponka-Privorotye, and 2nd SS-Panzer Grenadier Regiment was ordered to join up with it. The attack on Brusilov was cancelled. Peiper awarded the Iron Cross First Class to SS-Grenadier Toni Motzheim of the pioneer platoon, No 14 Company, and the No 13 Company medical orderly SS-Corporal Rudi Jentzsch. Seventeen men received the Iron Cross Second Class.[5]

At midday on 20 November, SS-Lt.Col Schönberger, commanding officer of the panzer regiment, fell at Ssolovyevka after being hit by splinters from an artillery shell whilst outside his tank. The divisional commander, SS-Colonel Wisch, appointed Peiper to replace Schönberger. This was a major new task: it amounted to a challenge to prove his ability as the commanding officer of a regiment. For Peiper it came as a blow to have to leave the APC battalion, of which he had been commander for over a year. He had reorganised it from an infantry battalion into an APC battalion and been extraordinarily successful with it. Peiper wrote: 'With its expansion, successes and quite unique vitality I have always considered it as the high point and fulfilment of my career as a soldier and felt inwardly a part of it as with no other unit.'[6] Because Peiper would be leading the division's armoured group as commander of the panzer regiment, the APC battalion remained tactically subordinate to him. He passed command of it to Paul Guhl, commander of No 11 Company.

On 21 November, 2nd SS-Panzer Grenadier Regiment attacked Brusilov from the south but encountered such determined enemy resistance that the attack was broken off at midday, to be followed by a night attack. During the night advance the Grilles came across a village in flames to the left and a Russian anti-tank position on the high ground to the right. In the ensuing exchange of fire the Grille of platoon-commander SS-Leading Grenadier Otto Brockmann was hit and set ablaze. Brockmann was killed.

Paul Guhl, SS-Sturmbannführer

b. 1 June 1916 Stuttgart-Zuffenhausen d.16 April 1997

German Cross in Gold 30 December 1943 as SS-Hauptsturmführer and commander 3rd Battalion, 2nd SS-Panzer Grenadier Regiment, 1st SS-Panzer Division LAH

Knight's Cross: 4 June 1944

1 August 1934 Entered LAH, 17 October 1934, No 11 Company

26 September 1939 Promoted to SS-2/Lt

1 November 1939 Awarded Iron Cross Second Class for bravery, Polish front, as leader of 2nd Platoon, the first of the LAH to be distinguished

1 November 1939–24 February 1940 SS Junkerschule, Bad Tölz, officers training: after passing out left 2nd Platoon, Western campaign

Autumn 1940 No 11 Company disbanded, Guhl sent to NCOs' School at Lauenburg

September 1942 Led No 11 Company, APC battalion

9 March 1943 Awarded Iron Cross First Class

11 July 1943 Kursk, wounded right thigh

1 September 1943 Awarded bronze Close-combat Clasp

9 October 1943 Passed battalion leadership course in Paris, only

---

representative of Waffen-SS amongst 126 candidates
20 November 1943 took command of APC battalion
5 December 1943 During night action received ricochet wound to face, lost left
eye
30 December 1943 Awarded German Cross in Gold
1 March 1944 Resumed command of battalion with glass eye
4 June 1944 In Flanders, awarded Knight's Cross
5 June 1944 Awarded silver Close-combat Clasp
After the Normandy invasion Guhl was ordered to take convalescent leave
at the regimental rest home.
September 1944 Commander, 2nd Battalion 1st SS-Panzer Regiment
30 August 1944 Awarded Wound Badge in gold
9 November 1944 Promoted to SS-Major

Next day the division received orders to link up with the southern group, 2nd SS-Panzer Grenadier Regiment, capture Divin, Ulsha and Jastrebenka and, after taking these, to attack Brusilov from the east and then halt. The northern group, 1st SS-Panzer Grenadier Regiment, was to attack Brusilov-West from Oseryany.

At 0555 hrs SS-Lt Col Hugo Kraas with the strengthened 2nd SS-Panzer Grenadier Regiment attacked Jastrebenka from the direction of Ulshka. SS-Captain Hans Beckers' 1st Battalion was in the lead, with SS-Major Rudi Sandig's 2nd Battalion following strung out behind it to the right: support came from eleven Tigers plus Nos 3 and 7 Artillery Batteries. Third Battalion waited initially at Divin as the intervention group until Jastrebenka fell, and would then advance.

The Soviets had established a very stout defence at Jastrebenka, and took the Leibstandarte under fire from so many weapons that the attack bogged down at 1005 hrs and both battalions took cover 1.5kms south of the position. At 1130 hrs, twenty-five Mk IV panzers of 2nd Panzer Battalion stood ready at Divin together with the APC battalion, both under the orders of SS-Lt.-Colonel Kraas, who set out with this battle group at 1304 hrs. Despite all the Russians could do, both on the flanks, at the rear and from tanks disguised as haystacks, the advance was successful and at 1450 hrs battle was joined at the south end of Jastrebenka from where the Soviets were firing with many anti-tank guns and artillery from extensive ground defences. Losses began to mount. No 13 Tiger Company accompanying the first wave took on the Russians on the flank and overpowered the anti-tank front south of Jastrebenka.[7] It was reported of the APC battalion:

When the Battle Group reached the southern end of Jastrebenka towards 1400 hrs, having set out from Ulshka an hour before, the panzers stopped on the outskirts in order to overwhelm the exceedingly strong anti-tank-front. On his own initiative SS-Capt Guhl detoured far to the right and left of the latter with the APC battalion and, at its head, made a surprise appearance in the locality, destroying large numbers of the enemy troops present and clearing it.[8]

Guhl's signals officer SS-2/Lt Hans Mahneke was killed. At 1615 hrs 2nd Regiment grenadiers entered the village and after bitter house-to-house fighting Kraas reported that Jastrebenka was in German hands. At Jastrebenka on 22 November 1943 as part of the full APC battalion I had my 36th Close-combat Day confirmed.

This first major attack as commander of the panzer regiment and the battle group was typical of Peiper's leadership in which the APC battalion often played a special role. Gührs, commander of No 13 Company, wrote: 'Peiper's transfer to the Panzer Regiment was not a problem for us: in a way we remained "his Battalion". Because the Panzer Regiment had not yet adapted itself to Peiper's often Hussar-like style of leadership, he would happily place "his Battalion" ahead of the panzers. I remember him saying then, "Fetch up the Battalion, we'll show them!"'[9] The initially stalled attack on Jastrebenka helped the APC battalion deployed by Peiper to success. The manner which the Battalion had of outflanking the frontal resistance on both sides and then storming into a locality at top speed with all barrels firing had been practised frequently by Peiper with success since Kharkov. He wrote: 'The APC battalion used to attack Russian villages like a cavalry unit: racing in from various sides and shooting from all barrels.[10] The new battalion commander, Guhl, also mastered the tactic. As commander of No 11 Company he had always set a high standard and led the battalion with élan and energy. On operations he was always to be found in one of the leading APCs and risked his life both there and in close combat unsparingly. Peiper called him 'Baby' because Guhl had been one of the youngest and smallest of stature in No 11 Company when they first knew each other in the Leibstandarte in 1936.[11] In the APC battalion Guhl could always be certain of Peiper's support.[12] The commanders of the four companies were SS-Lt Hans Schmidt, 31, from the Saar, recognised as a cool, self-assured leader; 23-year-old Georg Preuss from Danzig, a daredevil type whose personal bravery and very individual nature were known to all; Gührs, 23, from Hamburg, who had led No 13 Company since July 1943, and SS-Lt Otto Dinse, 31, leader of No 14 Company, who had been Peiper's adjutant at Kharkov. SS-2/Lt Werner Wolff was battalion adjutant. All commanders including Schmidt had at least the Iron Cross First Class and Close-combat Clasp.

An attack to the north-west against Lasarovka had been ordered for 23 November. The eastern and northern flanks of the division were to be protected from Ulshka to Jastrebenka. The strengthened 2nd SS-Panzer Grenadier Regiment was to make the attack. At ten minutes past midnight on 23 November the enemy reconnoitred the western approach to Jastrebenka and was met by a counter-attack by No 14 Company. In the general fighting for Jastrebenka/Dubrovka on 23 November 1943 I was awarded my 37th Close-combat Day. At 0600 hrs 3rd Battalion was attacked by enemy tanks from Starizkoye on the northern side of Jastrebenka, but held the field and destroyed one T-34. Werner Wolff was seriously wounded by a small-arms round to the upper right thigh. 'This time the Soviets gave me a nasty time . . . it was on 23 November and I went through a couple of dark hours. Then there were days when I wrestled with fate, because they wanted to amputate my right leg. But everything is OK now. It was not to be, because I am not that much indebted to fate,' he wrote a few days later.[13] The impulsive Wolff prevented the threatened amputation by firing his pistol at the feet of the medical orderly who arrived to take him to surgery.

The rain that night softened up the roads, delaying the movement out. APCs of 3rd Battalion left at 1130 hrs to join 3rd Battalion 1st SS-Panzer Grenadier Regiment. Peiper had fourteen Panthers, twenty-three Mk IVs and four Tigers operational. At 1230 hrs he headed towards Dubrovka for Lasarovka with the Panzer Group consisting of 2nd Battalion 1st Panzer Regiment and the APC battalion. Peiper took Dubrovka at 1400 hrs. At 1230 hrs on 24 November he set out again with the Panzer Group and west of Starizkoye stumbled across a strong Soviet anti-tank front, at the same time being attacked by tanks coming from Mal Karashin to the north. In the ensuing battle, Peiper destroyed six enemy tanks though suffering losses of his own and then kept going for Starizkoye. At 1540 hrs Guhl signalled that he was on the eastern outskirts of the village facing a strong anti-tank barrier which had halted him short of the expanded enemy positions on hill 185.4.

I was present with my Grille. My company comrade SS-Leading

Grenadier Franz Novotny fell east of Zhitomir on 24 November. For Starizkoye on that day I was awarded my 38th Close-combat Day. During the attacks Peiper was well forward with his panzer, numbered 055. He led the Panzer Regiment almost constantly with the APC battalion as an armoured group of the division, and perfected the operations of this tactical battle group. Even the men realised very quickly whom they had as commander: SS-Leading Grenadier Willi Micheluzzi, senior telephone operator at HQ, remembered: 'As regards the command of the Panzer Regiment it looked to us as though the whole regiment had been given a jolt and the panzer crews could realise their image of themselves as an attacking force.'[14]

On 26 November the Leibstandarte reached the area south of Negrebovka-Sabelotshye. It was planned to attack the southwards-advancing enemy on the flank at Radomyshl. On 27 November the next 'fire-brigade operation' of the Leibstandarte began: 3rd Battalion following 1st Regiment took the crossroads north of Guta Sabelozkaya. To our right a battle group from the Das Reich Division fought off several assaults by enemy tanks. SS-Colonel Wisch assumed that the substantial enemy forces north and west of Negrebovka and north-west of Sabelotshye were there to attack, and so veered north and north-east to deliver a surprise strike by the Leibstandarte.[15] For my involvement at Bulytchety on 27 November 1943 I was awarded my 39th Close-combat Day.

After the first few days of operations, Jochen Peiper had been accepted as commanding officer of the Panzer Regiment by the men. Finally the regiment was being led with the gusto usual to the Panzer Arm. SS-Grenadier Wilhelm Nusshag, HQ Main Signals Centre, confirmed this:

Once Peiper took over there was a certain change to be observed in the leadership of the Panzer Regiment. Schönberger was known as a rather anxious leader whereas Peiper was more or less the opposite. After a short time Peiper won the confidence of both officers and men. Because of his exemplary prowess on operations, his resolution of the most difficult situations, he was the ideal leader for our regiment. Personally I only had contact with Peiper when handing him the signals I had received. In his character he appeared to be a taciturn type, not very approachable.[16]

He was sure of himself and well aware of his responsibility for the

Panzer Regiment as the most powerful fighting force within the division. Most people in the regiment thought the 28-year-old blond Berliner to be the silent type, and it was not his style to spend time in conversation with everyone. His manner of speaking was forthright and clear, his explanation of a situation and his orders precise and well thought-out. His manner of expressing himself was often haughty, and sometimes his biting irony or even sarcasm would tend to flare up. Some suspected arrogance behind his generally tangible reserve. Peiper's operations officer SS-2/Lt Arndt Fischer set out this impression from his experience of Peiper as a military colleague and his later years of friendship with him: 'Whoever only knew him for a short time might have considered him arrogant, harsh and un-approachable, but whoever knew him longer, and as a leader of men, would confirm that he was a brave, fair and exemplary commander. Whoever knew him beyond that, personally and as a friend, knew that he was clever and well-educated, introverted, shy, unpretentious, loveable and very considerate.'[17]

On 28 November 1943 the APC battalion advanced over the Garbaroff Bridge erected by 1st Panzer Engineer Battalion. North of Guta Sabelozkaya enemy resistance was broken down and their extensive defences overrun. At 1045 hrs the battalion halted at the southern end of Garbaroff to refuel and re-ammunition at Bulytchety. Peiper's Panzer Group, now consisting of the Panzer Regiment and the reconnaissance half-battalion, headed west after re-crossing the river at 1120 hrs to take the Kotsherovo–Radomyshl road and advance northwards to the latter town. After running the gauntlet of enemy tanks and anti-tank guns he reached the fork in the road south of Radomyshl. At 1645 hrs Peiper's Group turned off at the Radomyshl fork for Garbaroff where a hedgehog defence was in place.[18] The APC battalion broke through the strong and large trench system south and south-east of Garbaroff, took the town and in so doing removed a large chunk of the opposition to the flank of the Panzer Group further west. Despite resistance the Battalion pushed forward into the forest north and north-eastwards and destroyed an underground camp with a large contingent of its personnel.[19] For my part in the fighting around Garbaroff on 28 November I was awarded my 40th confirmed Close-combat Day.

That afternoon the Soviets let us have their reply, first in regimental strength against 2nd Battalion of 2nd Regiment. This was blocked by one APC company of 3rd Battalion at the dam on the Belka. At about

1720 hrs the APC battalion drove off the enemy in a counter-attack. At 2032 hrs 3rd Battalion intervened to repel another attempt to break through against 2nd Battalion. In the night 2nd Parachute Division combed the woods between Belka and Teterev and then relieved the Leibstandarte.

Peiper gave APC battalion commander SS-Captain Paul Guhl a free hand in the management of the unit. They had known each other well for some years and each knew he could rely on the other. Guhl recalled that Peiper's maxim was: 'One man, one word.'[20] Peiper led the Panzer Regiment with the APC battalion attached almost daily on operations. The APCs merged outstandingly with the armour of the Panzer Group and Guhl, who saw himself as 'an APC man body and soul' considered the armoured personnel carrier as the most effective weapon after the panzers.[21] Of special significance therefore is undoubtedly Guhl's own impression of Peiper, obtained in daily contact on common operations: 'We had in Peiper an unimaginably brave and far-sighted commander.'[22] Peiper led with a marked outward imperturbability, and he remembered later: 'My men often used to say amongst themselves: "A thousand marks to anyone who can ruffle him".'

On 28 November SS-Brigadier Wisch recommended Peiper's promotion to SS-Lt Colonel:

He is a straightforward, level-headed and energetic personality. As commander of the armoured battalion he has proved his clever tactical thinking, accepting for the Division in fast, flexible thrusts whatever came its way. This special ability to sum up and take advantage of a favourable situation, his doggedness in counter-attacks and experience of leadership in the areas behind the enemy's frontline and the depth of their rear, together with his exemplary valour, make him appear especially suitable to command a Panzer Regiment. A leader of great vitality to have along the way.[23]

This assessment by his former regimental, and present divisional commander, Wisch, can be seen as a sound and apt description of Peiper the panzer leader. The introverted young regimental commander, who appeared unapproachable to many, concealed behind his almost impenetrable exterior all those attributes which a thoughtful unit leader should have. Yet only a few succeeded in getting close to the real man. One of these was his radio operator Fritz Kosmehl who recalled that Peiper '. . . behaved rather differently towards his panzer crew: in this special situation totally different relationships prevailed which differed very substantially from those of pure command. His personal warmth, which he showed repeatedly, appeared only occasionally like a flash of lightning and betrayed something of his true being, which he hid behind a cold, fully controlled mask.'[24]

The APC battalion supported by SP-guns arrived at 0530 hrs on 29 November at the edge of the forest west of Kol Tolstoye. A Russian attack stemming from the village was beaten off. Because the battalion was scheduled to take part in a second attack that morning with the Panther section, it was pulled back to the starting point. At 0915 hrs the APC battalion and Panthers led by SS-Major Kuhlmann set out for a fresh attack at the forest limits near Kol Tolstoye. Recognising the signs of an imminent Russian advance, Kuhlmann reacted quickly to destroy two enemy battalions. The German armoured group overwhelmed the extensive anti-tank defences and entered Tolstoye at 1300 hrs in a hail of anti-tank and mortar fire. The APC battalion sustained serious casualties. SS-2/Lt Walter Taferner, No 13 Company, died near Bulychety forest, to where the battalion pulled back at 1530 hrs. Next morning Peiper carried out his attack on Garbaroff with the Panzer Group and took the town at ten o'clock despite fierce resistance. For my part in the fighting at Kol Tolstoye on 29 November 1943 I was awarded my 41st Close-combat Day.

The APC company commanders now had the courage to take risks, knowing they had Peiper's full support. Their APCs, lightly armoured but fast and highly manoeuvrable across-country, could follow the Panthers, Tigers and Mk IVs anywhere, and the grenadiers would be able to secure the breakthroughs achieved by the panzers. To the panzer crews, the grenadiers of the APC battalion were reliable colleagues known generally for their lust for action. Guhl, commander of the APC battalion confirmed: 'The APCs were no appendages, but cooperated on an equal footing.'[25]

It is interesting that my No 14 Company was often commanded by NCOs – for example SS-Sgt Jochen Thiele – and that from 1943 it had no officer as platoon leader with the brief exception of the much-wounded Bernd von Bergmann. One of the reasons for the success of my unit was that every one of us could operate every weapon and drive all types of APC. Every NCO could lead a platoon.[26] For my own part I operated in action a heavy-MG on APCs and the Grille, an APC with the 7.5cm short gun, a flamethrower APC, the anti-tank Marder and even a Russian 7.62cm gun. During an attack, SS-Captain Guhl rode in the Grille of which I was the commander, and then nominated me platoon leader for that particular attack, something typical of the Leibstandarte but which it was difficult to imagine happening in other units. In these forays as Grille-captain I would change position after the first three or four rounds were fired. The Grille platoon had its own ammunition supply: a towing vehicle was attached to each Grille group, three in all, which supplied the heavy guns with shells during combat.

Orders came to clear the woods between Belka and Teterov on 30 November and 1 December 1943. On the morning of the 30th the Russians fired on Garbaroff especially with heavy artillery and mortars. They advanced to within 400m of the right-hand sector of the front and dug in. The left-hand sector remained quiet. Elements of 2nd Parachute Division had begun clearing the woods from 0600 hrs. The APC battalion was divisional reserve. Up to and including that date the Leibstandarte had 363 killed in action, 1,289 wounded and 33 missing. The frontline strength of the battalion on that date was eight officers, 24 NCOs and 131 men.[27] SS-Senior Sgt Bruno Wells, a platoon leader in No 12 Company, fell and SS-Senior Sgt Rudi Vieten, No 14 Company Grille platoon, had been seriously wounded and lost a leg. On 1 December 1943 2nd Parachute Division relieved the Leibstandarte. The Army armoured reconnaissance unit was also relieved and returned to 1st Panzer Division. SS-Colonel Wisch thanked them for their comradely cooperation.

Peiper transferred three flamethrower APCs of No 14 Panzer Pioneer Company of the Panzer Regiment to the APC battalion where they joined No 14 Company's pioneer platoon (SS-Lt Dinse). The vehicles came with their respective commanders, SS-Corporals Schuster and Richter, and SS-Leading Grenadier Schwambach. I remember an operation in which I was involved aboard a flamethrower APC. Surrounded by 700 litres of flammable fuel, Panzerfäuste and other ammunition I did not feel particularly mobile. From January 1943 only 347 medium armoured flamethrower vehicles (Sd Kfz 251/16) were manufactured. Initially they were built on a Model C chassis, later Model D. The armament was two 1.4cm calibre jet tubes with fast-locking vents and two MG 34s or 42s. (The earlier versions had additionally had a portable 0.7cm calibre flamethrower with a 10-metre long hose.) On operations 700 litres of fuel and 2,010 MG rounds were carried. The jet tubes laterally could cover a field of 160° each side. In order to engage the enemy effectively, either in trenches or in bunkers,

110

it was necessary to approach to within forty to fifty metres. The flamethrower APC was 5.8m long, 2.1m wide and 2.1m high. The armour forward was 1.45cm, at the sides and rear 0.8cm. Weight was 8.62 tonnes, propulsion being provided by a Maybach HL 42 – TUKRM 100-hp motor, maximum speed 50 km/hr.[28]

Three Marder III Model M self-propelled anti-tank guns were also transferred to No 14 Company. These proven Panzerjäger 38(t)s with the 7.5cm Pak 40/3 (Sd Kfz 138) were commanded from time to time by SS-Corporals Feldvoss and Jost, also by SS-Leading Grenadiers Rodenstein, Seberra and myself. The Marder gun-captains transferred in were SS-Leading Grenadier Karl-Heinz Fetzer and SS-Gunner Ludwig Clement.

Chapter Eleven

Operation Advent and the Fighting in the USSR to March 1944

The 1st Ukrainian Front had broken through to Zhitomir, and XXXXVIII Panzer Corps had attacked its flank to prevent its reaching the better road network south of the Pripet Marshes. The attack had not inflicted a disastrous defeat on the enemy, which had assembled Sixtieth Army north-east of Zhitomir to threaten the gap north of the town. XXXXVIII Panzer Corps had now received instructions to eliminate this threat by a surprise attack on enemy elements between the Teterev and the Zhitomir–Korosten highway. These elements faced the German XIII Army Corps. If successful, the German attack would enable XIII Army Corps to turn along the Teterev river and link up with LIX Army Corps to the north.

The attack would bring the Leibstandarte into unreconnoitred territory and so XXXXVIII Panzer Corps declined the order, citing problems of camouflage for reconnaissance. The only certain fact was that all bridges were down between Zhitomir and Korosten. On 2 December 1943, the Leibstandarte units arrived in the Zhitomir area and to the north of it and spent the time up to 5 December improving their operational readiness and in clandestine street reconnaissance. A decoy group had been assembled from the baggage-train and supply column whose purpose was to feint south-east via Zhitomir to deceive the enemy. The three panzer divisions moved off by night to their assembly areas north of Charnjachoff from where they intended to mount an attack to the east after crossing the Zhitomir–Korosten highway. Additionally, 7th Panzer Division was moving to Voldarsk, 1st Panzer Division to Federovka and the Leibstandarte to Sselyanshchina. Peiper prepared this important attack with great forethought and decided his Panzer Group should consist of his Panzer Regiment, the APC battalion, the reinforced panzer reconnaissance unit under SS-Major Knittel, No 2 Pioneer Company under SS-2/Lt Fellhauer, and 5th Flak Battery. On 4 December 1943 he had operational four Panzer Mk IIIs, thirty Mk IVs, twenty-eight Panthers and four Tigers, with a large number either reconditioning or under repair. The 2nd SS-Panzer Grenadier Regiment received orders to follow Panzer Group Peiper and take Korishevka and then Tortchin.[1]

SS-Colonel Wisch wrote of this attack by Panzer Group Peiper shortly afterwards:

On 4 December 1943, the Division was ordered to proceed from the area north-west of Chernjachoff across the Mokrenshchina–Pekarshchina line and attack the flank of the enemy facing XIII Corps, inflicting on the enemy a devastating blow: then, together with the other divisions of XXXXVIII Panzer Corps to facilitate the turning movement of XIII Corps towards the Teterev, linking with the advance of LIX Army Corps.

It was the task of Panzer Group Peiper to set out at 1500 hrs on 5 December 1943, detouring around enemy-held Chernjachoff to the west by night, then proceeding north of Chernjachoff on a broad front through Andreyev, the uplands either side of Styrty and later, without regard to any threat to the flanks, to gain territory in the direction of Radomyshl.

After the Panzer Group had taken Sselyanshchina at 2000 hrs on 5 December 1943 with its foremost elements, 3rd Battalion 2nd SS-Panzer Grenadier Regiment reconnaissance reported that the enemy was dug in west of Pekarshchina in an extensive trench system and had set up an all-round defence in the locality itself. Because it was not possible to go around the position on account of unfavourable terrain, and we had to capture the bridges there intact, Peiper took personal command of the APC battalion and carried out a night attack on the village with unprecedented verve, such that the enemy in the trenches and the village was taken completely by surprise, and was wiped out by gunnery and flamethrower fire from the APCs.[2]

Peiper led this night attack on Pekarshchina initially from Guhl's APC, and for the part Guhl played recommended him for the Knight's Cross:

SS-Captain Guhl recognised the importance of taking this village because the only 50-ton bridge had to fall into our hands undamaged. After a short discussion, SS-Captain Guhl headed his Battalion forward for the attack on Pekarshchina at moonrise. Paying no heed to MG and anti-tank fire, he entered the village at full speed, firing with all weapons, overwhelmed three trenches in front of the village and others inside it, set fire to large parts of the village with his flamethrowers, advanced into the eastern part of Pekarshchina, captured the bridge and, after wiping out large sections of enemy infantry established a bridgehead. He took only two APCs into the neighbouring village to reconnoitre and his vehicle was hit by light anti-tank fire on the MG protective shield. As a result SS-Captain Guhl received a serious head wound and lost an eye.[3]

In the darkness Guhl had first spotted the Soviet anti-tank gun by its muzzle flash and report of the discharge, and it had not been possible to avoid it. SS-2/Lt Gührs wrote:

During this night attack, Guhl and I were in the same APC when the shell from a light anti-tank hit our protective shield. We were standing together, observing the enemy. Guhl was at my left when he was hit. We placed an emergency dressing over the wound and I ordered the APC to go to the dressing station. Peiper was in another APC on the battlefield about fifty metres away. I ran over to him to report. Dinse took command of the battalion immediately and I climbed aboard his vehicle.[4]

The attack continued: 'SS-Major Peiper personally led another reconnaissance towards Andreyev and obtained important information for the attack by his Panzer Group.' As a result of the reconnaissance he set out at dawn on 6 December and after destroying an anti-tank battery took Andreyev at 0600 hrs and blocked the Chernjachoff-Korostern Rollbahn. For my participation at Andreyev on 5/6 December 1943 I was awarded my 42nd confirmed Close-combat Day. East of Andreyev the Panzer Group crushed a number of batteries and after destroying several anti-tank strongpoints reached the high ground either side of Styrty thus achieving the objective for the first day.

In an impetuous advance, the Panzer Group continued eastwards, overran and wiped out enemy batteries and anti-tank fronts, and then mopped up the command posts of 121st Rifle Division at Kisselevka, 322nd Rifle Division at Seliyzshy, 148th Rifle Division at Kamenny Brid and 336th Rifle Division at Kaitanovka, where a halt was made to refuel. For my participation at Kaitanovka, I was awarded my 43rd confirmed Close-combat Day. On this day the Panzer Group captured or destroyed twenty-two field guns, seventy-six 7.62cm anti-tank guns, thirty-eight light anti-tank guns, forty-nine MGs, forty motor vehicles, seventy-one horse-drawn vehicles and the enemy lost 1,450 men dead. 'Despite the extraordinary difficulties of orientation and progress across the terrain, the Panzer Group advanced thirty kilometres into the enemy's rear, destabilised the entire Russian front along that length of territory and enabled XIII Army Corps divisions to advance.'[5]

At 1630 hrs Peiper arrived with the Panzer Regiment and reconnaissance unit at Chaikovka via Tortchin.[6] SS-Colonel Wisch continued:

Because the enemy had temporarily cut the supply road during 6 December 1943, it was not until the afternoon of 7 December that the Battle Group was able to proceed, first to Chaikovka. Here the Russians had gone to extraordinary lengths to install obstructions and set up an anti-tank front brought up from elsewhere, and in order to avoid casualties, SS-Major Peiper had decided not to leave until nightfall, but to go around Chaikovka northwards and then head east again. Towards 1900 hrs the Battle Group was already behind the enemy's back, overcame some anti-tank resistance and pushed east for ten kilometres. The Battle Group was then ordered by Division to bear north, where it took Chodory and then went further north into the heavily defended Sabolot. After fierce house-to-house fighting, SS-Major Peiper had the village in our hands by 1000 hrs. In this night attack, Battle Group Peiper captured or destroyed one T-34, eight field guns, one 4.5cm anti-tank gun, sixty-one 7.62cm anti-tank guns, twenty-one light anti-tank guns, fifty-five MGs and five lorries. 930 Russians were killed, three taken prisoner. This nocturnal advance by his Battle Group, once again operating far behind the enemy's back, created a breach in the extensive defensive system of strongpoints, and prevented an operational bridge head being set up over the Teterev. SS-Major Peiper achieved an extraordinary success by his personal bravery and also the tactical leadership of his powerful unit. His personal dash, his battle plan, the determined execution of the same, as well as his lightning-fast appreciation and manipulation of favourable opportunities, helped his Battle Group, and with it the Division, achieve this great success. Moreover 1st SS-Panzer Grenadier Regiment destroyed or captured in the short period between 21 and 24 November 1943 under his leadership: 100 T-34s, eleven field guns, 124 anti-tank 7.62cm, twenty-four light anti-tank, sixteen lorries, fourteen towing tractors, seven AA guns and two IL2 aircraft.

On account of his repeated extraordinary personal bravery and outstanding leadership of his regiment, I consider the award of the Oak Leaves to the Knight's Cross of the Iron Cross as worthy and request that this high distinction be granted to SS-Major Peiper.
Signed, Wisch, SS-Colonel and Divisional Commander.[7]

On the basis of the citation quoted above, Peiper received the Oak Leaves on 27 December 1943. For Chodory on 7 December 1943, and Kovotka Sabolot on 8 December 1943, I received the grant of my 44th and 45th confirmed Close-combat Days respectively.

Whenever complicated tasks arose, Peiper was always happy to attempt to carry them through with the APC battalion, his particular speciality being his highly successful night attacks with the Panzer Regiment. Gührs, commander of No 13 Company, voiced the general opinion of the officers in the Battle Group when he wrote:

Peiper was the eternal model of the German officer. For us all he had charisma and an unusual aptitude for the profession of soldier. Moreover throughout the entire war he was accompanied by the famous luck of the soldier, and he was very brave. He simply pulled everything off. We had faith in him in the most audacious operations. About his luck. He was already commander of the Panzer Regiment. We were on a night attack with the entire armoured force of the Division, that is, the Panzer Regiment, the SP-guns including the Grilles, the APC battalion – therefore more than 150 tracked vehicles. We were given Marschzahl [route heading] 9. After half an hour I drove up alongside Peiper's command panzer to tell him that the whole Battle Group was going in the wrong direction. It was hardly possible to change it now and shortly afterwards we became embroiled in a major tank battle. Two days later Peiper told me that he had been ordered to report to the Army General. He expected a major dressing down, but it was something else, typical for Peiper. The General thanked him for veering aside and so being positioned to attack the flank of a powerful Soviet thrust.[8]

Together with 2nd SS-Panzer Grenadier Regiment, Peiper's Panzer Group took Meshiritshka towards 1930 hrs on 9 December 1943 after fierce Soviet resistance, and advanced units reached Teterev. For Meshiritshka on 9 December I received my 46th confirmed Close-combat Day.

(TOP) Men in an APC watch a direct hit close by.

(BOTTOM) Jochen Peiper decorates a young panzer grenadier during the Kursk offensive. Behind is his adjutant Werner Wolff, awarded the Knight's Cross shortly afterwards.

(TOP) SS-2/Lt Erhard Gührs was the author's company commander in No 14 Company during the Kursk offensive in July 1943. He wears the Iron Cross First Class and Close-combat Clasp in silver. Behind him is Georg Preuss, to the right Hans Schmidt.

(BOTTOM) An APC with a 3.7cm anti-tank gun. This APC would usually be the platoon commander's vehicle.

(TOP) Italy, August 1943. The author's Grille, in the foreground the gun commander, SS-Leading Grenadier Gerhard Kendzia.

(BOTTOM) Awards of the Iron Cross First Class by regimental commander Hugo Kraas on 16 September 1943 in Italy. From the left, Peiper, Kurt Israel (Guhl's APC driver), and the author's company colleagues – nearest the camera SS-Leading Grenadier Günther Vogel and Erich Jost, both of whom destroyed a Soviet tank in close combat. Receiving the Iron Cross Second Class is SS-Sergeant Johannes Häckel, acting CSM, No 12 Company.

(TOP) Fritz Schuster of No 12 Company (fell, Eastern Front, 21 November 1943).

(BOTTOM) The APC battalion marching through Reggio-Emilia with a song. In the foreground Paul Guhl (Knight's Cross 1944), Jochen Peiper and Werner Wolff.

SS-Leading Grenadier Werner Kindler fought on the Eastern Front in the winter of 1943 as commander of a Grille, of a flamethrower APC and gunner of a Marder SP anti-tank gun. He was wounded for the sixth time on 21 December 1943.

(TOP LEFT) On 15 March 1944 in the rank of SS-Leading Grenadier, the author was awarded the Iron Cross First Class.

(CENTRE) On 5 June 1944 the author was decorated with the Close-combat Clasp in silver.

(RIGHT) On 6 June 1944 the author was decorated with the Wound Badge in gold. He was wounded on six occasions.

(BOTTOM) On 5 June 1944 a number of soldiers of the APC battalion received the Close-combat Clasp in silver for service on the Eastern Front. From left to right: SS-Lt Hans Schmidt (commander, No 11 Company), Heinz Tomhardt (platoon commander, No 13 Company), Heinrich Meyburg (signals officer), Gerhard Babick (commander, No 13 Company), SS-Captain Paul Guhl (commander APC battalion), SS-Lt Georg Preuss (commander, No 12 Company), SS-2/Lt Erhard Gührs (adjutant) and senior surgeon (Luftwaffe) Dr Gustav Haarmann (Iron Cross First Class).

(TOP AND BOTTOM) Training on the new APCs delivered before the invasion. The rear exit doors are clearly visible in the upper photo.

(TOP) In Bree, Belgian Flanders, before the invasion. Back to the camera, right, SS-Captain Wilhelm Haferstroh, extreme right SS-Corporal Paul Pfalzer, hidden Helmut Feldvoss, Toni Motzheim, Klose.

(BOTTOM) In July 1944 the author's platoon was equipped with six APCs armed with 7.5cm guns.

Regarding the operation in this area, SS-Captain Kling's loader wrote:

After Panzermeyer, Major Peiper was undoubtedly amongst the most resolute and daring commanders of the Leibstandarte. We Tiger crews were proud and happy when Peiper took command of the Panzer Regiment after Colonel Schönberger's soldier's death. As commander of 3rd Battalion, 2nd SS-Panzer Grenadier Regiment (the so-called 'blow-lamp battalion') Peiper already belonged amongst those commanders with whom one could feel safe even on foolhardy operations.

In December 1943 near Radmyshl an armoured group consisting of four to five Tigers, some SP guns, Panzer Mk IVs and a number of APCs and amphibious vehicles came along a Rollbahn. A 'Rollbahn' was an unpaved highway which had been bulldozed up to fifty metres wide. In dry weather it looked like a bowling alley, in slush and rain it became a quagmire. This was the approach, or rather the 'moving up for the attack' under Major Peiper.

The leading group was two or three Tigers commanded by SS-2/Lt Wendorff and led by APCs of the reconnaissance unit. We passed through a wooded region a good twenty kilometres behind enemy lines and then – as Peiper confirmed in his memoir – sneaked along the horizon. Towards evening on the second day we regained the German lines. During this operation I was loader in SS-Captain Kling's panzer. I found this very interesting and also lucky for me. Interesting insofar as Kling's panzer was approximately in the middle of the Battle Group, which was proceeding in a fan-shaped order, and immediately behind us was Peiper in a heavy cross-country car. Peiper was perched on the mudguard of this car nursing a submachine gun. I could overhear many of his orders. The forest roads and paths were extremely thickly mined. The mines looked like wooden fish crates with a yellow explosive, and were very well camouflaged. At least three of the leading Tigers ran over mines on those two days and received serious damage to the tracks and suspension. They stood immobile in the woods protected by an APC with half a dozen panzer grenadiers. It really was a stroke of luck for me not to be one of the crews stuck twenty kilometres behind enemy lines. We were all on edge, wondering what would happen that evening once it got dark. That was typical of Peiper: 'Form a hedgehog.' The terrain was some way from the woods with

SS-Corporal Molly's mined Tiger, Peiper's car and Kling's Tiger at the centre. In a radius of 100m the entire Battle Group formed up into this all-round defence.

It was the most nerve-wracking situation in my career as a soldier, but Peiper and Kling, who were close by me, radiated a peculiar confidence despite the fact that we skirmished all night with enemy scouting parties. Apparently the Soviets were confused by the defence and could not work out where the front and back of it was. Grenadier Wenzel, loader of a mined and immobilised Tiger, recounted later that they had gone into a hut in search of food and stumbled across a Red soldier, apparently there for the same purpose. Startled, he dropped his eating utensils and the Tiger people – unarmed – seized the opportunity to take to their heels.

Towards midday on the second day we had to go through the enemy lines from the rear. As far as I remember only Kling's Tiger was still operational. Behind a shack we took up position to destroy an anti-tank gun. We were moving up closer to the hut to align the gun when we received a hit which made the gun shake. I think Bobby Warmbrunn was the No.1 gunner. I opened the breech and as Kling suspected we had a hit on the barrel which we could see from inside it. If we had fired, our shell would probably have exploded in the barrel, killing us all. Peiper, behind us, ordered an SS-Corporal of the reconnaissance section to take out the anti-tank gun. We looked on as these magnificent reconnaissance men hurled hand grenades and then fell on the Russian gun crew. In the late afternoon we reached our own lines and collapsed in exhaustion in the Russians' huts. Now Bubi Wendorff did something typical of him: he went from crew to crew asking for volunteers to help the men stranded with the mined panzers.

Aboard a three-tonne towing tractor loaded with replacement track parts, wheels, ammunition and rations we returned to the two Tigers, and with the assistance of the panzer grenadiers of the reconnaissance section, who meanwhile had occupied forward positions, got them mobile. Yes, there were many reasons why such officers as Michael Wittmann, who was not present at this incident, and Bubi Wendorff, received such respect and admiration in No 13 Company 1st SS-Panzer Regiment.[9]

On 10 December 1943 the Panzer Group set out from Meshiritshka to attack Krasnoborki, but was halted by heavy anti-tank fire at the eastern end. The panzers which engaged these anti-tank positions suffered casualties. The APC battalion was in close combat on ridge 154.2. The attack on Wel.Ratcha via Krasnoborki was resumed by the Panzer Group next day, supported from the north by 1st Panzer Division. For Hill 154.2 on 10 December I was granted my 47th Close-combat Day.

The 2nd SS-Panzer Grenadier Regiment war diary for 11 December 1943 relates:

The hour of attack for the assault on Wel.Ratcha is ordered for 1200 hrs and the following battle plan has been worked out. Assemble in the gullies 2.5kms west of Meshiritshka. 1st and 2nd Battalions will attack together, to the right near 1st Battalion the Grilles, left near 2nd Battalion the Panzer Regiment securing the left flank. Behind the Panzer Regiment, 3rd Battalion. Attack will commence after ten minutes' bombardment. Using this, capture east end Krasnoborki at the earliest moment. Re-form, immediate crossing of the bridge there by panzers and Grilles. After re-formation, Hill 170.2 is to be taken, grenadiers to follow up with attack on Wel.Ratcha, taking advantage of the stream flowing into the north end of Wel.Ratcha. At this point penetrate the village and after turning south, mop up, with support of 3rd Battalion occupy hill at 171.1 and secure.[10]

The attack began at midday. Krasnoborki and Hill 170.2 were taken. The Russian tanks were waiting at the western end of Wel.Ratcha, but all the same, the Panzer Group occupied it at 1650 hrs. For Wel.Ratcha on 12 December 1943 I was granted my 48th Close-combat Day. However, it was not possible to take Chudin because of the strength of the occupying force, and additionally the Russians had heavy guns installed along the raised east bank of the Teterev.

SS-2/Lt Gerd Jahn, platoon leader in No 2 Panzer Company (Panthers) under SS-Lt Hans Malkomes wrote of the commanding officer:

For me, Jochen Peiper was one of the most capable panzer leaders of the Wehrmacht – and during that long war there was opportunity enough for comparison. His high decorations were justly received. But not only for his great example as a military leader, but for something much more – his outstanding personality! A man of great intellect, straightforward and clear in his manner, in his orders, in the execution of his ideas. No blind daredevil to whom success was more important than people – of those we got to know quite a few – but somebody who could analyse, plan and carry out without overestimating his own capability nor underestimating that of the enemy. Unpretentious, modest. We had a great respect for him, all of us.[11]

On 12 December 1943 3rd Battalion under SS-Lt Dinse, reinforced by one Tiger and five Grilles, attacked Badyalovka at around 1430 hrs in order to get to the banks of the Teterev and blow up the bridge. After the APCs and Grilles had broken through the first defences and passed through the village, the Panzer Group received heavy fire from an anti-tank front which, together with the artillery fire from the east bank of the Teterev, made any further progress impossible.[12] Accordingly the Group withdrew to the western end of Badyalovka, while 1st Regiment remained in Sabolot. The commander of 2nd SS-Panzer Grenadier Regiment, SS-Lt-Colonel Kraas, wrote to his wife that day: 'The best of it is that I can tell you I am still hale and hearty – that is something with us! I am writing you these lines quickly in some hut or other here in the countryside: we are in the midst of the most bitter fighting, five days and nights without a break facing the enemy in unimaginably fierce combat. It will soon overwhelm our strength.'[13]

The regimental war diary recorded: 'The men of the units are totally exhausted and therefore apathetic as a result of the enormous demands made on them in the last few days of fighting.' With their attacks against XXXXVIII Army Corps in the Teterev-Irsha river delta the Soviets were aiming to hold the Kiev–Korosten railway line and gain the ground they needed for a major troop build-up. Holding the bridgeheads over the Teterev and the Irsha was therefore very important for them.

At 1130 hrs on 14 December 1943 the Panzer Group attacked, captured Iskra and reached the Weprin–Fedorovka highway, wheeled to the west and followed the bed of the stream to the fork in the highway 1km south of the eastern part of Fedorovka. Two panzers were lost there for three T-34s destroyed. Since there was no possibility of re-crossing the stream before Vyrva, Peiper wanted to cross at Federovka-East. For Iskra on 14 December 1943 I received my 50th Close-combat Day.

At 2100 hrs, on orders from Corps, the Panzer Group disengaged from the enemy and retired to the Sabolot-Chodory area. For a planned panzer attack in the area south of Korosten, meeting the Soviets north-west of Malin, the panzer divisions reorganised. The Leibstandarte was sent west of Meleni. The attack by XXXXVIII Panzer Corps against the Russian Sixteenth Army had given the latter the chance to launch its own offensive.[14] For the action on Hill 179.6 on 15 December 1943 I was granted my 51st Close-combat Day.

The new orders for XXXXVIII Corps envisaged their uniting with 7th Panzer Division from the Janovka-Budilovka area to the north, while 1st SS-Panzer Division and 1st Panzer Division initially to the north-east and later, wheeling south-east, east of Chepovitshi, would meet up with 7th Panzer Division there. The Leibstandarte and 1st Panzer Division moved to the departure point in two legs by night, the LSSAH into the area west of Meleni. On 18 December there was a conference of commanders regarding the attack on Chepovitshi. The goal was the Malin–Korosten road north of Sovchose. On 19 December 1943 at 1043 hrs Peiper set out with the Panzer Regiment consisting of thirty-three Mk IVs, twelve Panthers and seven Tigers operational. The SP-gun batteries would lead the attack with thirteen SP-guns and five 10.5cm howitzers with Peiper and the 2nd SS-Panzer Grenadier Regiment. To their right 1st SS-Panzer Grenadier Regiment with the APC battalion was to capture the area north-west of Sovchose for a further thrust to the south-east. After the two-pronged attack went well and the Russians were ejected from Meleni railway station, the leading vehicles were west of Sovchose at 1335 hrs, and at 1520 hrs Peiper, followed by 1st SS-Panzer Grenadier Regiment, took Balyarka station after a tank battle at Stremigorod in which two T-34s were destroyed.

Virtually the entire 2nd SS-Panzer Grenadier Regiment was involved in close combat at Balyarka. At 1830 hrs the vanguard of the Panzer Regiment entered Peremoga but was stopped by an anti-tank front 1.5km to the east. For Balyarka on 19 December 1943 I received my 52nd confirmed Close-combat Day. XXXXVIII Corps mentioned in its assessment that 'the rapid advance of the LAH threatens the Soviet forces in the Chepovitshi-Meleni area with encirclement'. The commander of XXXXVIII Corps Staff, Colonel von Mellenthin, wrote: 'That type of cooperation in attack from several different directions could only have been achieved by fighting units of high quality. The two panzer divisions [1st Panzer Division and LAH] involved in this attack belong beyond doubt to the best German divisions'.[15]

During this period of fighting without rest, SS-Lt Otto Dinse, commanding the APC battalion had a strange experience. During the struggle for a village he burst into a house and found himself facing a tall Russian officer. He had no chance to go for his weapon. Without speaking the two officers looked each other in the eye. Then the Russian raised his hand and gave Dinse a military salute. Dinse returned it, did an about-turn and left the house.[16]

At daybreak on 20 December 1942 the Leibstandarte panzers were forced by the terrain to pull back 400m from the enemy. 2nd SS-Panzer Grenadier Regiment followed the Panzer Regiment and secured the two crossroads north of Chepovitshi facing to the southward. At 1445 hrs, Peiper's panzers were locked in battle for Chepovitshi railway line which lasted until 1800 hrs when it fell into German hands, assistance having been forthcoming from the Bradel Battle Group meanwhile. For Chepovitschi on 20 December 1943 I was granted my 53rd Close-combat Day. The railway crossing and crossroads north of the village were secured and protected. Because of the heavy Russian anti-tank fire, against which there was no effective defence, the APC battalion was forced to pull back to the point from where it had started that morning. One APC was destroyed by a direct hit. At 1930 hrs the APC battalion reached the level crossing of the railway and Rollbahn and secured to the east and north.[17]

A war correspondent reported the attack of the massed panzers on Chepovitshi thus:

It is now almost dark. We see the muzzle flash from the anti-tank guns, which seem to poke up out from the earth, but they do not see us well. We have to keep a good watch, for the Soviet infantry runs under cover of the dark shadows around the houses and can be dangerous. In the blast of a shell one of the dark huts collapses. A great hole gobbles up the exterior wall and the roof lifts up like a tousled straw-coloured wig flying off a bald head. Something inside is glowing, a flame stabs out and in a few seconds the house is burning like a torch. Now we are in the centre of the village. The commanding officer's panzer rolls quickly down the illuminated street seeking the darkness between two houses. At the other end of the street something explodes with a reddish-yellow fire, and a black cloud of smoke – that was a T-34! A second disappears into a thousand fragments behind it.[18]

The 2nd Battalion of the 2nd SS-Panzer Grenadier Regiment, which entered Chepovitshi from the west, had to clear every dwelling while

122

under anti-tank, tank and mortar fire. 1st and 2nd Battalions, sent to the assistance of Peiper's Panzer Group, reached the outskirts at 2330 hrs and linked up with the Panzer Group at the railway level crossing two kilometres east of the station, but were prevented from achieving their objective by fierce resistance. Seventeen T-34s, four SP-guns and forty-four field guns were destroyed on 20 December 1943.

During the night, Peiper was waiting with the Panzer Group to refuel at the railway embankment east of Chepovitshi. After midnight he noticed numerous Soviet tanks taking on fuel on the other side of the embankment and which appeared not to have seen the German panzers. Relying on the element of surprise he led his panzers skilfully into the attack. In this night attack, numerous Soviet tanks were destroyed.

Hans Oeser wrote about this experience thus:

On the other side of the embankment, outside Chepovitshi, we noticed a lively vehicular traffic. When it got a little lighter we saw that the train with the T-34s had been unloaded and the tanks were being refuelled and taking on ammunition between the houses. At that moment Peiper came up behind the railway embankment in the command panzer with a Mk IV and asked me what was going on. I said we were going to take on the T-34s. At that he enquired, 'What ammunition have you got?'

'Another five or six rounds.'

'Good, I'll give you mine from my panzer,' he said, and gave me seven panzer shells. 'Take care! Three SP-guns are coming up from the south-west to support you. Make sure you don't fire on me!'

Peiper drove off and we got into a firing position. We were three panzers, one of the commanders was SS-Corporal Hans Ahrens from No 5 Company. We opened fire and hit so many of the tanks that later we argued who hit what. We destroyed a total of thirty-two of their tanks and they never fired back. We hit them all broadside-on and they then burst into flames. It would have been difficult to hit us because only our gun barrels would have been visible above the embankment, After that there was concentrated rifle fire from the embankment. At least twenty to twenty-five of our men were shot in the head. At that the company commander of the grenadiers told us: 'I have lost so many people, I'll leave it to you. Those over there must be Siberian snipers. I am going back.' His people got aboard and he headed off for Chepovitshi.

We stood there and had no idea what we were supposed to do next.[19]

I was on the railway line with other Grilles of No 14 Company. On the night of 21 December 1943 the APC battalion had to defend against strong enemy attacks. The Soviets laid mortar and tank fire on all roads, and their tanks on the railway tracks north of Peremoga disrupted our traffic on the Rollbahn. On the morning of 21 December 1943, the Russians harassed the Bormann Battle Group with tanks and infantry.

Despite pressure from the enemy the Battle Group security line was recaptured as far as the row of houses south of Chepovitshi. '1050 hrs: Battle Group Bormann fighting off enemy from all sides. Position held with the utmost effort.' At 0700 hrs SS-Grenadier Wolfgang Günther No 19 Pioneer Company, 2nd SS-Panzer Grenadier Regiment destroyed an enemy tank in close combat. I was present when Grilles from my No 14 Company destroyed two T-34s.[20]

At 1300 hrs elements of 1st Panzer Division arrived from north of the railway lines to support Group Bormann and to join forces. At 1330 hrs Peiper withdrew the Panzer Regiment from the railway embankment because of incessant enemy fire from the railway station. The elements of the APC battalion on the embankment near Chepovitshi suffered heavy casualties. Gührs recalled: 'He' – meaning SS-Lt Dinse, commanding officer of the Battalion – 'was no more than forty metres away from me and was hit by a bullet. He dropped, but then to my surprise rose again. He was wearing a greatcoat over leathers and the bullet had been stopped by them.'[21]

My No 14 Company was fighting alongside No 13 Company. I was commanding a Grille. There was an APC with eight to ten wounded near my Grille on the railway embankment. When the Battle Group was ordered back to the outskirts of Chepovitshi, I took over from the wounded driver of the APC. Shortly before reaching our lines the APC took a hit and I received my sixth wound, a shell splinter into the lower right arm which forced me to report to the battalion dressing station. It put me out of action until 14 January 1944. On 21 December 1943 at Chepovitshi, SS-Leading Grenadier Walter Schott and SS-Grenadier Karl Zander lost their lives. SS-2/Lt Gührs' No 13 Company, which arrived at Chepovitshi with eight APCs and sixty men escaped from this precarious situation with only seven grenadiers unwounded. Seventeen had lost their lives and thirty-six were wounded including Gührs, who was wounded three times.

On that day the Leibstandarte destroyed a total of twenty-three T-34s and two anti-tank guns. The Soviet intention to break out of the Chepovitshi–Meleni area *en masse* to attack Zhitomir to the south-east was frustrated by the Leibstandarte. Our orders to wipe out the enemy troops in this region were accomplished to some extent. Between 8 November and 20 December 1943 the Leibstandarte destroyed 258 enemy tanks.[22] For my part in an action at Ossefovka on 21 December 1943 I was granted my 54th confirmed Close-combat Day.

In the APC battalion, SS-Lt Otto Dinse and SS-2/Lt Gerhard Babick were wounded, and in December amongst others the commander of No 12 Company SS-Lt Georg Preuss, SS-Lt Rudolf Möhrlin and SS-2/Lt Gührs. In these last weeks in difficult situations the Leibstandarte pulled off some remarkable achievements and was constantly at the centre of the XXXXVIII Corps' struggle, the wedge of Fourth Panzer Army. Two of the three major Soviet groups which had crossed the Dnieper in November 1943 were knocked out near Brusilov, the third was deprived of its ability to attack south-east of Korosten[23] but the losses suffered by the Leibstandarte in this endless fighting weighed heavily.

The LAH and 1st Panzer Division transferred within XXXXVIII Corps to the region south of Zhitomir. The Soviets were massing east of Zhitomir to attack XXXXVIII Corps and stood north-east of Kotsherovo. The region was reached on Boxing Day 1943. 2nd SS-Panzer Grenadier Regiment held the line Voliza–Stepok and reconnoitred to Popelnya. At 1230 hrs a T-34 carrying infantry which broke through at Voliza was destroyed by young SS-Grenadier Willi Pfeifer of 2nd Platoon No 14 Company. He was rewarded with special leave and the Tank Destruction Badge on 5 May 1944.[24]

On the grey morning of 2 January 1944 at 1040 hrs the APC battalion with a detail of Panthers beat off an enemy attack from the north against Gorodishche, destroying two T-34s. The whole battalion was locked in close combat at Rudnaya-Gorodishche. The No 11 Company and 3rd Battalion commanders, SS-Lts Schmidt and Dinse respectively, were wounded.

On 14 January 1944 I rejoined my company. I had ten weeks of constant major engagements behind me. The Leibstandarte had spent six weeks attacking and four weeks defending. That the German Eastern Front withstood the enormous pressure from the Red Army, and that Army Group South was not encircled and ripped apart was also due entirely to the Leibstandarte. The severely reduced APC battalion was now commanded by SS-2/Lt Heinz Tomhardt.

The Leibstandarte, attached to XXXXVIII Panzer Corps as from 22 January 1944, moved north of Vinniza on 24 January. There was a thaw and the roads were a mass of mud. Next day the Leibstandarte attacked with Battle Group Kuhlmann south of Rotmistrivka and linked up with heavy Panzer Regiment Bäke. The APC battalion was involved in close combat at Janovka. On 29 January it took Morosovka.[25] During the attacks by Battle Group Kuhlmann between 25 and 29 January, 116 enemy tanks, eighty-nine anti-tank and eleven field guns were destroyed. On 27 January Peiper was awarded the Oak Leaves to his Knight's Cross. SS-Captain Paul Guhl received the German Cross in Gold on 30 December. After his wound on 5 December when he lost an eye, and convalescent leave from 22 January to 15 February 1944, he was ready again for duty, and having been fitted with a glass eye in Berlin resumed command of the APC battalion on 2 March 1944.[26] For my participation at Rotmistrivka on 25 January, at Janovka on 26 January, at Rossoshe on 27 January and Morosovka on 29 January I was credited my 55th to 58th Close-combat Days inclusive.

The Leibstandarte daily bulletin of 7 February 1944 reported that the APC battalion was only available 'as infantry as a result of all its vehicles being out of service'. On 13 February 1944 its serviceable small-arms amounted to two light MGs, one submachine gun, five pistols and four rifles. The remainder of the APC battalion, led by SS-Lt Georg Preuss at that time, headed for the Cherkassy operation. 'The Battalion left by night. We still had six panzers. The rain was torrential. We made slow progress forwards. By morning we still had four panzers. The mud made the roads almost impassable. Then came the real bad luck. A track came apart eight times in three hours. On the way we saw lorries and even Tigers stuck fast'[27] wrote SS-Grenadier Gert Quarthammer of No 13 Company in a field-post letter of the time.

The APC battalion was officially still only a Battle Group and on 9 March 1944 consisted of one officer, four NCOs and seventeen men, less than a platoon.[28] Between 5 and 13 March 1944 I was awarded six confirmed Close-combat Days for actions at Basalia (5th), Kupel (8th), Manatchin (9th), Losova (10th), Voitovzy (11th) and Svaljik (13th) bringing my total to 64. From 23 March 1944 the Leibstandarte was encircled with First Panzer Army, the westwards-wandering Hube pocket. Those elements of the APC battalion not encircled were at Vinniza where SS-2/Lt Gührs was in charge of training.

March 25th 1944 found me at Proskurov, which we abandoned next day. I left town aboard the last vehicle, a motor-cycle with sidecar, and rejoined my company, led by SS-Sgt Haferstroh, at Stanislau. Parts of it went to make up a Battle Group under SS-Sgt Thiele, but Haferstroh sent me off to an NCOs' course at Debica.

SS-2/Lt von Bergmann was detailed to take charge of two Grilles at Tarnopol. Upon arriving at the railway station there he discovered four more Grilles on the transport train. He decided at once to take them all so that in Flanders the Company had six Model M Grilles again.[29]

In constant fighting the exhausted battle groups of the Leibstandarte, long down to the last sweepings, kept up the rearguard. On 14 April 1944 Battle Group LSSAH was finally relieved, and shipped out by train to re-form in Belgium.

Chapter Twelve

The Reorganisation in Flanders, April to June 1944

After a long train journey the men of the APC battalion were found billets in Flanders. Whether panzer grenadiers or panzer crewmen, all soldiers of the Leibstandarte had the worst of the fighting to date behind them.

The APC battalion led by SS-Captain Guhl lay in and around Bree. No 11 Company was at Opitter, No 12 Company at Gardingen (called 'Preussingen' by the men, a play on the term 'Prussian Guard'), No 13 Company at Gruitrode and my No 14 Company at Bree itself. Reorganisation began at once and the companies subjected the new arrivals to intensive training. Every day men were returning from convalescence, several officers came back or were transferred in from elsewhere.

My NCOs' course continued at Lommel. On 10 May 1944 I had to go to Bree where my company was based. Two Grilles had rolled up and some of the battalion paraded in the marketplace of the Flemish village. SS-Captain Paul Guhl decorated a number of men who had especially distinguished themselves in the operations in Russia with the Iron Cross First Class. I had been advised of the award on 15 March 1944 in Russia, and now received it from Guhl's hand.[1] Other recipients were SS-Lt Heinz Tomhardt, commander No 13 Company, SS-Corporal Rudi Knobloch, No 12 Company, and SS-Leading Grenadier Rudi Schwambach, No 14 Company. After this I did not resume the NCOs' course but remained with my company in Bree where I celebrated the award with my comrades at a Belgian tavern. Many Eastern Front veterans were present. During the festivity a man spilt a glass of wine over the breeches of SS-Lt Georg Preuss. The daredevil company commander simply took off his trousers and continued the party in his underpants. I quote this as an example of the closeness existing between the officers and men of the division.

Training was dogged by the difficulties inherent in the fifth year of war and the shortage of fuel. Accordingly we undertook no large-scale exercises with the Panzer Regiment. The reorganisation of the APC battalion continued along those lines, new APCs arrived and the training of the new arrivals showed promise. Nos 11, 12 and 13 Companies were re-equipped with APCs (Sd Kfz 251) armed with the MG 42. The heavy platoons received APCs with light MGs and mortars. My No 14 Company at Bree had six Grilles in the infantry-gun platoon. Grille-commander Heinz Klose transferred out to No 13 Company. Once the Normandy invasion began, however, the Grilles were handed over to the regimental infantry gun company.

Until that time the existence of an SS-paratroop battalion was not generally known in the Waffen-SS, and now it received applications from volunteers in all branches of the Wehrmacht. At No 14 Company, one evening Fuchs the CSM read out an order following which nearly all NCOs of the fighting companies volunteered. Only the forceful intervention of the company commander, SS-Captain Dinse, prevented it being deprived of its battle-hardened NCOs at the time of the invasion. I had also volunteered.

On 4 June 1944 the battalion commander SS-Captain Paul Guhl was awarded the Knight's Cross. The tough Swabian had always led the APC battalion on the Eastern Front from the front, being wounded in the head and losing an eye in the process. On 5 June 1944 I was awarded the Silver Close-combat Clasp for 'more than thirty' confirmed Close-combat Days on the Eastern Front, although by then I had already sufficient confirmed Close-combat Days (64) for the gold clasp as well. The silver clasp also went to Grille commander SS-Corporal Rudi Rayer, flamethrower APC-commander SS-Leading Grenadier Rudi Schwambach, No 14 Company, SS-Corporal Albert Krüger, and SS-Leading Grenadiers Max Schmale, Georg Irmler and Gerhard Sieling of the pioneer platoon. In all the silver clasp was awarded to only thirty-six officers, NCOs and men of the APC battalion: the officers including Guhl, and Hans Schmidt, No 11 Company: Preuss, No 12 Company, Tomhardt and Gührs, No 13 Company and SS-Lt Babick.[2] On 2 June 1944 my company commander SS-Captain Dinse was recommended for the award of the Gold Close-combat Clasp: I was awarded the Gold Wound Badge on 6 June 1944 for being wounded six times in action. Still in the rank of SS-Rottenführer (Leading Grenadier, a non-NCO rank since I had not completed any qualifying course for NCO rank), I wore the Iron Cross First Class, the Silver Close-combat Clasp, the Gold Wound Badge, the Bronze Infantry

Assault Badge and the Ostmedaille, and for some time I numbered amongst the most experienced veterans of my company who in the long months of combat in the East had become the irreplaceable pillars of their unit. It may not be amiss to claim that through our rich experience and uncompromising will to fight we laid the foundations for the successes of the APC battalions of the Leibstandarte. In the front units it was the Rottenführer who were the backbone of every company.

At this time the group leaders and APC commanders were given close-combat daggers. I wore mine on the belt at the rear, right-hand side. The hand-held weaponry was an MG, submachine-gun, bolt-action carbine and pistol. Our company had no automatic rifles. When within the battalions of the two SS-Panzer Grenadier Regiments of the Leibstandarte the MG companies had been disbanded, and absorbed into the heavy armoured companies, the company numbers had changed. On 16 June 1944 the companies of the APC battalion were renumbered. 3rd Battalion (Armoured) 2nd SS-Panzer Grenadier Regiment was now composed of companies numbered 9 to 12 inclusive instead of the former companies numbered 11 to 14. My Company was now No 12 Company.

Gührs had been appointed adjutant to Guhl, signals officer was SS-2/Lt Heinrich Meyburg. The respective commanders of Nos 9 to 12 Companies were SS-Lts Hans Schmidt, Georg Preuss, Gerd Babick and SS-Captain Dinse. SS-Captain Siegfried Wandt took over the APC battalion's supply company.

Peiper led and trained the Panzer Regiment with his distinct personality. One of the most charismatic Waffen-SS officers, his bearing on and off duty – inasmuch as such clearly defined periods existed in the fifth year of war – was considered exemplary by his men. SS-2/Lt Stiller of No 7 Panzer Company remembered him thus:

For me, to my as then unimpressive powers of judgement, Peiper was the most cultured officer in the Division, in substance, as from the heart. My generally very reserved Company commander Werner Wolff once spoke of his time as adjutant to the APC battalion and the long conversations he had with Peiper, which could be considered purely as private tuition in all areas of general personal development. Because he always demanded good bearing of his officers, he was naturally no friend of so-called 'gentlemen's evenings'. Departures of whatever kind from proper bearing, even under the influence of alcohol, provoked his disapproval and he would react accordingly.

At the end of the refresher course at Hasselt, the NCO corps decided to have an evening of merriment to which they also invited the officers and commanders of the regiment. A troupe with dancers, singers and a small band provided entertainment. There was no lack of alcohol and many overdid it. As the evening wore on the mood grew livelier. Suddenly the curtain was raised, an officer, highly decorated, appeared in dancer's costume and pranced a few steps. Rousing applause. Peiper? His mouth was a firm line, no other reaction. Next day the dancer was on report. Confined to quarters, draft a full situation report within three days! An episode which had been relatively harmless but probably showed that Peiper abhorred fun of this kind and binges in general. Peiper knew no compromise with regard to continence.[3]

Chapter Thirteen

Invasion: Securing the Mouth of the Scheldt, 6–17 June 1944

On 6 June 1944 the Allies landed on the coast of Normandy. German intelligence knew that the invasion would come in the first week of June 1944. The greatest armada in history set out from southern England with 6,500 ships, and at 0015 hrs on 6 June British paratroop landings began north-east of Caen. Although the fact of the invasion, and the presence of enemy forces, was confirmed, even at ten that morning OKW was still refusing to allow 12th SS-Panzer Division Hitlerjugend to move, and not until after much telephoning and urging by the Supreme Commander West did OKW finally act at 1430 hrs with regard to Hitlerjugend. At 1507 hrs I SS-Panzer Corps was released from the OKW reserve.

While the German divisions at the invasion front were involved in fierce fighting with the invaders, numerous German divisions in other areas of France and Belgium were ordered to remain inactive. Because the Department of Foreign Armies West was expecting further Allied landings in the Pas-de-Calais, on the night of 9 June the Leibstandarte was moved east of Bruges in order to prevent a push along the coast should the enemy put troops ashore in the Scheldt Estuary.[1] The Division was transferred into the area of LXXXIX Army Corps: Peiper moved the Panzer Regiment east of the Scheldt. All operational elements of the division moved up east of Bruges. The APC battalion was ordered: 'In the event of enemy landings in the Scheldt Estuary, prevent by immediate counter-attack a break-out along the coastal front. Secondly, operate against enemy landings from the air.'

The 2nd SS-Panzer Grenadier Regiment reached Ijzendijke via Lommel–Geel–Westerlo–Bosch–Mechelen–Termonde–Zaffelare–Zelzate–Oosteeklo–Kaprijke. The Leibstandarte took up station south of the Western Scheldt positions, 1st (Panther) Battalion of the Panzer Regiment lay south-east of Knockke-Heist, 2nd Battalion in the Ursel area. The APC battalion occupied positions around St.Margriete guarding the Leopold Canal from the Kaprijke–Ijzendijke road. The APCs and other vehicles were camouflaged against aerial reconnaissance and partially dug-in. Reconnaissance was operated along the

No 12 (Heavy Armoured) Company, 2nd SS-Panzer Grenadier Regiment LSSAH

The principal posts on the invasion front 6 June–1 September 1944 were occupied as follows:

Company commanders: SS-Captain Otto Dinse, SS-Sgt Jochen Thiele

HQ NCO: SS-Corporal Walter Malek

Signal unit: SS-Corporal Adalbert Klein

CSM (acting): SS-Corporal Eduard Funk

Harness-master: SS-Sgt Siegfried Menner

APC Repairs: SS-Corporal Erich Strassgschwandtner

Paymaster: SS-Corporal Roog

Quartermaster: SS-Corporal Springmann

Tank gun platoon:

SS-2/Lt Bernd von Bergmann (wounded 7 August 1944): SS-Corporal Helmut Feldvoss.

Platoon runner: SS-Leading Grenadier Otto Rohmann

Gun-captains of the six APCs equipped with 7.5cm tank guns:

SS-Corporals Helmut Feldvoss, Emil Knappe and Paul Pfalker: SS-Leading Grenadiers Sepp Pointner, Otto Stenglein, Werner Kindler, Karl-Heinz Fetzer, Karl-Heinz Rodenstein, Herbert Exner, Kurt Wiemann, Erich Händel: SS-Grenadiers Ludwig Clement and Fritz Wrede.

Ammunition carriers: 1 APC and three lorries.

Mortar platoon:

SS-Senior Sgt Wilhelm Haferstroh

Four APCs with 12cm mortars

Section commanders: SS-Corporal Max Schmale, SS-Leading Grenadier Walter Götz.

Pioneer platoon:

SS-Senior Sgt Wilhelm Haferstroh

Platoon troop leader SS-Corporal Willi Schneider (fell 18 July 1944)

Section Leader:

SS-Corporal Willi Pluschke

APC commanders:

SS-Corporals Toni Motzheim, Albert Krüger (fell 27 July 1944), Georg Irmler, Günther Ludwig.

assumed area for enemy landings from the sea.

On 19 June 1944, SS-Senior Junker Ensign Luis Brandmeier, leading No 11 Company pending the return of SS-Lt Heinz Tomhardt, wrote:

We spent fourteen days in a region of wild country. This was supposed to be where the main strike of the enemy would fall, paratroopers dropping straight down on top of us, etc, but nothing happened. You can imagine how the appropriate fighting spirit gripped us, but now it has all calmed down. In a few days we are leaving this hospitable region. Rumours abound that we are going to somewhere which last saw us two years ago. Well, that's not so bad, is it? . . . Guhl is commanding the Battalion again, he has got his Knight's Cross at last. His motto is: 'With the help of my glass eye, I shall give them a wooden leg!' Now we have the number of his old company. Dinse is commanding the heap he had previously as are the others, Preuss and Schmidt.[2]

In my No 12 Company an armoured mortar platoon had been newly formed to replace the infantry gun platoon. SS-Sgt Hans Fuchs came from Guhl's Company to take it over. Fuchs (Iron Cross First Class and bronze Close-combat Clasp) was acting CSM. He came from Franconia and had been with me in Vienna in 1940 with another unit. The mortar platoon was to have heavy 12cm mortars aboard APCs, but the latter had not yet arrived. The Battalion having relinquished its Grilles, now I was to command a section of two within a platoon of six APCs fitted with 7.5cm tank guns.

On 15 July 1944 the authorised strengths for armoured SS-Panzer Grenadier Regiments were changed by the War Budget of 1 April 1944. In the case of my company, Otto Dinse's No 12 (Heavy Armoured) Company, a troop was nineteen men: the tank-gun platoon consisted of one officer, seven NCOs and twenty-four men. Of the seven NCOs, six were tank-gun commanders and APC commanders plus the nominal platoon commander. The heavy mortar platoon under SS-Sgt Fuchs consisted of eight NCOs and thirty-seven men, section leaders amongst others being SS-Corporal Max Schmale and SS-Leading Grenadier Walter Götz. The pioneer-platoon remained unchanged under the experienced SS-Sgt Haferstroh. No 12 Company had two officers, twenty-nine NCOs and ninety-five men. Under the new regulations Companies Nos 9 to 12 were supposed to have each three officers, thirty-six NCOs and 144 men.

The German divisions fighting on the invasion front since 6 June 1944, amongst them the Hitlerjugend, sister division to the Leibstandarte, urgently required reinforcements. On 17 June 1944 the Leibstandarte loaded up the APC battalion at Eeklo and were moved by rail overnight to Rheims from where they made their way via Verneuil overland to Normandy. I remained behind at Chaise Dieu chateau with two platoons waiting for the missing equipment and weapons to turn up.

Chapter Fourteen

Action in Normandy, 30 June–20 August 1944

The transfer of the division was completed by 6 July 1944. It located south of Caen under cover of extensive woodland. The panzers dug in at Cinglais Wood. On 6 July 2nd SS-Panzer Grenadier Regiment reached Bretteville-le-Rabet, Quesnay, Ouilly-le-Tasson and Tassily east of the N158 between Caen and Falaise.

On 28 June 1944 Albert Frey led 1st SS-Panzer Grenadier Regiment with HQ and 1st and 2nd Battalions to Venoix on the west side of Caen. At midday two battalions headed either side of the Caen to Villers-Bocages highway for Mouen in order to cut off enemy forces which crossed the Odon near Tourville. Despite heavy resistance the regiment reached Verson and Mouen. Next day the British launched counter-attacks. The elements of 1st Regiment involved occupied positions at Verson, Eterville and Maltot. On 7 July 1944 the sorely-tried town of Caen was the target of a heavy Allied air raid prior to the British-Canadian attack.

The APC battalion (2nd Regiment) moved further south to St André-sur-Orne as divisional reserve. Shortly before it had come as a surprise to us when SS-Captain Josef Diefenthal took command, since he had never served with the battalion previously. He had long been the adjutant to the commanding officer of the division, SS-Major-General Theodor Wisch in his battalion at 2nd Regiment. SS-Captain Guhl departed for the regimental convalescent/rest home at Steinach on the Brenner.[1]

The APC battalion remained understrength in the Orne operational area. When the battalion headed for the invasion front, No 12 Company's mortar and tank-gun platoons had stayed behind to await their APCs. At the front itself Dinse had only the pioneer platoon operational under SS-Senior Sgt Wilhelm Haferstroh. In the chateau Chaise Dieu at Verneuil-sur-Avre I waited for the APCs armed with short-barrelled 7.5cm tank guns to turn up. Six of them finally arrived in the first week of July. I had been appointed section commander within the new tank-gun platoon which meant I commanded two APCs. The platoon commander was SS-2/Lt Bergmann, his No 2 SS-Corporal Feldvoss. The training of the new arrivals on the tank guns and APCs began at once. In contrast to the earlier APCs the new ones were not fitted with radio, instead the platoon commander in the field would have a medium-size radio panzer (Sd Kfz 251/3) at his disposal. The ammunition squad leader had one APC (IG) (Sd Kfz 251/1) for munitions and an open 3-tonne lorry for ammunition and equipment.[2] At the same time the expected APCs with 12cm mortars for SS-Sgt Hans Fuchs' platoon arrived at Chaise Dieu and the mortars were calibrated.

On 22 July 1944 I celebrated my 22nd birthday and the following night the tank gun and mortar platoons set out for Normandy, reaching the company at the front without incident. I was thinking on the way, only a year ago I was in the great offensive at Kursk in Russia. Now I found myself 3,000 kilometres farther west in order to come face-to-face with the Anglo-American invasion force at Caen in Normandy in our attempts to prevent it making inroads towards the Reich. I had not defended Germany on all sides in a gigantic circle, in the East, South and now the West.

On the invasion front things were ablaze. SS-Leading Grenadier Traugott Schmidt (Close-combat Clasp in gold, 1945), 1st SS-Panzer Grenadier Regiment, faced the British and left his impressions for posterity in a field-post letter:

After a six-hour artillery bombardment the British attacked. The sun was blotted out, everything was grey and black, the earth trembled under the impact of endless artillery shelling. Then they attacked, thinking nobody could have survived that. In fighting man-to-man they were repulsed with heavy casualties, without artillery preparation we pursued them at once through hell and advanced. We had not slept for three days and nights . . . in a sector mentioned every day in the Wehrmacht communiqué. We are 1st Regiment Leibstandarte. Either we win, or we die for the Fatherland.[3]

On 11 July 1944 the defended sector south of the national highway Caen-Falaise was transferred to the Leibstandarte between Caen-South and Maltot, thus relieving the Hitlerjugend Division, which had been in action without a break since 7 June. At St André-sur-Orne the APC battalion lost in action SS-2/Lt Albert Baur and three men. The commander of No 9 Company, SS-Lt Hans Schmidt, and twelve men were wounded.[4] On 12 July the battalion lost two men in action at St André, one of them the commander of 1st Platoon in Preuss' No 10 Company, SS-2/Lt Fritz Böcker: seven men were wounded. On 13 July the battalion came under persistent attack from fighter-bombers using bombs and MGs.

On 15 July the Leibstandarte occupied its new area of operations on either side of the N158 which lay ruler-straight north to south between Caen and Falaise. Elements of the Panzer Regiment, such as Nos 5 and 7 Companies, moved eastwards later. The APC companies remained for the time being at St André, Preuss' No 10 Company went to Percauville. SS-Grenadier Helmut Hoffmann of the pioneer-platoon in my Company fell on 18 July 1944.

SS-Corporal Rudi Knobloch of No 10 Company remembered that before a German night attack two or three days after the LAH arrived at the front near Caen, a runner came to him with news that on account of his tally of Close-combat Days he had to leave his unit immediately. At that time he had over fifty. He reported to his battalion commander and, issued with a leave pass, set off for the regimental rest home at Steinach on the Brenner in Tyrol. At Innsbruck station the field police gave him the third degree but eventually he convinced them that his leave was bona fide.[5] SS-Corporal Karl Menne of the mortar group was wounded. Later he led the motorcycle reconnaissance platoon of 24th SS-Panzer Grenadier Regiment Danmark, 11th SS-Panzer Grenadier Division Nordland on the Eastern Front. Possibly he was unique in that he received the Iron Cross First Class from this division after already having been awarded the Iron Cross First Class by the Leibstandarte on 16 September 1944. He was also a recipient of the Close-combat Clasp in gold.[6]

Rudi Knobloch, SS-Hauptscharführer (Senior Sgt)
b. 23 September 1919, Pulsnitz, Kamenz/Saxony
Awards: Gold Close-combat Clasp, 1 April 1945: German Cross in Gold, 20
    April 1945 as SS-Corporal and section leader, No 10 Company, 2nd SS-
    Panzer Grenadier Regiment, 1 SS-Panzer Division LSSAH
October 1933 Joined Hitler Youth
1 February 1937 Entered 9th Sturm, 46th SS-Standarte at age 17
1 October 1939 Transferred to No 2 Company, Leibstandarte Reserve Battalion
    and then to IV/LAH, the guard battalion in Berlin where he was often at

the Reich Chancellery and stood guard outside Hitler's study there
July 1941 With No 17 Company LAH to the Russian Front
2 November 1941 In rank of SS-Grenadier was awarded Iron Cross Second
   Class, and later the Infantry Assault Badge in bronze, and in August 1942
   the Ostmedaille
1 July 1942 Promoted to SS-Corporal
January 1943 led section in No 12 Company, Kharkov area
1 September 1943 Awarded bronze Close-combat Clasp, later silver clasp, and
   the black Wound Badge.
5 May 1944 Awarded Iron Cross First Class.
July 1944 at Caen sent on special leave to the rest home at Brenner (tally of
   over fifty Close-combat Days). After his return to unit was assigned to APC
   battalion supply.
1 October 1944 Promoted to SS-Sgt. Before the Ardennes offensive took over
   1st Platoon of No 10 Company at the request of Preuss.
17 December 1944 Ardennes campaign, Büllingen, received facial wound.
   Awarded silver Wound Badge.
February 1945 Went to Bad Tölz for officer training but no course running:
   Preuss had recommended him for promotion to officer based on his
   personal bravery.
1 March 1945 Promoted to SS-Senior Sgt (Hauptscharführer)
1 April 1945 Awarded gold Close-combat Clasp
20 April 1945 Awarded German Cross in Gold.

On the night of 20 July 1944 the APC battalion left St André and Bully
for a position at Tilly-la-Campagne. SS-Lt Hans Schmidt's No 9
Company at Troteval fought off a tank attack there that afternoon.
Because of constant pounding by artillery and the fighter-bomber
attacks, the company was forced to abandon Troteval. In mist and rain,
Nos 5 and 6 Panzer Companies attacked Canadian anti-tank positions.

APC battalion HQ and No 9 Company arrived at Verri'res while the
remainder waited as before at Tilly. On 24 July the commander of 2nd
Platoon, No 10 Company, SS-Sgt Egmont Eichler, fell. He had been my
heavy MG section leader in the fighting for Kharkov in 1943. The
adjutant of the APC battalion, SS-Lt Gührs reported:

I passed through the main front line by motorcycle and sidecar to an
advanced post of No 9 Company, platoon of 2/Lt Walter Kern, who
wanted to withdraw temporarily because of the bombing. In this
sector the Allies were using bombs and artillery almost exclusively to
conquer the territory. For us it was a battle of man against steel, but

also cat and mouse. After every bombardment we re-occupied our trenches. In the prevailing situation no opportunity presented itself to Peiper to intervene personally with the panzers in the fighting and mostly he stayed put in his command post in the Garcelles-Secqueville chateau.

Chapter Fifteen

Tilly-la-Campagne, Caen and Falaise to the Westwall: 25 July–November 1944

My tank-gun platoon leader SS-2/Lt von Bergmann was transferred from the invasion front to the Führer-reserve after three days. SS-Corporal Feldvoss took command of the tank-gun platoon and I became his No 1 and half-platoon leader. No 9 Company had two wounded and two missing at Verrières. On the right flank of the division, the enemy attacked Tilly-la-Campagne on 26 July 1944 at 0330 hrs after tremendous artillery fire but they were held off by panzer grenadiers of the APC battalion and No 7 Panzer Company under SS-Lt Werner Wolff, former adjutant of the Battalion. SS-2/Lt Gerhard Stiller, commander of No 1 Platoon, reported on No 7 Company's battle at Tilly as follows:

The balloon went up on the night of 25 July 1944. It was no longer harassing fire over an entire sector, Tilly was being churned up for their assault. The infantry cowered in their holes, the panzer crews took shelter under their vehicles. Mortar and artillery fire plastered us. The individual vehicles had clear instructions in the event of attack. Daybreak came. We were fortunate that the sun was so low, the Canadian tanks coming up from the north-west had it in their eyes. Let them come closer, was the word. They lowered their barrels at our forward positions. Finally a white flare – fire at will! The panzers fired tracer from concealment. Round chased round from our barrels while more panzers joined our concealed ranks. Less than five minutes of this and the Canadian attack came to a standstill. When would the second wave arrive to push the stalled attack forward? They had nothing. From behind us we heard a roaring and a booming. Heavy mortars, and 500m ahead of us all hell was let loose. How those boys cleared out the Canadians from our sector of territory![1]

On this day of fighting at Tilly, the APC battalion sustained thirteen dead and twenty-six wounded. SS-Lt Heinz Tomhardt's No 11 Company was hit especially hard. It fought off several Canadian incursions, including one with tanks, by immediate counter-attacks and took thirty-six prisoners and two wagons, but suffered four dead and nineteen wounded. My company comrade SS-Corporal Willi Pluschke was attached to Tomhardt's company with his section from the pioneer platoon. In an enemy assault Pluschke captured sixteen Canadians single-handed. When he arrived at Tomhardt's command post, he was told to take them to the battalion command post. When Pluschke reported the details to SS-Captain Diefenthal there, the latter immediately removed his own Iron Cross First Class and fastened it to Pluschke's breast pocket. However, a recommendation for the award of the Honour Roll Clasp for this brave front soldier was not acted upon.[2]

In SS-Senior Sgt Haferstroh's pioneer platoon, SS-Corporal Willi Schneider, SS-Grenadier Ernst Arlt and 35-year-old SS-Grenadier Fritz Mitschke fell on 25 July 1944, and also SS-Grenadier Karl-Heinz Küllgans. The pioneer platoon was very valuable to the APC battalion in Normandy. When not clearing landmines they often fought on foot. During this fighting on the Caen–Falaise highway a confident mood began to develop in the APC battalion because the enemy was being consistently fended off.[3] Despite a massive investment in men and material, the Canadians had not prevailed in the face of the determined resistance of the Leibstandarte and abandoned their Operation Spring.

The APC battalion was able to use its mobility and firepower in these skirmishes because in the characteristic hedge country of Normandy the panzer grenadiers had mostly to fight on foot. Careful camouflage for the APCs and the men was of great importance. Allied air supremacy was a constant menace to every individual soldier and every move and movement had to be carefully thought about before acting. Refuelling was done at night. Because the 7.5cm tank-gun APCs could no longer be directed by radio, the section leaders and gun commanders were subject to greater demands on their decisiveness and personal decision-making. In action in the APC I would sit behind the driver. We would be in the midst of loud noises, shells bursting all around, the bark of our own cannon and the roar of the motor. I found it convenient to tap him on the left or right shoulder with a riding crop to indicate which way to go. When we attacked with our vehicles, we had to make lightning-fast decisions or we would be lost. SS-Corporal Albert Krüger (Iron Cross First Class 20 April 1943, Close-combat Clasp in silver), aged twenty fell on 27 July 1944, SS-Corporal Toni Motzheim was wounded. For Tilly on 25 July 1944 I was awarded my 65th confirmed Close-combat Day. SS-Captain Michael Wittmann (Knight's Cross, Oak Leaves and Swords), the most successful German panzer commander, wrote on 30 July 1944: 'The war has become very hard. One would think it hardly possible what our grenadiers, for long periods without rest and exposed to the greatest stress, have achieved.'[4]

The battalion's APCs were camouflaged and partially dug-in in orchards. Fresh reserves arrived. At Tilly, SS-Grenadier Helmut Neumann remembered:

In my scanty schoolboy French there was one indispensable phrase: 'Bonjour Madame, avez-vous quelques oeufs a vendre?'. Every morning I would set out on a tour of local farms and buy the eggs with our soldiers' pay. I would usually return to our panzer with ten to fifteen and first fry a couple with the blow-lamp to give the men a taste. Next we would dig out a lump of earth, lay three bricks around the edges in a horseshoe shape and put the frying pan on top. That was our stove and the blow-lamp beneath it the fire source.[5]

The enemy persisted with attacks against Tilly on 31 July and 1 August, but we managed to hold on to it in fierce fighting. For my participation at Tilly on 27 and 31 July, and 1 and 2 August 1944, I was awarded my 66th, 67th, 68th and 69th Close-combat Days respectively. For the brave resistance of No 7 Company at Tilly, company commander SS-Lt Werner Wolff (Knight's Cross) was recommended by Peiper on 2 November 1944 for a mention in the German Army Honour Roll:

In the heavy defensive struggle south of Caen, Company Wolff at Tilly was an extraordinarily important pillar of the entire front line against an enemy attacking constantly with unparalleled material superiority. The course of the main front ran back both sides of Tilly village and provided a flanking effect against enemy positions. Every day and night the incessant enemy attacks highlighted the significance of this extremely important position. Had the enemy taken Tilly, a withdrawal of the whole front in the sector of I SS-Panzer Corps LSSAH would have been unavoidable. The endless heavy artillery bombardments and numerous attacks by enemy fighter-bombers and low-level fighters led one to believe that this important position might have to be abandoned. SS-Lt Wolff organised a basis of defence which repulsed every attack of the numerically superior enemy.

On 21 July 1944 strong Canadian infantry forces in regimental strength supported by ten tanks pierced our front line, which had again been under the heaviest artillery bombardment for three hours. This reduced the village of Tilly to rubble. After breaking down the resistance of our own infantry, forced to pull back before the enemy pressure, the enemy entered the village with infantry and armour. SS-Lt Wolff kept his deeply dug-in panzers in their positions and organised defensive fire based on strongpoints. At the same time other enemy forces arriving from the south-east had approached the unprotected rear of Company Wolff and were threatening to wipe out the defence. SS-Lt Wolff decided at once to emerge from cover in his command panzer, forced back the advancing enemy in bitter house-to-house and street fighting and stabilised the German defence. During this battle nine of the ten enemy Sherman tanks were destroyed.

On 31 July the enemy succeeded again in breaking through the main front line to attack the Company from the rear. Here again SS-Lt Wolff was successful, by means of a skilful counter-attack with his own panzer and without any support, in wiping out the enemy infantry in a battle lasting an hour and a half, and destroyed two of the enemy's five Sherman tanks. A further three enemy attacks were disposed of similarly by SS-Lt Wolff. In this fighting, his unit suffered only a small number of casualties for the following successes: thirteen enemy tanks, two lorries, two armoured MTPs, two towing tractors, and two anti-tank destroyed, one lorry captured and thirty prisoners taken. The enemy lost about 200 men dead and wounded. These successes and the fact that the entire defence by 1st SS-Panzer Division LSSAH, which depended on whether Tilly was held or fell, was exclusively the personal contribution of this outstanding soldier. Under artillery fire day and night, that kind of exemplary will to fight and the cold-bloodedness of Company Wolff was due entirely to its always imperturbable and outstanding Company commander. SS-Lt Wolff was wounded for the fifth time in this fighting in Normandy. He is worthy to be mentioned in the Honour Scroll of the German Army.[6]

The defence of Tilly by No 7 Company was very similar to the operations by the APCs and Peiper's Panzer Regiment. In Normandy no major attacks were possible, apart from that of the Panther Battalion on 18 July 1944. After that there were only local forays while the routine of the panzer crews was defensive. Well camouflaged, often half-buried, they awaited the attacks of the British and Canadians, destroyed attacking tanks from positions of cover and having separated off the infantry, would usually bring the attacks to a standstill.

The artillery concentrated on the panzers was unbelievable, and additionally the Allied air forces were everywhere. Wolff's platoon leader SS-2/Lt Stiller wrote:

At least the greater part of the fighting received its stamp in the bocage countryside and was a defence aimed at a delaying resistance. This meant that the company never fought as a uniform task force, forcing the company commander to make a purely tactical assessment on two or more levels. Because the majority of No 7 Company's operations in Normandy were as infantry support in defence, basically a dug-in and concealed defensive arrangement by platoon, or mostly even in half-platoons, Wolff's orders were mainly of an anticipatory nature. At Tilly he was hardly able to influence the fighting at all, but even the most experienced panzer commander could not have done any better. Flares and messengers were used to transmit the orders because radio signals from the entrenched and practically immobile panzers would have betrayed their positions. Once triangulated, a panzer would have been exposed to concentrated artillery fire. In any case, as regards the situation at Tilly, Wolff acted correctly. In my opinion he could not have done any different, so that his presumably minor panzer-tactical experience played practically no role. His pronounced self-confidence always allowed him to present himself as master of the situation. Never for an instant did I ever detect a weakness of leadership in him.[7]

The Canadian Army historian C.P. Stacy wrote '1st SS-Panzer Division kept to the task, evidence of their inflexible resolve not to give up'.[8] On 1 August 1944 the APC battalion transferred out of Tilly to Rocquancourt and May-sur-Orne, one company going into trenches on the blood-soaked ridge 112. The APC battalion adjutant Gührs wrote:

In that location, a small village with a tall church spire, we were totally tucked away and positioned with the companies at the edge of the village in trenches under orders neither to fire nor let ourselves be provoked. The mortar spotter sat in the church spire. This went on for three days. It deceived the Canadians into believing the village was unoccupied. So along they came in the bright midday sun without any protection, and when they were close enough to our village mortar fire sealed off their retreat and all we had to do was round them up. The youngsters were terribly worried at being in the hands of the SS, of whom their propaganda had fed them so many fairy stories of atrocities. Our field kitchen had just turned up with coffee and we were really pleased at being able to invite them to join us. The we handed them over to the regimental HQ.[9]

On 19 July 1944 the Americans had succeeded in capturing St Lô on the western flank of the German northern front, and after that broke through the German front near Avranches to the south. Seventh Army led by SS-General Hausser now planned a counter-attack from east to west towards Avranches on the coast in order to cut off the advanced enemy force from its lines to the rear. XXXXVII Panzer Corps with 2nd SS-Panzer Division Das Reich, 17th SS-Panzer Division Götz von Berlichingen, 1st SS-Panzer Division LSSAH, 2nd Panzer Division and 116th Panzer Division were to lead this attack. The Leibstandarte's move to the west on the night of 5 August 1944 was hampered and the complete division could not make the date ordered, 7 August. The Leibstandarte would now attack St Barthélemy north of Montain, and then continue west.

On 7 August, SS-Major Kuhlmann had about sixty panzers at his disposal. The Leibstandarte would now be fighting US troops for the first time. At 0200 hrs that day the German Operation Lüttich (Liège) began. The Panther Battalion headed for St. Barthélemy via St Clément, but was delayed by the burning wreckage of a crashed bomber on the approach route. In thick fog the Panthers headed north for Barthélemy but went past to the south of it, recognising their error around the Le Bourlopin Hill. Then the skies cleared. Fighter-bombers and Typhoon fighters dived as if demented on the German panzers. After hours of repeated low-level attacks the progress of the Panzer Regiment came to a halt. Contrary to what is alleged in various publications, this Panzer Regiment attack was led by Kuhlmann and not Peiper.[10]

Elements of 2nd SS-Panzer Grenadier Regiment fought around St Barthélemy. Gührs described the fighter-bomber attacks: 'It looked to me as though there were about two hundred aircraft. One for each of our vehicles. We baled out quickly into the roadside ditches and gnashed our teeth as we watched our column being taken apart. It was a dreadful jumble.'[11] SS-Lt Georg Preuss, commander of No 10 Company, stated:

It is probably true that a shot-down fighter-bomber crashed into a panzer and nobbled it, but most of the other panzers and APCs became victims of these extremely intensive hours of low-level attacks. The grenadiers, insofar as they were still able, sought cover left and right in a countryside rich in hedgerows: they were quite happy when the swarms of fighter-bombers sought more rewarding targets than individual soldiers. As was I. I heard that Peiper had had a heart attack. Diefenthal had lost his hearing after a bomb went off in his immediate vicinity and Kuhlmann did not succeed in getting any farther forward. My brave despatch runner Grenadier Horst Reinecken fell while bringing a report to the superior Army panzer unit that its commanding officer and adjutant had fallen not far from my hedgerow.[12]

After a hard fight the panzer grenadiers of the APC battalion forced the Americans out of St Barthélemy. Preuss' men fought relentlessly: 20-year-old SS-Corporal Eduard Maron (Iron Cross First Class 16 September 1944, Close-combat Clasp in silver, Tank Destruction Badge, silver Wound Badge) destroyed an enemy tank in close combat. SS-Corporal Hans-Günther Bergerowski (Close-combat Clasp in silver) fell on 8 August 1944. For my participation at St Barthélemy on 7th and 8 August 1944 respectively I was awarded my 71st and 72nd confirmed Close-combat Days.

No 9 Company headed west of St Barthélemy to La Fresne Poret. SS-2/Lt von Bergmann, returned to my Company, was wounded by fire from fighter-bombers: the pioneer-platoon lost SS-Grenadier Helmut Lusar, fell on 7 August 1944 at St Barthélemy, and also APC battalion surgeon Luftwaffe-Stabsarzt Dr Eberhard Lucknow: SS-Captain Dinse took command of the battalion. My company colleague, 18-year-old Officer-Aspirant Helmut Neumann, recalled: 'For the counter-attack on Avranches elements of our company were included; my friend Roderich Schneider was there, I was not. The tank guns on our APCs were not really the right weapon against American Shermans. All the same we did knock out some, as we noted with pride.'[13]

Mental, as well as physical, exhaustion now began to spread through the ranks of the APC battalion. Gührs wrote:

Our battalion command post was a hole in the ground. There were Americans ahead of us and we had a constant artillery barrage all day. In the evening a messenger arrived from Regiment with the order to attack. SS-Lt Hans Schmidt and I exchanged glances, then we got a direct hit in the trench. What remained of Schmidt stuck to my tunic. I lost consciousness and when I came to noticed that blood was spurting in my face from my upper arm. I tied it off with a belt and then probably lost consciousness again. Found by messengers searching for the Battalion command post, I was taken by panzer to the main dressing station. The tent was full of wounded, everybody laid out on the straw-covered floor waiting to be operated on. When my turn came the surgeon told me I should remove my wristwatch because he had to amputate the arm . . . [14]

It was on this day east of Gaumesnil on the far side of the Caen-Falaise highway that the most successful panzer commander of the war, SS-Captain Michael Wittmann, lost his life when his Tiger received a direct hit and blew up in a field, the death of a panzer soldier.

My company was reinforced by the discovery of three abandoned APCs with 7.5cm tank guns, so that my platoon now had nine such vehicles. SS-Corporal Hans-Joachim Redecker (Close-combat Clasp in silver) of Preuss' No 10 Company, fell at Joué-du-Bois on 14 August 1944. On 17 August SS-Captain Otto Dinse, strengthened by two Panzer Mk IVs, crossed the Orne in order to hold the road for the retreat over the Nécy crossroads. In the course of the fighting, the Leibstandarte had become caught up in the encirclement at Falaise. On 20 August the mixed battle-groups of the division attempted to break-out to the east near Chambois. During this operation the divisional commander, SS-Major-General Theodor Wisch, was seriously wounded but was brought out in an APC. Otto Dinse was wounded for the fifth time this same day. He refused to give himself up to captivity as per his motto: 'The Leibstandarte does not surrender.' A vehicle of his company found him at the last moment.[15] For my participation in the fighting inside the Falaise pocket between 18th and 20 August 1944 I was awarded my 73rd, 74th and 75th Close-combat Days respectively.

The division broke out of the Falaise pocket en masse, losing nearly all its equipment and weaponry in the process. However, my tank-gun platoon of No 12 Company got away with all nine APCs intact and crossed the Seine at Rouen. From there on the sixty-one dispersed groups of the division, constantly harassed by the Americans and their aircraft, moved east across France until they reached Belgium. The division was commanded by SS-Lt.Colonel Franz Steineck, commanding officer Panzer Artillery Regiment, until SS-Colonel Wilhelm Mohnke took over on 30 August 1944.[16] On 4 September 1944 the Leibstandarte received orders to proceed to Germany to reorganise. After crossing the Reich border the Division set up a signals centre at Siegburg. The APC battalion was at Heidelberg, my No 12 Company at Schwabenheimerhof.

Previously, at the end of August, my tank-gun platoon plus the pioneer and mortar platoons of No 12 Company had been at Charleroi in Belgium for a short time. On 1 September Battle Group Diefenthal was set up, consisting of my company, No 12, 2nd SS-Panzer Grenadier Regiment, one platoon of No 9 Company, elements from 1st Battalion 1st SS-Panzer Grenadier Regiment and the 7.5cm-Infantry gun/Anti-tank Company, also known as the Testing Company, under SS-Lt Otto Woelky. Commanding officer was the commander of the APC battalion Diefenthal, adjutant SS-2/Lt Wolfgang Lüdeck. For an incident at Charleroi in early September 1944 I was awarded my 77th Close-combat Day. There were now twelve 7.5cm tank-gun APCs in my No 12 Company. Nine of them went to Battle Group Diefenthal while the other three were taken to Germany shortly after by Helmut Feldvoss, Erich Händel and another for training the new intake.[17]

Originally I was supposed to return with them to the Reich, but remained on the express order of Diefenthal as commander of a tank-gun section (two APCs) and half-platoon commander of the tank-gun platoon. I was given a new APC and Händel's crew. My gunner was SS-Leading Grenadier Oskar Niessner, loader SS-Grenadier Grenzer and driver SS-Leading Grenadier Ernst Höppner. No 12 Company's tank-gun platoon was commanded by SS-Corporal Emil Knappe. His gunners were all SS-leading grenadiers: Donnhäuser, Herbert Exner, Karl-Heinz Fetzner, Husen, Fritz Müller, Karl-Heinz Rodenstein, Fritz Wrede and myself. The task of Battle Group Diefenthal was to block the entry into Belgium of the advancing armour wedge of the US VII Corps.

Towards 2300 hrs on 1 September 1944 the APCs arrived in the small French town of Avesnes-sur-Helpe near the Belgian border and took up positions in the town and its outskirts. I did not arrive until the following morning because of technical damage and had to wait for the breakdown crew. I was shown to a position in Avesnes near the entrance to the town. Early on the morning of 2 September we heard the rattle of tank tracks and some American armour appeared. Both sides opened fire at once. Where the road forked I had placed my vehicle behind a wall close to an alley which passed a church and then curved out of sight. The other APCs were beyond this bend so that I could not see them, although I heard them firing, and driving past they shouted something about tanks being hit. Suddenly two Shermans appeared in the alley at the far end. They had to negotiate the bend, which forced them to reduce speed, and this gave me the chance to knock them both out at a range of 200m. Now I had to change location since I was alone in the open.

Sgt Braasch told me where I should reposition my APC. Hearing this, a comrade warned me that the Americans were already there. I did not think this was likely, moved up and stood on the gun to observe. I could see the Americans at the crossroads. I had no idea where the other APCs had gone. I had no maps although Feldvoss had detailed me as the leading APC. I had destroyed two American tanks, the other vehicles of my platoon destroyed five more. The 7.5cm gun fitted to an APC was only suitable for engaging enemy tanks at close range and in good conditions. It was used earlier in SP-guns, but was not the weapon for employment against Shermans in 1944. You had to have a good position and hit the tank in the right spot or you could not expect much. Everything was luck. But even if the gun was not properly calibrated, its trajectory was so flat that you were bound to get a hit at 200m.

Immediately after this battle APC commander SS-Corporal Helmut Feldvoss wrote:

In the early morning of 2 September we occupied Avesnes where we were to intercept the leading enemy tanks and destroy them. When as expected they appeared at first light, they encountered stiff resistance. Our platoon destroyed seven of them. Then more of them came up and we were threatened with encirclement. Accordingly we beat it out of there. During this withdrawal, Fritz Wrede's APC was hit. Fritz and his crew got out and sought cover between the houses. We succeeded in salving and repairing the APC. Meanwhile Fritz and his men made their way back from the eastern end of the town where other comrades picked them up. During our withdrawal the Americans attacked and broke up the company, but most of us managed to escape.

When the company was scattered, the grenadiers of the mortar platoon under SS-Sgt Hans Fuchs could not be accounted for and it was assumed they had been outflanked and then encircled. These men were taken prisoner, as were SS-Corporal Max Schmale and SS-Leading Grenadier Walter Götz.

After the battle I had been left alone on guard behind Avesnes with my APC. Suddenly a 2/Lt came past in a lorry and told me I was the last outpost, beyond me were only Americans. At my back was a village. I had noticed armed partisans infiltrating it. I left at once, crossed a bridge and met my company commander, SS-Senior Sgt Thiele. I held up in a farm. Pioneer-platoon commander SS-Senior Sgt Haferstroh decided to reconnoitre in an amphibious vehicle. Despite my warning that there were Americans in the vicinity he left anyway and shortly afterwards I saw him being captured. It is not known what happened to him next in American hands, but on 3 September 1944 the Americans shot him at Binche. His grave is in the German War Cemetery at Bourdon, France.[18]

In the following days I often drove on reconnaissance on Diefenthal's orders to establish where the Americans were, and almost every day I called in at his command post to report. We fought our way to the Reich border and then along the Westwall defences between Bitburg and Aachen. Of my tank-gun APC crew, my gunner SS-Leading Grenadier Oskar Niessner received the Iron Cross First Class and was promoted to SS-Corporal, gunloader Grenzer received the Iron Cross Second Class. For my engagement at Avesnes on 2 September 1944 I was awarded my 76th Close-combat Day: for incidents at Fleurus on 4 September, at Ohey on 7th and at Modave on 8th I was awarded my 78th, 79th and 80th Close-combat Days respectively.

Between 11 September 1944 and the beginning of October 1944 my colleagues and I guarded the frontline along the Westwall from Neuerburg in the Eifel mountains towards Aachen. We did not use the bunker complex but worked as an armoured unit with a seated crew ready for mobile engagements. The Americans attacked the Westwall here and there but failed to penetrate it and so it held out as the German main front line. During these operations, on 1 October 1944 I became an NCO when promoted to SS-Unterscharführer (Corporal). For my part in the fighting at Vibrin on 11 September 1944 I was awarded my 81st Close-combat Day.

On 9 October 1944 I was ordered to assist Battle Group Diefenthal in ejecting enemy forces from the village of Würselen which had been attacked by the Americans at 1220 hrs and German forces driven out. The Battle Group held the area south of the Gouley colliery overnight facing ten Shermans. Although the order had been received to transfer to Aachen, on 10 October Battle Group Diefenthal intervened at Würselen to relieve hard-pressed units of 116th Panzer Division Windhund. The Americans abandoned the western end of Würselen, losing two tanks to Panzerfäuste in the process. On 12 October, when I took my crew to occupy a house as quarters, we were inspecting the cellar when an artillery round hit the inside of my APC parked outside and destroyed it. After that I proceeded to Hofen near Düren to the Company supply and baggage train and from there back to No 12 Company which was reorganising at Rulle near Osnabrück. For my participation in the fighting at Würselen on the three days 10–12 October 1944 I was granted my 82nd to 84th confirmed Close-combat Days. I have not been able to discover if any further Close-combat Days were credited to me between 12 October 1945 and the end of the war.

The remainder of the Battle Group transferred to Aachen on 13 October, from where until 22 October only nineteen men escaped after heavy house-to-house fighting. Amongst these survivors was tank-gun platoon leader SS-Sgt Emil Knappe.[19] The APC battalion lay at Engter, No 12 Company at Rulle. The battalion commander was SS-Major Siegfried Wandt. By the end of October 1944 not even half of the authorised complement of panzers had arrived and so Peiper had only thirty-two instead of ninety-six Mk IVs and twenty-four instead of seventy-three Panthers, and no command panzer. Nos 3 and 4 (Panther), 5 and 8 (Mk IV) Companies, lacking tanks, were amalgamated into 2nd Battalion of the Panzer Regiment. Peiper appointed the former commander of the APC battalion, SS-Captain Paul Guhl, as commanding officer. Both battalions were formed into a training company each: that for the Panthers was led as from 2 November 1944 by SS-Lt Werner Wolff, recovering from his serious leg wound sustained in France.[20]

The German Reich found itself in a desperate situation. At the eastern borders, the unswerving Soviet armies had reached East Prussia. The American advance from the west had been held at the Westwall. The German cities lay under a deluge of American and British bombs day and night. The armaments and fuel industries had suffered losses which could not be made good. The German forces knew the war aim of the Allies, repeated over and over again: the unconditional surrender and occupation of Germany, which would mean a Reich unarmed and defenceless, its population deprived of the protection of national and international law. What would come to pass in the German Homeland if the final battle were to be lost had been shown clearly by the enemy Powers. In some parts of East Prussia where the Red Army had penetrated, the Soviets had already shown the world their face in murder and rape.

Despite all the difficulties inherent in this fifth year of the war, with all its severe psychological stresses, training continued in the Leibstandarte. Peiper described it thus:

Really outstandingly good when you remember it was the fifth year of the war. Of belief in victory, enthusiasm, fanaticism there was naturally no longer any sign, rather there was a mood of defeat mixed with defiance and gallows humour. That the Waffen-SS could expect nothing good from the Russians was clear to everyone and, after hearing the filthy lies and slander regularly broadcast by the evil Soldatensender Calais operated by the BBC, even the dumbest of us knew what was being cooked up for us in the West. Before they tipped us over, however, there were a few things we wanted to try out beforehand.

Chapter Sixteen

The Führer-Escort Company, the Gold Clasp and Preparing for the Ardennes

I was with my company at Rulle involved in training the new arrivals when my company commander SS-Senior Sgt Thiele informed me that I had been recommended for the award of the Close-combat Clasp in gold, and the German Cross in Gold on the basis of fifty-six confirmed Close-combat Days. Actually I had far more than fifty-six, which I had earned exclusively in Russia. Those at the invasion front and with Battle Group Diefenthal had not been entered in my Soldbuch. On the basis of the entries in the Soldbuch of SS-Captain Herbert Rink, who had commanded Battle Group Diefenthal at Aachen and had also been recommended for the gold clasp and German Cross in Gold, I was able to reconstruct my confirmed Close-combat Days in those operations subsequent to my 56th (on 26 January 1944 at Yanovka).

I was the first Leading Grenadier (my rank as at 26 January 1944) of the Leibstandarte to be recommended for the Close-combat Clasp in gold. According to an order of the Führer, these soldiers were to be withdrawn from direct frontline operations. Now to my surprise I found that I was to be transferred to the Führer-Escort Company. In the summer of 1944, two of these had been set up within the Waffen-SS which took turns protecting the current Führer-HQs or in being at the front. No 2 Führer Escort Company was an APC company operational in 1944 under the Army's Führer Escort Brigade.

I went off to the Leibstandarte's divisional HQ at Lübbecke, where I found other NCOs available for selection. The conditions were that the applicant must hold at least the Iron Cross First Class, be an NCO at least 1.8m (5ft 9in) tall. Since my objective was to avoid selection, and I was only 5ft 7in, I placed myself between one man over 6ft 5in tall and another 6ft 2in. Thus I achieved my aim. I met SS-Captain Georg Bormann, my former company commander, and after a conversation he gave me a bottle of schnapps and then I returned to my company.

In October 1944 at Rulle my company had been equipped with three tank-gun platoons and now had available eighteen APCs armed with 7.5cm guns. Six of these made up a platoon. I took over 3rd Platoon, the other platoon leaders were SS-Corporal Helmut Feldvoss and SS-Sgt Paul Pfalzer. SS-Senior Sgt Jochen Thiele led No 12 Company again: he had commanded it several times in Russia and for a longish period in Normandy. Officer-Aspirant Helmut Neumann remembered:

Amongst ourselves we called Thiele 'Uncle Jochen' – that seems to me an apt description. My duties brought me into contact with him at Schwabenheimerhof. The Company had had losses in Normandy: there were letters to write to relatives. This was a job given to me as No 2 clerk. These letters had a margin in which some personal lines would be added. This was done by the company commander. Therefore every morning at a particular time I had to go to Thiele and he would dictate five or six letters to me. Then I would return to my typewriter and prepare them all. I recall of these hours of dictation that Uncle Jochen did it with a personal involvement, so that the memory of this or that man from his company was clear to him. It was not always easy to see that, because he tended to stutter.[1]

SS-Sgt Rudi Knobloch of Preuss' No 10 Company, my comrade in the company from the end of 1942 to June 1943, was also recommended for the Close-combat Clasp in gold and accordingly was transferred to the refuelling company to keep him out of harm's way.[2] My company commander in Normandy, SS-Captain Otto Dinse, wounded in Normandy, had already been notified of the award of his gold clasp on 1 September 1944. On 12 December 1944 he received the decoration from the hand of Reichsführer-SS Heinrich Himmler at the Council Chamber, Ulm. Dinse had fifty-six confirmed Close-combat Days. In my own company on 27 October 1944 SS-Corporals Toni Motzheim, Willi Pluschke, Georg Irmler and Günter Ludwig – all from the pioneer platoon – received the Close-combat Clasp in silver.[3]

The silver clasp – the visible distinction of a proven veteran front-line soldier – was awarded throughout other companies of the APC battalion, and on 27 November 1944 gold and silver clasps were applied for at OKH on behalf of a number of officers of the Division.[4] Apparently within the Leibstandarte at this time the procedure involved in getting these awards made was unclear, for, as is known, initially the only recipients were Rudi Knobloch and myself, and the separate recommendation for SS-Major Gustav Knittel. The notification of the award was made by Battalion (for Knittel by Division), for the presentation of the decoration was supposed to be only from the hand of Adolf Hitler. In the same letter Division asked about the award of the silver clasp to a regimental commander which had been recommended seven months before!

After the APC battalion's return from operations as part of the Battle Group named after him, SS-Captain Diefenthal (German Cross in gold 29 October 1944, Close-combat Clasp in silver, silver Wound Badge) resumed command of it. In October 1944 the battalion had been authorised nine new APCs which the drivers collected from Spandau. No 12 Company commanded by SS-Senior Sgt Thiele had three tank-gun platoons each with six APCs, platoon leaders being SS-Sgts Paul Pfalzer, SS-Corporals Helmut Feldvoss and myself. Nos 9, 10 and 11 Companies were commanded by SS-Lt Dieter Kohler, Georg Preuss and Heinz Tomhardt respectively.

Josef Diefenthal, SS-Sturmbannführer
b. 5 October 1915 Euskirchen, d. 10 April 2001
Awards: German Cross in Gold, 29 October 1994 and Knight's Cross 5 February 1945 as SS-Captain and commanding officer 3rd Battalion, 2nd SS-Panzer Grenadier Regiment – 1st SS-Panzer Division LAH.
Matthias Josef Diefenthal was the son of a Reichsbahn Secretary
15 October 1935 After leaving school with the Abitur served with 5.Company Leibstandarte
24 September 1939 One of the first soldiers to be awarded the Iron Cross Second Class
28 May 1940 Wounded in the West
8 June 1940 Awarded Iron Cross First Class
7 September 1940 Promoted to SS-2/Lt
Late 1940 Transferred to 10.Company LAH, took command of motor-cycle reconnaissance platoon II Battalion LAH
June 1941 Battalion adjutant
5 July 1941 Regimental adjutant to 'Teddy' Wisch
20 April 1943 Promoted to SS-Captain
1 September 1943 Awarded Close-combat Clasp in bronze, commanding No 1 Company, 2nd SS-Panzer Grenadier Regiment
10 November 1943 Seriously wounded
1 July 1944 Took over APC battalion
1 September 1944 Led Battle Group Diefenthal in Belgium and at the Westwall

29 October 1944 Awarded German Cross in gold
12.1944 Ardennes offensive
5 February 1945 Awarded Knight's Cross for Stavelot operation
28 March 1945 Seriously wounded and suffered amputation of a leg, Raab, Hungary.
After the war: In a trial held by the US victors at Dachau sentenced to death for the alleged Malmédy massacre, sentence commuted, released 1956.

In November 1944 I received the Wound Badge in gold after getting the Soldbuch entry in June. On 9 November 1944 eleven members of the Battalion were handed their Iron Cross First Class, amongst them my driver, SS-Leading Grenadier Ernst Höppner, tank-gun commanders SS-Leading Grenadiers Karl-Heinz Fetzer and Karl.-Heinz Rodenstein, my Company commander SS-Senior Sgt Jochen Thiele and Kwk-platoon commander SS-Sgt Emil Knappe.[5] The APC battalion was at Poll and Gladbach. The command post of SS-Captain Jupp Diefenthal was located in a farm at Gladbach. The APCs were dug-in up to the top of the track. The battalion was now fully equipped with APCs and new weapons, including triple-flak guns and twin MGs from Luftwaffe stocks.

At the beginning of December 1944, the APCs in my platoon were transferred out to create tank-gun sections, each of two vehicles, in the heavy platoons of other APC companies. These were replaced by a new triple-flak platoon. Triple-flak APCs were also present in the other APC companies. On all fronts, veteran officers led the companies in Diefenthal's APC battalion. Commander of No 9 Company was now SS-2/Lt Max Leike, a 33-year-old who previously commanded the company's heavy platoon. Since April 1943, No 10 Company had been led by SS-Lt Georg Preuss, also known as 'tricky Preuss', one of the boldest officers in the battalion. SS-Lt Heinz Tomhardt had led No 11 Company since 1943. All wore at least the Iron Cross First Class, Close-combat Clasp in silver and a wound badge, as did many of their NCOs and men. No 12 Company was commanded by SS-Senior Sgt Jochen Thiele, in the SS-Leibstandarte since 21 June 1933, and who had led the company on several occasions in 1943/44 as an NCO. Young officers and veteran NCOs commanded the platoons.

In this waiting area the men were witnesses to an American air-raid on Düren which caused a heavy death toll amongst the civilian population and transformed the town into a heap of rubble. Jochen Peiper wrote of it:

A damp and cold December day as all the previous ones had been. Towards 1000 hrs we heard the only too-well-known droning in the air, the earth began to tremble and on the western horizon we saw the clouds arise from detonating bombs and fires. Düren was the Allied target. Endless formations of four-engined bombers unloaded 2,703 tonnes of HE and incendiaries and within minutes destroyed 95 per cent of the town. 1030 hrs: Division rang, 1st Panzer Regiment set out with all available vehicles for Düren for the job of saving lives and salvaging what we could. A smog made up of dirt, smoke and brick dust hung over the hapless town. Upon our approach we saw only senseless destruction. What had been the highest was now underfoot, electricity cables hung down, rubble covered the streets and water poured out from ruptured mains. Putting out the fires was impossible. The local fires had already developed into major conflagrations which mocked all human rescue attempts. Nevertheless the panzer crews walked into the inferno, at the risk of their lives freeing people trapped beneath wreckage, carrying others out, leading women and children to safety and everywhere administering first aid. The destruction they saw was worse than anything they had experienced at the front, and above all the worst thing about this catastrophe was an upwelling of impotence and helplessness. Nevertheless the men kept going until they dropped from exhaustion, heeding neither burns nor wounds. Exhortations and orders were entirely superfluous. Everybody wanted to help – out of horror, compassion – and anger! 'These swine!' one heard often. 'Wait till we get them! This is not war, but mass murder.[6]

On 3 December 1944 1st (mixed) Battalion of the Panzer Regiment consisted of thirty-seven Mk IVs and thirty-eight Panthers. The 50th (heavy) SS-Panzer Battalion which arrived at Weilerswist the same day had thirty-four Tiger IIs and was still not up to strength.

Chapter Seventeen

The Ardennes Offensive, 16–24 December 1944

It was the objective of Sixth SS-Panzer Army to disperse the American positions between Hellenthal and Ormont, after which 1st SS-Panzer Division would reach the Meuse between Liège and Huy, holding the bridgeheads there until II SS-Panzer Corps had assembled for the push on Antwerp. Peiper's Panzer Group had the most important role in the offensive: without paying heed to any threat on the flanks, he had to use the element of surprise to penetrate the American rear areas behind Losheimergraben and reach the Meuse between Liège and Huy as quickly as possible.

After his return from this conference, Peiper assembled the leaders of the Panzer Group he would command in the coming attack in his command post at the Blankenheimer Wald forestry lodge. His Panzer Group was composed as follows: alongside 1st Battalion (mixed), 1st SS-Panzer Regiment (SS-Major Poetschke), in place of the missing 2nd Battalion, the 501st Heavy SS-Panzer Battalion (SS-Lt.Col von Westernhagen) was attached to the Panzer Regiment. Third Battalion 2nd SS-Panzer Grenadier Regiment (SS-Captain Diefenthal) belonged – as previously in Russia – to the Panzer Group.

On the afternoon of 14 December 1944, Peiper summoned the commanders of his subordinated units to discuss the offensive and subsequently the company commanders briefed their men and informed them of the impending operation. Because I was awaiting the presentation of the Close-combat Clasp in gold, I was transferred to 2nd Tank Gun Platoon as deputy platoon commander under SS-Corporal Helmut Feldvoss. The role of this platoon during the offensive was as reserve and to guard the fuel and ammunition transports. At the request of SS-Lt Georg Preuss, SS-Sgt Rudi Knobloch, also waiting to be presented with the gold clasp, took command of 1st Platoon in his company.[1]

Peiper had a powerful fighting formation of Mk IV panzers, Panthers, King Tigers, APCs, flak-APCs, infantry guns, artillery and a Luftwaffe flak unit. At its head would be a specially selected panzer vanguard led by SS-Lt Werner Sternebeck of No 6 Company consisting of two Panthers, five Mk IVs and two APCs of No 9 (Pioneer) Company, 1st SS-Panzer Regiment. Peiper assembled the units under his command into the most favourable tactical order. Therefore the panzer and APC companies were not to set out as individual companies, but were separated up into platoons and inserted here and there across the force as appropriate. On the night of 16 December 1944 all was ready, and the German offensive in the West, long prepared in great secrecy, began.

No 12 (Heavy Armoured) Company, 2nd SS-Panzer Grenadier Regiment LSSAH

The principal posts during the Ardennes Offensive for No 12 Company were occupied as follows:

Company commander: SS-Senior Sgt Jochen Thiele

Troop leader: SS-Corporal Rudi Vogt

Signals section: SS-Corporal Adalbert Klein

Messenger (tracked motorcycle): SS-Ldg Grenadier Otto Rohmann, SS-Grenadier Helmut Neumann

Senior medical orderly: SS-Corporal Heinzelmann

CSM (acting): SS-Sgt Eduard Funk

Harness-master: SS-Sgt Siegfried Menner

APC and Repairs: SS-Corporal Erich Strassgschwandtner

Armourer: SS-Corporal Günter Lehmann

1st Tank-Gun Platoon (six APCs with 7.5cm tank guns)

SS-Sgt Paul Pfalzer

Gun commanders: SS-Corporals Sepp Pointner, Schuster and Siegfried Sebera: SS-Ldg.Grenadiers Leo Binke, Eduard Moser (fell 19 December 1944) and Kurt Wiemann

2nd Tank-Gun Platoon (six APCs with 7.5cm tank guns)

SS-Corporal Helmut Feldvoss

Gun commanders: SS-Corporal Werner Kindler and Rudi Schwambach: SS-Ldg.Grenadiers Karl-Heinz Rodenstein, Karl-Heinz Fetzer, Herbert Exner, Fritz Müller: SS-Grenadier Ludwig Clement.

III Triple-flak-Platoon (three tank guns and three flak)

SS-Corporal Toni Motzheim

Gun commanders: SS-Corporals Erich Händel, Schumacher, Stenglein: SS-Grenadier Günther Weiss.

Pioneer Platoon (four APCs)

SS-Corporal Willi Pluschke

APC commanders: SS-Corporals Günther Ludwig, Georg Irmler

On that icy cold evening many men of the Panzer Group were unable to sleep. All knew the terrible danger confronting Germany and that in the East, Soviet troops were at the border of the Reich and some had already crossed it. Immediately before leaving the Blankenheimner Wald assembly area between 0100 and 0200 hrs, SS-Lt Heinz Tomhardt addressed his No 11 Company of the APC battalion: 'I explained the importance of the impending offensive for Germany's future. I appealed for the total personal commitment and bravery of every man. I spoke of the responsibility we had to the Homeland, which had given us this opportunity once from amidst the terror bombing. Then I gave some tactical details, as for example the infantry and artillery preparations to open the offensive, I spoke of a major Luftwaffe involvement and of the objectives of the armoured group.'[2]

On 16 December 1944 at 0530 hrs concentrated artillery fire began the Ardennes offensive. At 0800 hrs the units of Panzer Group Peiper drawn up behind 12th Volksgrenadier Division headed off to attack the American positions at Losheim and Losheimergraben. Peiper accompanied the commander of 3rd Battalion, 2nd SS-Panzer Grenadier Regiment, SS-Captain Jupp Diefenthal, behind the advanced troop. Following a conference with his commanders early on 17 December, Peiper had arranged the Panzer Group for the attack by having two Panthers lead, followed by Rudi Knobloch's APC platoon from No 10 Company (SS-Lt Georg Preuss) and behind it two triple-flak APCs of Preuss' company. At 0400 hrs together with the paratroopers of 2nd Battalion 9th Parachute Regiment under Major Taubert he headed for Büllinger Wood. At the end of the woods the leading panzers under SS-Lt Sternebeck came across the first Americans, who fled at once into the darkness. At 0430 hrs the panzer spearhead arrived at Honsfeld, taking the Americans there totally by surprise, as Peiper recalled:

As we roared into Honsfeld with the first rays of the sun we awoke an American reconnaissance battalion. The anti-tank guns at the entrance to the village were not manned, and the streets, alleys and farms were packed with armoured vehicles, jeeps and lorries. The sleepy eyes of hundreds of speechless GIs looked at us from the windows. We drove through, fired MG bursts into the houses and kept going for Büllingen. The paratroopers were to clear the village.[3]

Only after Peiper's formation had stormed through Honsfeld did the surprised Americans recognise the disaster. They managed sporadic fire at the rearmost Panthers and paratroopers. About fifty recon-naissance vehicles and armoured personnel carriers were captured at Honsfeld.[4]

Shortly after 0600 hrs the panzer spearhead pressed on. As the previously unhindered advance proceeded, about 2km south of Büllingen the spearhead came upon an American airstrip to the left of the road. Reconnaissance aircraft stood waiting with propellers turning. Twelve of these aircraft were destroyed by the heavy platoon of Preuss' No 10 Company under SS-2/Lt Klaus Aschendorff,[5] although one aircraft was scrambled before the APC arrived. SS-Lt Werner Sternebeck reported:

On the road into Büllingen, a few hundred metres from the entrance to the town, the Mk IV ahead of me was ambushed and destroyed by close combat weapons. The crew was shot down as they abandoned the vehicle. There were no survivors. At full speed and firing with all weapons, the remainder of the panzer spearhead roared into Büllingen. The enemy was in total confusion, we had achieved surprise again. The enemy offered no organised resistance.[6]

Of the entry of Sternebeck and Preuss' No 10 Company Peiper commented: 'Despite crazed AA, MG and rifle fire, Preuss caused havoc with only two APCs and made possible the capture of the village by the armoured group.'[7]

The open APCs sustained losses at Büllingen from heavy fire issuing from the houses. SS-Sgt Rudi Knobloch, a veteran with over fifty Close-combat Days commanded the leading APC through the hail of bullets at Büllingen. He was standing in the APC when suddenly his driver warned him, 'Take care, they are shooting at us from the houses!' At that moment Knobloch was struck in the face and felt the blood stream-ing into his mouth and running down his chin. He had been hit on the upper lip. He reported to Preuss who sent him to a paratrooper military hospital where the lip was operated on.[8] Peiper wrote that SS-Corporal Karl Übler, commander of the tank-gun section in Preuss' No 10 Company 'in personal involvement, without any thought for himself, not heeding the murderous American defensive fire from all directions, drove into the village of Büllingen where, in bitter street and house-to-house fighting, bastion by bastion, he put down the defences.'[9]

Near the western exit of Büllingen an American fuel depot was found. The German vehicles stopped and despite the increasing artillery fire the crews hauled fuel drums to their panzers and APCs, fuelled up and then moved on. The morale in Peiper's Panzer Group rose as they rolled on and had even managed to refuel. The messenger in my No 12 Company, SS-Grenadier (Officer candidate) Helmut Neumann, wrote:

> Recalling the days of that advance, above all I remember that we captured a lot of material. American lorries were parked at the side of the road, inside were cases of bean coffee which we had not had for years, and chocolate. We stuffed ourselves full of chocolate. Our people liked the American laced boots and yellow leather gloves, and the panzer drivers made good use of the captured fuel drums. All in all in those few days of the advance we were very buoyed up after always having been on the retreat in the past.[10]

Numerous prisoners were taken at Büllingen. SS-Lt Georg Preuss drove flat out through the village to escape the hail of bullets and came upon an American column. With nerves of steel, Preuss inveigled himself in amongst them. The Americans failed to notice that German APCs had slotted into their ranks. He detached from them in woodlands, killed a sentry in close combat and returned hours later to the Panzer Group. For his feat in taking Honsfeld and Büllingen so swiftly, Peiper recommended him for the Knight's Cross.

Sternebeck's spearhead rolled through Möderscheid, Schoppen and Ondenval to Thirimont where Preuss' No 10 Company veered west over field paths and pasture heading for the N23 Malmédy–Engelsdorf (Ligneuville) road in order to clean out the US 49th AA-Brigade Staff at the latter. Because of the difficult terrain, the Panzer Group could not take this short cut and had to continue on the road to the north-west as far as the crossroads at Bagatelle, then turning south-west at the intersection along the N32 from Weismes. After a short stretch, the N32 met the N23 at Baugnez road junction, from where the N23 led into Engelsdorf.

Beyond Thirimont the panzer spearhead opened fire at 700 yards on a column of American lorries approaching Baugnez road junction from the north, 4km south-east of Malmédy. Eighteen months later the victors fabricated an accusation and condemnation of Peiper and seventy-three members of the Panzer Group, Corps and Army. As leading vehicle of the Panzer Group spearhead, SS-Lt Sternebeck arrived first at the column of lorries. They formed part of B Battery of

285th Field Artillery Observation Battalion. Sternebeck recalled:

> On the road from Thirimont to the north-west, about 800 to 1200m east of the Baugnez crossroads, I made a stop to observe and saw a column of enemy lorries going through the crossroads heading south. The spearhead opened fire (AP rounds) on the column when about 200 to 300m south of the crossroads. Some of the lorries caught fire immediately and confusion broke out in the convoy. The crews jumped out and sought cover. This was the moment to advance across the Weismes–Baugnez road to the crossroads. Just before reaching it we came under MG and rifle fire from the occupants who had sought cover. We returned fire with our panzer MGs and headed at speed for the standing convoy. When my leading panzer had got to within 60–70m, the Americans came out of the roadside ditches and the terrain, raised their hands and surrendered. I reduced speed and came up to the convoy slowly. By arm signals I indicated that the US soldiers should go back towards the crossroads. I contacted Panzer Group by radio and reported the encounter, the skirmish and the outcome. I received orders to proceed without delay to Englesdorf. There was a time gap of ten minutes between my armoured spearhead and the vanguard in which the command group was travelling.[11]

I cannot provide closer details of what happened subsequently. My platoon was given supply protection duties, and therefore was neither caught up with Panzer Group Peiper in the encirclement at La Gleize nor in direct fighting for that reason.

The next objective was the town of Stavelot. On 17 December, the SPWs and panzers advanced along the narrow road to Stavelot. It had a mountain to one side on the right which dropped steeply beside the town. In the darkness the first attack was not successful because the approach to the bridge over the Amel had been effectively blocked by two anti-tank guns. During the night a dismounted APC complement from No 11 Company made its way through the forest to the left of the road downhill into Stavelot and took out an American patrol in a jeep.[12] SS-Lt Heinz Tomhardt's No 11 Company, which had two platoons forward in the formation, was ordered to take the bridge over the Amel. Towards 0200 hrs on 18 December 1944, Tomhardt and his men – dismounted from the APCs of 1st and 4th Platoons under SS-2/Lt Willi Horn and SS-Sgt Rudi Rayer, reached the Stoken district of the town and quickly took the Amel bridge despite heavy defensive fire. 'The Company set up an all-round defence in front of the bridge,' SS-Sgt Rayer wrote, 'because at the time it was in a difficult situation. Enemy tanks were constantly rolling by and we expected a counter-attack. We were receiving fire from all sides without being able to do much about it in the darkness.'[13]

The American tanks were rolling along the road uphill. From the terrain left of the road, No 11 Company troop leader SS-Sgt Walter Quinten fired a Panzerfaust at a tank which failed, but then destroyed the tank with a limpet mine. Although the bridge was in German hands, it was under fire from all sides and could not be held by a weak company on only one side of it. SS-Lt Heinz Tomhardt was wounded, SS-2/Lt Willi Horn and others fell. On Diefenthal's orders SS-Sgt Rudi Rayer took over the company.

At first light German panzers arrived and the attack proper began. Panzer pioneers worked to support No 11 Company and secure the bridge against being blown.[14] A group from No 11 Company occupied the flat roofs of the first houses in Stavelot and observed from there sniper activities being conducted by Belgian civilians. Shortly afterwards the attack on Stavelot commenced. Peiper had appointed the Panther of SS-Sgt Erich Strelow of No 1 Company as the lead panzer.

On reaching the town, Strelow rounded a bend and suddenly saw fifty metres ahead two anti-tank guns protecting the important bridge at the entrance to town. SS-Sgt Strelow recognised at once that the bridge was of the greatest importance for the advance of the Abteilung and had to be captured at all costs. The enemy opened a withering fire on the leading panzer with anti-tank guns, 2cm cannon and infantry weapons. Without hesitation Strelow rolled up to the two anti-tank guns, waltzed over them, laid smoke to blind the flanks, crushed another anti-tank, took the bridge and thereby opened the way for the company into town.[15]

While the Panthers were still fighting on the bridge, the panzers and APCs of the entire Panzer Group were lined up one behind the other on the sloping road outside Stavelot waiting to attack. The Americans made a flanking attack from the wooded terrain to the left of the Panzer Group. The APC battalion beat off this dangerous effort after which the commander, SS-Captain Diefenthal, put himself at the head of the battalion and immediately set off downhill to the bridge and held it open. For this action Jupp Diefenthal was awarded the Knight's Cross.

Belgian civilians took part in the defence of Stavelot. From windows and attic lights they fired on German soldiers from the rear and into the crew compartments of the open APCs.[16] Each vehicle had to run the gauntlet of the road through Stavelot. Because the bridges over the Amel and Salm had been blown, Peiper had to continue his advance to the north. Towards 1300 hrs on 18 December 1944 via Coo he reached La Gleize where it bore away towards Cheneux since he was heading for Werbomont. That evening the Panzer Group decided to push on west because the bridges via Stoumont were down. In the morning mist of 19 December the panzers attacked Stoumont while No 9 Company under SS-2/Lt Leike, mounted up through the woods, approached Stoumont from the south. No 11 Company under SS-Sgt Rayer followed the Panthers but remained on the road as a reserve on standby. Elements of 1st Tank-Gun Platoon, No 12 Company, led by SS-Sgt Pfalzer also assisted in the attack on Stoumont, which was taken after breaking down substantial anti-tank fire. Twenty-year-old SS-Ldg Grenadier Edi Moser, commander of a tank-gun APC in my company, fell: the triple-flak APC of SS-Corporal Toni Motzheim was hit and caught fire. Motzheim baled out, his driver SS-Grenadier Leo Moser, suffered burns.

The panzers resumed rolling west and came upon a farm called 'Zambompré', where two Panthers were destroyed and the No 11 Company APCs following behind sustained losses to artillery fire. Peiper and Poetschke brought back the remaining panzers and APCs to Stoumont due to shortage of fuel, and from 21 December Peiper withdrew his Panzer Group to La Gleize. A triple-flak APC of my No 12 Company shot down a US artillery spotter aircraft.[17] SS-Leading Grenadier Friedrich Wittwer of the pioneer platoon fell. While the Panzer Group was still in La Gleize without fuel, the units of 2nd SS-Panzer Grenadier Regiment and 1st SS-Panzer Reconnaissance Battalion at Stavelot were obliged to fight off heavy American attacks. I was there with the tank-gun platoon of SS-Corporal Helmut Feldvoss, which was the reserve platoon guarding supplies.[18]

After surviving all attacks, Peiper broke out of La Gleize at 0200 hrs on 24 December 1944. Following a long trudge on foot through the snow-covered woods, the men still had to cross the Salm in full spate. Here they came under heavy fire from the Americans. While swimming the Salm, a non-swimmer grabbed Peiper's leg in panic; during this incident, Peiper was shot in the hand. During the crossing of the river, the especially strong comradeship in the Waffen-SS was exemplified by the incident in which SS-Corporal Erich Strassgschwandtner of my company carried No 12 Company troop leader SS-Corporal Rudi Voigt across the Salm after his left arm was paralyzed.[19]

After thirty-three hours cross-country, on the morning of Christmas Day 1944 Jochen Peiper reported to the divisional command post at the chateau of Wane and in his typical ironic manner explained to SS-Colonel Mohnke: 'What a pitiful performance by three US divisions which failed to wipe out a small German battle group lacking fuel or ammunition, allowing them to blow up all their vehicles and heavy weapons before marching off, fearless and unbroken, through the sleeping enemy.'[20] Mohnke recommended Peiper for the Swords to his Knight's Cross with Oak Leaves: immediately after Christmas, Peiper recommended Diefenthal and Preuss for the Knight's Cross, and SS-Corporal Karl Übler, tank-gun section leader in Preuss' Company, for the Honour Scroll Clasp. On 11 January 1945, Peiper was awarded the Swords by Mohnke.

Chapter Eighteen

Transfer to Hungary, January–February 1945

At the beginning of 1945 Soviet divisions were on the outskirts of Königsberg, at Ebbing and the Baltic coast, and now threatened to cross the river Oder between Stettin and Breslau. The bestiality of Soviet troops in the regions of eastern Germany they had conquered appalled people. Countless streams of refugees, veritable columns of wretchedness, mostly women, old people, the infirm and children found themselves heading west in order to save their lives and honour before what was surfacing in their homeland from the Soviet steppes. Not only Germany but Europe was being swept into deadly danger. Meanwhile the Western allies were at the western border of the Reich, and had already crossed it at a few places.

The APC battalion was at Siegburg, where new APCs had been delivered fitted either with 2cm triple-flak or MG 81s. No 12 Company now consisted of two tank-gun platoons, the triple flak platoon and the pioneer platoon.[1] SS-Sgt Dieter Kohler took over No 9 Company in place of the fallen SS-2/Lt Leike. Battalion commander Jupp Diefenthal was promoted to SS-Major on 30 January 1945: the commander of my No 12 Company, veteran SS-Senior Sgt Jochen Thiele, was made an SS-2/Lt.

Following the Ardennes offensive, 1st SS-Panzer Regiment and the heavy 501st SS-Panzer Battalion had been in the Buhl, Bonn and Euskirchen areas since January 1945 to rest and replenish with new tanks. Around 20 January 1945 the transfer by train to the Eastern Front in Hungary began. The companies of 1st (Mixed) Battalion 1st SS-Panzer Regiment travelled via Central Germany–Linz–Vienna and unloaded at Raab (Gyor), from where they continued via Bacsa-Venek across the Danube to quarters at Kisbajcs, between the old and new beds of the Danube.

On 5 February 1945 the commanding officer of the APC battalion, Jupp Diefenthal, and the commander of No 10 Company, Georg Preuss, were awarded the Knight's Cross. Of Preuss it was Peiper's assessment: 'He was prominent repeatedly for his aggressiveness and unique gallantry in the field.'[2] By then Preuss already had fifty-three confirmed Close-combat Days and had been recommended for the award of the Close-combat Clasp in gold. His platoon leader SS-Sgt Rudi Knobloch, wounded in the Ardennes, had been recommended for this award six months previously.

Georg Preuss, SS-Hauptsturmführer

b. 24 April 1920 Danzig-Neufahrwasser, d. 3 February 1991 Clenze

Awards: Knight's Cross 5 February 1945, Close-combat Clasp in gold, 1 April 1945, German Cross in gold, 20 April 1945 as Obersturmbannführer (SS-Lt-Col) and commanding officer No 10 Company, 2nd SS-Panzer Grenadier Regiment, 1st SS-Panzer Division LSSAH.

1 April 1939 Joined 1/LAH

February 1941 Concluded officer training course, Staff officer 4th Battalion LAH in Russia

1943 Platoon-leader No 13 Company, 2nd SS-Panzer Grenadier Regiment

April 1943 Commanding officer, No 12 Company, 2nd SS-Panzer Grenadier Regiment

20 April 1943 Promoted to SS-Lt

1 July 1943 Awarded Iron Cross First Class. Received neck wound before Kursk.

1 September 1943 Awarded Close-combat Clasp (bronze)

December 1943 Wounded in Russia

February 1944 Led APC battalion until wounded again

5 June 1944 Awarded Close-combat Clasp (silver)

5 February 1945 Awarded Knight's Cross

28 March 1945 Commanding officer, APC battalion in Hungary until the end of the war

1 April 1945 Awarded Close-combat Clasp (gold)

20 April 1945 Awarded German Cross in Gold

1946: sentenced to death by US military tribunal for his part in the alleged 'Malmédy massacre', sentence commuted to life imprisonment, released from Landsberg, 1956.

The men of the Panzer Regiment at Raab read the Wehrmacht communiqués very thoughtfully. The development of the situation on the fronts was assuming ever more threatening features. The men with family in the east of Germany were always very relieved when news came through that they had reached the West, but few had this certainty. The Volksdeutsche had already lost their homeland, many remained without anything: several had lost parents, wives and fiancées in nights of bombing by the American and British air forces. Inwardly afflicted, they all waited for the coming operations. Hitler wanted to secure the oilfields at the confluence of the Danube and Drau for Germany's fuel needs. For this, a well-thought out offensive had been prepared which it was hoped would draw the Soviets away from Berlin into this region. All preparations were cloaked in the greatest secrecy.

In December 1944, the 3rd Ukrainian Front had broken through to Lake Balaton and occupied the region between the Danube and Drais. Therefore the last oilfields were in acute danger. On 24 December 1944, Budapest, with a strong German garrison, had been encircled by the Russians. In January 1945 west of the Gran, the Soviets had built up a bridgehead 17km deep. The bridgehead represented a major threat to the planned German offensive codenamed 'Spring Awakening', because it enabled a Soviet advance to the south across the Danube which would place the Soviets at the centre of the German advance. Therefore 1st SS-Panzer Division had the job of advancing from Farnad to Bart, crossing the Parizsky Canal and capturing Nana and Parkany.

On 12 February 1945 the Leibstandarte moved. The Panzer Regiment transferred from Raab via Komorn to Neuhäusel. On 15 February 1945 SS-Major-General Otto Kumm took over command of the Division from SS-Colonel Mohnke. On 17 February 1945, Peiper set out to attack the Soviet bridgehead at Gran.

No 12 (Heavy Armoured) Company, 2nd SS-Panzer Grenadier Regiment LAH

The principal posts from the arrival in Hungary to the end of the war, 1945, were occupied as follows:

Company commanders: SS-2/Lt Jochen Thiele (wounded circa 18 February 1945): SS-2/Lt Günther Wagner (27 March – 17 April 1945, wounded), SS-Lt Kruse (missing): SS-Sgt Werner Kindler (? May–10 May 1945).

Company HQ section commander: SS-Sgt Rudi Voigt (fell 2 April 1945)

Messenger: SS-Leading Grenadier Otto Rohmann (tracked motorcycle)

Senior medical orderly: SS-Corporal Richter

CSM (acting): SS-Sgt Eduard Funk (fell 7 March 1945): SS-Sgt Paul Pfalzer.

Harness-master: SS-Sgt Siegfried Menner

APC formation leader: SS-Corporal Erich Strassgschwandtner

Armourer: SS-Corporal Günther Lehmann (fell 10 March 1945)
1st Tank-Gun Platoon
SS-Sgt Paul Pfalzer, platoon-troop leader and runner
Gun commanders of the six APCs with 7.5cm tank guns: SS-Corporal Karl-Heinz Rodenstein, SS-Leading Grenadiers Kurt Wiemann (fell 7 March 1945) and Erich Händel, SS-Grenadier Ludwig Clement.
2nd Tank-Gun Platoon
SS-Sgt Helmut Feldvoss, platoon troop leader and runner
Gun commanders of the six APCs with 7.5cm Kwk: SS-Corporals Werner Kindler, Siegfried Sebera, Leo Binke, Sepp Pointner, Fritz Müller, SS-Leading Grenadier Karl-Heinz Fetzer.
3rd Triple-flak Platoon (3 tank-guns and 3 Flak)
SS-Corporal Toni Motzheim, SS-Grenadier Nico . . . (?)
Pioneer Platoon
SS-Corporal Willi Pluschke
Commanders of the four APCs: SS-Corporals Rudi Schwambach, Günter Ludwig: Georg Irmler

Because of my award of the gold Close-combat Clasp – with which I had still not been presented – to my surprise I was plucked out of the assembly area at Veszprem on 18 February 1945 and sent on leave to the regimental rest home at Steinach on the Brenner. SS-Corporal Sepp Pointner took over my APC to the 'long faces' of my crew . . .

Steinach was the rest and convalescent retreat of 2nd SS-Panzer Grenadier Regiment. There I met my commanding officer at regimental level, SS-Lt.Colonel Rudi Sandig and the regimental adjutant SS-Captain Fritz Bremer. We were soon joined by my company commander SS-Sgt Jochen Thiele, who had been wounded in the hand during the fighting at the Gran bridgehead. I spent three weeks resting in the Tyrolean mountains at Steinach. On the occasion of the marriage of my company comrade, SS-Corporal Erich Händel, I made the trip to Innsbruck to present him with a gift on behalf of the company.

On 11 March 1945 in company with SS-Corporal Hans Brakensieck of No 9 Company I headed back to my unit. On the way in Hungary, without a weapon, I was waylaid by an Army Battle-Group at Stuhlweissenburg, whose idea it was to fit me into their threatened sector at the front. My finely developed instinct for danger warned me against being lured into some unknown Army unit to fill gaps in their front line. At this stage of the war there were many field police in evidence who would string you up as soon as look at you for any deviation from your orders, but I arranged it with them to travel back to Steinach where I waited four days for fresh orders to be drafted. Finally in the last week of March 1945 I headed for my unit once more together with SS-Captain Bremer.

Chapter Nineteen

Operation South Wind, 17–24 February 1945, and the Retreat from Hungary

D uring my sojourn at Steinach, my colleagues had attacked the strong Soviet bridgehead at Gran. By night a bridgehead was made over the Parizsky Canal and extended southwards on 18 February against fierce Russian opposition. The 21-year-old platoon leader of Preuss' No 10 Company, SS-Captain Eduard Maron (Iron Cross First Class, silver Close-combat Clasp, Tank Destruction Badge), distinguished himself in these operations, was under consideration for the Knight's Cross but was seriously wounded, as a result of which he died at Ramsau on 11 April 1945.

SS-2/Lt Günther Borchers (No 9 Company, 1st SS-Panzer Regiment) stated:

It was an attack out of our best days. King Tigers, Panthers and APCs rolled at speed and unhaltingly towards the enemy positions. The first of them were mined. Despite fire from either side, the mines were cleared and we carried on. Szögyen, Batorkeszi, Köbölkut, Muzsla and other villages were wrested from the Soviets. The populations cheered us. They had suffered grievously under Soviet occupation. The Russians raped women and children of all ages, dragging them off to their trenches. At Nemet Szögyen we stopped and set up an all-round defence.[1]

Our own losses were irreplaceable, amongst them the commander of No 9 Company, SS-Lt Dieter Kohler and platoon leader SS-2/Lt Kuno Balz from No 11 Company, both wounded (19 February): Balz eventually had to be ordered by Diefenthal to report to the military hospital. The Soviet Gran bridgehead was thus destroyed.

In Berlin, my company commander SS-Captain Otto Dinse begged Peiper for a return to the Division. Together with SS-Major Gerd Hein (Knight's Cross/Oak Leaves) he drove an amphibious car through the

172

Reich and then via Prague into Hungary, where he reached the Leibstandarte on 1 March 1945. The divisional commander, SS-Major-General Otto Kumm (Knight's Cross/Oak Leaves/Swords), his old comrade from 4th SS-Standarte at Hamburg-Altona, took him onto his staff.

The Lake Balaton offensive planned during Operation South Wind had as its objective the recapture of the Drau-Danube confluence in order to secure the Nagy Kamisza oilfields and simultaneously establish bridgeheads on the Danube as a departure point for further operations. Sixth SS-Panzer Army was to attack south between Lake Balaton and the Sarviz Canal in order to seize the high ground at Fünfkirchen. On 7 March 1945 the tank-gun APC of SS-Leading Grenadier Kurt Wiemann of No 12 Company was hit at Kaloz. Wiemann was killed. The Russians fled. Peiper now set his panzers to the north for an attack on Soponya and towards evening ejected the Russians from there, forcing them into the park of the chateau.

On 16 March 1945 the Soviets launched their offensive between Lake Velencz and Bicskje in the sector of IV SS-Panzer Corps. The 3rd Ukrainian Front extended from Tatabanya to Stuhlweissenburg. Soon the Russians were approaching Komorn, having split General Balck's Sixth Army at the seam between 3rd SS-Panzer Division Totenkopf and 2nd Hungarian Tank Division. The report of the Russian counter-attack motivated General Guderian to request the immediate transfer northwards of I SS-Panzer Corps. After passing through Polgardi, the APC battalion entered enemy-occupied Inota on the morning of 19 March 1945. Its commanding officer Diefenthal recalled: 'Heaviest house-to-house fighting. Dismounted. The village was freed with heavy losses: secured east of Inota. Individual assault troops successfully beaten off. Enemy movements north of Inota.'[2]

On 20 March 1945, the commander of No 1 Panzer Company, SS-Lt Werner Wolff (Knight's Cross), was seriously wounded at Inota while standing in the turret of his panzer, and died ten days later at the reserve hospital, Götzendorf barracks. He had been Peiper's adjutant in the APC battalion in 1943. Peiper wrote: 'Werner Wolff had a short meteoric career. He rose up shining for a short while only to fall back into the darkness equally as fast.'[3]

Between Inota and Varpalota the APC battalion formed the rearguard. SS-Major Diefenthal reported:

In the evening, the divisional commander personally gave the order

173

to leave because Varpalota was already occupied by the enemy, and was ablaze. We went south of Varpalota for Öskü. Also occupied by the enemy. Apparently the Russians had boxed us in. We cleared the retreat route in the direction of Veszprem. Third Battalion formed the rearguard for the Division ... the Battalion, with grenadiers mounted up, proceeded north and south of the Rollbahn with APCs still intact so as to engage any enemy flowing past left and right. Isolated contacts with enemy. Width of battalion front about 800m. Information passed by open radio telephony. The Russians were mainly overhauling our own troops to the north of us heading west. On the Veszprem–Devecser Rollbahn German Army units in disorderly retreat.[4]

The Division had now to cross the river Raab, where some Russian units had preceded them. At Nuczk the APC battalion engaged a number of tanks. On 27 March 1945 on the west bank of the Raab, Diefenthal was wounded for the seventh time during a briefing with SS-Major-General Kumm, and lost a leg. SS-Lt Preuss now assumed command of the APC battalion.

SS-2/Lt Günther Wagner, formerly with No 13 Company, reached Division with 1,350 men, reinforcements from the Kriegsmarine, Luftwaffe and Army, of whom half had been sentenced by courts-martial:

When I had them parade in a square formation in a meadow, I was very surprised when Lt Preuss appeared to hear my report. After a brief welcoming speech in his sarcastic way he stood them at ease. I made a short report regarding the content of the personal files ... as I had express orders to return to Leschau for another purpose and Preuss quickly gave me an outline of the situation, I requested leave to remain with the APC battalion. Next morning I drove with some of the reinforcements to the front on the Raab. In my search for the APC battalion I met Lt.Colonel Peiper at his command post. It was in a tall building with a view over the river banks. I reported my reinforcements to him and my desire to remain at the front. Peiper told me where I could find my former company, now No 12 Company. He would report my transfer by telex to SS-FHA.[5]

At the same time as Wagner arrived, SS-2/Lt Adolf Sellmeier, leader of my MG half-platoon in 1942/43, came to the battalion and relieved

Preuss of No 10 Company. It was about now that I returned to my unit from Steinach. Preuss took me into his staff to set up an MG platoon. However, since there were neither weapons nor personnel available, I departed for my Company a few days later and reported to SS-Sgt Paul Pfalzer, who was now acting CSM.

The company had suffered bitter losses in Hungary. The former CSM, SS-Sgt Eduard Funk, was killed by friendly fire from a triple-flak on 7 March at Polgardi. As reported, Leading Grenadier Kurt Wiemann fell at Kaloz the same day, and armourer SS-Corporal Günther Lehamn was fatally wounded on 10 March at Soponya while defusing a Russian hand grenade. Many others had been wounded or killed.

SS-Sgt Helmut Feldvoss remained in command of the tank-gun APCs. He introduced me to the new company commander, SS-Lt Kruse, who sent him a bottle of schnapps. Kruse had come from an office and had not previously been at the front anywhere. On the evening of 29 March 1945 the order came for German units to return to positions protecting the Reich. On 31 March 1945 Panzer Group Peiper crossed into the Reich at Sopron. The Panzer IV Group reached the area east of Wiener-Neustadt, at Pöttsching-Sauerbrunn. The Division now stood on the soil of the Reich.

On 1 April 1945 a messenger brought me an order to report to the battalion command post where my battalion commander, SS-Lt Preuss, formally handed me the Close-combat Clasp in gold. I was twenty-two years of age and thus was one of only 630 soldiers of Army and Waffen-SS who were ever to receive it. The entry was made in my Soldbuch the same day. By October 1944 I had been accredited 84 Close-combat Days. Preuss received his own gold clasp the same day.[6] Preuss and I had fought in the same battalion since 1941, and since 1943 Preuss had been from time to time my Company commander and training course leader. We had often been thrown together in action and understood each other well. On 31 March 1945 Preuss' native city of Danzig had fallen to the Soviets. SS-Sgt Rudi Knobloch, platoon commander in Preuss' company after being wounded in the Ardennes, also received the gold clasp.[7] Preuss, Knobloch and I were therefore three of the fourteen soldiers of the LSSAH to receive the highest award to which a frontline soldier could aspire.

Chapter Twenty

The Fighting on Reich Soil, 1 April–8 May 1945

On 2 April 1945, No 12 Company troop leader SS-Sgt Rudi Voight was fatally wounded by a shell splinter in the stomach. SS-Leading Grenadier Eckedrt, the commanding officer's driver, was also killed. On 5 April Peiper transferred the Panzer Group to Pottenstein to confront Soviet attacks from the west and north. On 7 April the Soviets attacked Pottenstein with infantry and armour and entered Ödlitz. Elements of the Panzer Group and APC battalion launched a counter-attack to force the Russians to withdraw, destroying eleven of their tanks. On 10 April the APC battalion was at Steinberg: on 12 April Preuss' command post was located at the crossroads south-east of Weingartenweg outside Grabenwegdörf.[1]

On the morning of 13 April 1945, No 2 (Mixed) Battalion 1st SS-Panzer Regiment led by SS-Major Paul Guhl arrived at Weissenbach. The mixed battalion consisted of Nos 3 and 4 Companies of 1st Battalion, and Nos 5 and 8 Companies of 2nd Battalion of the Panzer Regiment which had been left behind in the sheltered area at Rahden in the autumn of 1944 before the Ardennes offensive. Now it attacked Pöllau. On 14 April 1945 the APC battalion, which had been known for three years as 3rd (Armoured) Battalion, 2nd SS-Panzer Grenadier Regiment was renumbered 1st (Armoured) Battalion, 2nd SS-Panzer Grenadier Regiment.[2]

I remember well a situation near Wilhelmsburg. A road was receiving Russian fire. One of the APCs had been hit and was burning, blocking the way for the rest. It caused a major hold-up. I wanted to go around the column to the left over a hill, but company commander Kruse decided to continue along a nearby stream. Kruse bogged the APCs down and was not seen again. Shortly afterwards SS-Corporal Erich Strassgeschwandtner arrived on a motorcycle with orders from Preuss that I was to take command of No 12 Company. Thus I led it in the last days of the war.

In a fighter-bomber attack on 23 January 1945, the former divisional adjutant SS-Captain Heinz Meier (German Cross in Gold) received splinters in both eyes, losing the sight in his right eye. He discharged himself and turned up at Peiper's Battle Group. 'What drove me on,' he wrote, 'to discharge myself from a military hospital in the Homeland and, bypassing official channels, return to Division, or what remained of it? Perhaps it was despair and an unconscious need to protect. My immediate native town – Graz – was threatened by the Red Army, women and children evacuated to the mountains . . . it was desperation, and the minds of the men had mutated to the concept of Homeland!'[3]

Peiper put Meier, who had been his No 11 Company platoon-leader in 1941, to work knitting together the fractured parts of the defensive front. Regarding the fatal situation and the inner, psychic state of mind of the officers, Meier wrote:

In the fighting arm we were all as if sheltered in a family, which also explains the preparedness, up until to the obviously recognisable final collapse, to risk our lives for it. What else really remained in this comradeship? In officers' circles we never discussed other possibilities. It was as though we were all gripped by the same psychosis, that we must just keep on fighting. Hardly anybody considered how it would look at the end, let alone mentioned it openly . . . a phenomenon that can only be explained by the German mentality and the natural inclination for loyalty. A mental attitude which became irrelevant for the next generation and who therefore do not understand us today. It is certain that even in the last hopeless days there was no question of our laying down our weapons. For every SS man, the struggle was an affair of the heart; from the world of Germanic mythology the doctrine to protect Homeland, wife and children.[4]

On 17 April the men of SS-Major Kling fought alongside elements of the APC battalion in a clash with the Russians at Wilhelmsburg, and ejected them from the northern part of the town. Eleven enemy tanks were destroyed. During this battle I was involved in close-combat with a Russian tank and affixed a hollow charge to it which slipped off. I went to cover allowing SS-Corporal Eduard Stadler, No 2 Company, 501st SS-Panzer Battalion to destroy the tank with his King Tiger. SS-Grenadier Werner John of the pioneer platoon fell. During the night hand-to-hand fighting took place. SS-Lt Tomhardt's No 11 Company command post was in flames, his men lay facing the Russians at close quarters. After that he set up another command post in the spa hotel Sonnhof at Schwarzenbach. His company, which broke out of the encirclement in the afternoon, suffered heavy losses and holed up in the woods.

On 20 April 1945 I was summoned to the battalion command post where regimental adjutant SS-Captain Fritz Bremer awarded me the German Cross in Gold and gave me a promotion to SS-Sergeant. My battalion commander Preuss was present and received the German Cross in Gold and promotion to SS-Captain.[5] SS-Sergeant Rudi Knobloch was awarded the German Cross in Gold in his absence.[6] Afterwards in the bunker we removed our steel helmets and drank to each other in schnapps. The ceremony was interrupted when the front flared up again.

A number of veteran NCOs and men of the APC battalion were also close to the required fifty Close-combat Days for the award of the gold clasp. These included the commander of the pioneer platoon of No 12 Company, SS-Sergeant Willi Pluschke (49 days), SS-Corporal Günther Ludwig (49 days) and from Pluschke's platoon Rudi Schwambach (48 days): SS-Corporal Günter Janzen (48) and the commander's driver SS-Corporal Paul Zwigart (48) of No 9 Company: SS-Corporal Helmut Urbat of No 10 Company and quite a few more well over the forty-day mark.[7] SS-Lt Tomhardt must also have had more than fifty confirmed days at this point.

On 22 April 1945 the Leibstandarte moved further south and the APC battalion became the corps reserve at Kleinzell. The next few days passed in trench warfare, assault troops and Soviet artillery bombardments. On 1 May 1945 we received news of the death of Adolf Hitler in Berlin. This report came as a blow to our morale, already at rock-bottom. Worst of all were the concerns of those men with family in the east of the German Reich where Stalin's hordes were wreaking havoc. How the troops of the Red Army were likely to treat the German civilian population in the territories they conquered was only too clear from our own experiences at where we drove them out of localities in Hungary and Austria. In April 1945 the Americans defined their war aims: 'Germany will not be occupied with the aim of liberating it, but as a conquered nation for the fulfilment of Allied interests.'[8]

At this time the Leibstandarte Panzer Regiment was equipped with the latest version development of the Tiger II, the Jagdtiger. Peiper's last command post before the move to Enns was at Annaberg, north of

178

Mariazell, where he received the last two signals from Division. Their content was roughly: 'Capitulation 9 May 1945 0001 hrs. Retire to the West crossing the Enns at Steyr up to 8 May 1945 2359 hrs.'[9] The Enns was the demarcation line and had to be crossed before one minute past midnight on 9 May so as to fall prisoner of the Americans. Whoever failed to make it would become a prisoner of the Soviets. On 8 May Peiper assembled all members of the Panzer Regiment Staff on parade to address them: then the battle groups set out in different directions because the roads were very congested. The last command post of the APC battalion at Lilienfeld was evacuated and SS-Captain Preuss, its commanding officer, paraded the battalion at Türnitz, announced the ceasefire, remembered the fallen and wished the men good luck.

I was the last man of the company who had been a member of it in Russia in July 1941. All the others were either dead, wounded or in other units. According to my company commander Jochen Thiele, up to 1945 a total of 985 men had served with the Company, and I had known twenty-five different company commanders. I was located with my APCs at the eastern end of the convoy. The other elements of No 12 Company, amongst them SS-Sergeant Feldvoss, were up front with Preuss at the head of the Battalion. Together with a 2/Lt of the 1st SS-Panzer Reconnaissance Battalion with his five armoured reconnaissance vehicles we made up the rearguard of the Division, our task being to hold off the Russians and prevent their blockading the roads. 9 May 1945 dawned. In various villages through which we drove I advised the girls to come with us to escape the Russians. They declined. Later we heard their screams and could see the Soviets raping girls in the village of Scheibbs. It was a depressing situation for we were not allowed to shoot. Now we saw what unconditional surrender meant – to be defenceless before the enemy and at his mercy.

After we had reached Scheibbs over field paths we headed next for Ternberg. The lieutenant and I were now racing desperately for the Enns, the Russians hot on our heels but holding fire. On 10 May we got to there. I covered the retreat as the last soldier of the Leibstandarte. At the Enns I drove the last APCs into the mountain river. Thus I did my duty, obedient to the very last. SS-Corporal Erich Strassgschwandtner remembered those last hours of our common struggle:

Now we were alone there. Our last company commander was Werner Kindler. The last NCOs and men of No 12 (Heavy Armoured) Company were assembled in two tank-gun vehicles and three APCs.

We set off towards Annaberg. We got through the pass leaving some vehicles behind. The Russians pursued us on 9 May. Our last 7.5cm gun fired once and peace fell over the entrance to the pass. Then we went full out past Scheibbs, Waidhofen and Weyer to Ternberg, where we arrived on 10 May. There we drove the APCs on to the slope and at full speed into the Enns. We were probably the last of our forgotten battalion. We went into a bitter captivity.[10]

What captivity was going to be like I discovered on the bridge over the Enns. I asked a 17-year-old soldier, an apprenticed tailor in civilian life, to shorten my tunic at the hem and cover the collar with a dark green material. I was searched on the bridge over the Enns by a black US soldier who discovered my dagger under the shortened uniform jacket and confiscated the weapon.

I was interned by the Americans in prison camps at Ternberg, Steyr-Wald, Ebensee I and II and Babenhausen. I was not happy in captivity and decided to escape. I drew lots with four other NCOs for the order of departure. On 19 November 1945 one cut a gap in the wire, another carried his hand luggage. We crept through the hole to freedom.

Now each began his new life in an occupied Germany ravaged by the victors. I still had no information as to the fate of my family in Western Prussia. After the Soviets came they took my father away. He fell ill in captivity and was brought home to die. My parents' farm at Gotenfelde was occupied by Poles who ejected my family. They spent a while in emergency accommodation at the Insthaus, a lodge which had once been home to agricultural labourers. In the summer of 1945 my mother had fled with the three children to Mecklenburg and later to Western Germany. West Prussia was re-annexed by Poland and I could no longer return there. I got work and started a family.

Not all members of my company, nor the commanders, escaped US captivity so easily. SS-Corporals Rudi Schwambach, Toni Motzheim, Axel Rodenburg and SS-Grenadier Günther Weiss were all sentenced to death by the American victors on 16 July 1946 in the Malmédy war crimes trial. My battalion commanders Jochen Peiper, Georg Preuss and Jupp Diefenthal were also sentenced to death. Much has already been written about the 'facts' offered as 'evidence', and the methods of torture and mock executions staged by the Americans to extract statements. In this connection one should refer to the biography of Jochen Peiper by Patrick Agte.

From the beginning, the Americans set out to have statements to lay before the tribunal to the effect that before the Ardennes offensive orders had been issued that prisoners were to be shot. The NCOs and men, and also the officers, were supposed to have admitted the existence of these non-existent orders to facilitate the manufacture of a case against the platoon and company commanders. Particularly in Peiper's case the American prosecutors assembled a mountain of paperwork to get a conviction. Since there was no actual proof against Peiper or anybody else, when the confessions extracted under duress were recanted in the court at Dachau by the accused the tribunal convicted without any evidence. Some ten years or so after the sentences of death were handed down but soon commuted to life imprisonment, my company colleagues were released. Former SS-Lt Sternebeck, sentenced to death, was accepted into the West German border protection police in the rank of full lieutenant and rose to be a Lt-Colonel in the Bundeswehr. Preuss and Diefenthal left Landsberg in 1956: after eleven years and seven months in captivity Jochen Peiper was the last of those convicted at the Malmédy trial to leave Landsberg. He stepped out to freedom on the afternoon of 22 December 1956. I found success in my private and professional life after the war. I soon re-established contact with the colleagues from my company, met them regularly over decades and attended various reunions of my old units.

Notes

Foreword
1. For a masterly debunking of the Soviet offensive thesis see David M. Glantz, *Stumbling Colossus: The Red Army on the Eve of World War* (Lawrence, Kansas: University Press of Kansas, 1998).

Introduction
1. Führerbefehl 25 November 1942 in Allgemeine Heeresmitteilung bulletin, 7 December 1942.
2. OKH, 3 December 1942.
3. OKH, 26 March 1944.
4. OKH, 30 August 1944.
5. OKH, 30 August 1944.
6. The calculations are based on the officially confirmed close-combat days which 2nd SS-Panzer Grenadier Regiment LAH advised to Kindler's battalion. The various dates listed are taken from the regimental war diary. The author's close-combat days in Normandy are from officially confirmed schedules from Normandy in 1944 and are reconstructions from confirmed close-combat days of various LAH companies and casualty lists. Kindler's close-combat days with Battle Group Diefenthal are taken from the Soldbuch of SS-Captain Herbert Rink, who commanded the battle group at Aachen.

Chapter One: From a Farm in Danzig into the Leibstandarte-SS Adolf Hitler
1. Bernhard Lindenblatt and Otto Bäcker, *Bromberger Blutsonntag* ('Bloody Sunday in Bromberg') (Kiel: 2001), p 56.
2. Kurt Lück, *Der Lebenskampf im deutsch-polnischen Lebensraum*, quoted from Bolko von Richthofen and Reinhold Robert Oheim, *Die polnische Legende, part 2, Polens Marsch zum Meer: Zwei Jahrhunderte Teilungen und Expansion* (Kiel: 2001), p 209.
3. From a Note on the conversation between Reich Foreign Minister von Ribbentrop and Polish ambassador Lipski, 24 October 1938 in

Auswärtiges Amt 1939, No 2 Dokumente zur Vorgeschichte des Krieges (Berlin: 1939), pp 178f.

4. Kurjer Polski, 10 August 1939, quoted from von Richthofen, *Die polnische Legende, part 2*, p 212, and Maier-Dorn, Emil, *Alleinkriegsschuld* (Grossaitingen: 1970), p 284.

5. Report by Heinrich Julius Rotzoll, 1939, Wachtmeister (Sergeant-Major), 57th Artillery Regiment.

6. At the end of April 1940, 1st and 2nd Battalions were sent to Norway and attached in January 1941 to SS-Kampfgruppe Nord. Later reformed as the 11th SS-Mountain Regiment Reinhard Heydrich within SS-Mountain Division Nord they spent a long period fighting the Soviets in the Karelian forests of Finland.

7. After fighting alongside Army Group North it was reconstituted as a motorised regiment at Cracow in December 1941. XIII Army Corps co-opted 1st Battalion for the Soviet winter offensive of 1941 while 2nd Battalion fought alongside 19th Panzer Division from Juchnov. 3rd Battalion arrived at Kaluga. In these bitter defensive battles in the icy cold, the regiment bled out down to 180 men. This remnant did not return until April 1942 when it was awarded the honour suffix and cuff title Langemarck on Hitler's birthday that year. It was reformed as the fast SS-Motorcycle Regiment Langemarck and incorporated into the SS-Panzer Grenadier Division Das Reich. The major contingent of the old Ostmark soldiers went into II Battalion. When 2nd Battalion of the new SS-Panzer Grenadier Division Das Reich was formed in October 1942, Langemarck Regiment was absorbed into it and fought in Das Reich until the end of the war. The name Langemarck was later given to the Flemish SS-Assault Brigade.

Chapter Two: Russia 1941–1942: My First Ten Close-combat Days

1. *Pravda*, 11 June 2002. See also: Viktor Suvorov/Dmitrij Chmelnizki (German translation). *Der Eisbrecher – Hitler in Stalins Kalkül and Überfall auf Europa. Plante die Sowjet Union 1944 einen Angriffskrieg?* (Stuttgart: 1989). Joachim Hoffmann, *Stalins Vernichtungskrieg 1941-1945: Planung, Ausführung und Dokumentation* (Munich: 1995).

2. For these actions in 1941/42 see the divisional history: Rudolf Lehmann, *Die Leibstandarte*, Vol 1 (Munin Verlag: 1978).

3. Lehmann, *Die Leibstandarte*, Vol 1, p 215.

Chapter Three: I Become a Panzer Grenadier

1. Heinz Guderian, *Erinnerungen eines Soldaten* (Wels: 1952; Stuttgart: 2003).

2. War Diary, 2nd SS-Panzer Grenadier Regiment LAH.
3. Günter Gaul, letter 29 March 1991. Formerly commander, No 11 Company, 2nd SS-Panzer Grenadier Regiment.
4. Erich Schöbel, formerly of No 11 Company, 2nd SS-Panzer Grenadier Regiment, letter 4 October 1996.
5. Jochen Peiper, personal files.
6. Paul Guhl, statement 1 July 1995.
7. War Diary, 2nd SS-Panzer Grenadier Regiment LAH.
8. Franz Neuendorff, letter 10 November 1990.
9. SS-FHA, secret document 24 November 1942.
10. Telex 2 January 1943, War Diary 2nd SS-Panzer Grenadier Regiment LAH.
11. Günther Wagner, formerly of No 13 Company, 2nd SS-Panzer Grenadier Regiment, letter 13 June 1995.
12. Günter Gaul, formerly of No 12 Company, 2nd SS-Panzer Grenadier Regiment, letter 7 December 1996.
13. Walter Spillberger, *Halbkettenfahrzeuge des deutschen Heeres* (Stuttgart: Motorbuch Verlag, 1984).
14. Gustav Becker, letter 13 May 1996; Martin Säuberlich, letter 30 September 1996; Günter Gaul, letter 7 December 1996. All were attached at that time to No 12 Company, 2nd SS-Panzer Grenadier Regiment.
15. Martin Säuberlich, letter 30 September 1996.
16. Gustav Becker, letter 13 May 1996; Kuno Balz, letter 29 March 1995; Günter Gaul, personal statement 30 May 1997.
17. Kuno Balz, letter 29 March 1995.
18. Martin Säuberlich, letter of 10 April 1995.
19. Günter Gaul, letter 7 December 1996.
20. Günther Wagner, letter of 13 June 1996.
21. Fritz Schmautz, formerly of No 11 Company, 2nd SS-Panzer Grenadier Regiment, letter of 11 September 1995.
22. Günther Wagner, letter 13 June 1996.
23. Paul Gaul, personal statement 1 July 1995.
24. Erich Schöbel, letter 1 February 1994.
25. Franz Neuendorff, letter 18 October 1990.
26. Günter Gaul, 6 September 1995.
27. Joachim Peiper, personal files.
28. Erhard Gührs, then SS-2/Lt and platoon commander, No 14 Company, 2nd SS-Panzer Grenadier Regiment, diary entry.
29. War Diary, 2nd SS-Panzer Grenadier Regiment LAH.
30. Erhard Gührs, diary.
31. Ibid.

32. H.D.V.298/3a *Ausbildungsvorschrift für die Panzertruppe – Führung und Kampf der Panzergrenadiere, Part I: Das Panzergrenadier-Bataillon (gep.)*, 5 August 1944

Chapter Four: The Battle for Kharkov, 27 January–29 March 1943
1. Erhard Gührs, diary.
2. Ibid.
3. War Diary, 1st Battalion, 2nd SS-Panzer Grenadier Regiment LAH.
4. War Diary, 2nd SS-Panzer Grenadier Regiment LAH.
5. War Diary, 1st Battalion, 2nd SS-Panzer Grenadier Regiment LAH.
6. War Diary, 2nd SS-Panzer Grenadier Regiment LAH.
7. Ibid.
8. Ibid.
9. Heinz Glenewinkel, then of No 13 Company, 2nd SS-Panzer Grenadier Regiment, diary.
10. War Diary, 1st Battalion, 2nd SS-Panzer Grenadier Regiment LAH.
11. War Diary, 2nd SS-Panzer Grenadier Regiment LAH.
12. Erhard Gührs, diary.
13. Ibid.
14. Recommendation for award of German Cross in Gold to Jochen Peiper, 26 February 1943.
15. Erhard Gührs, diary.
16. Ibid.
17. Ibid.
18. Jochen Peiper, 10 April 1976 in Lehmann, *Die Leibstandarte*, Vol III.
19. Paul Guhl, personal statement 1 July 1995.
20. Rudolf von Ribbentrop, then of 7th Company 1st SS-Panzer Regiment 1, letter 4 October 1995.
21. Recommendation for award of German Cross in Gold to Jochen Peiper, 26 February 1943.
22. Paul Guhl, personal statement 1 July 1995.
23. Ibid.
24. Jochen Peiper, 10 April 1976 in Lehmann, *Die Leibstandarte*, Vol III.
25. Günther Wagner, letter 13 June 1995.
26. War Diary, 2nd SS-Panzer Grenadier Regiment LAH.
27. Erhard Gührs, diary.
28. Günther Wagner, letter 13 June 1995.
29. Erhard Gührs, diary. All quotes from Gührs in the main text without a footnote reference come from his diary.
30. Paul Guhl, personal statement 1 July 1995.

31. War Diary, 1st Battalion, 2nd SS-Panzer Grenadier Regiment LAH.
32. Recommendation for award of German Cross in Gold to Jochen Peiper, 26 February 1943.
33. Günther Wagner, letter 13 June 1995.
34. Kuno Balz, letter 29 March 1995.
35. Confirmed Close-combat Days, 2nd SS-Panzer Grenadier Regiment LAH, War Diary.
36. Otto Dinse, then adjutant 3rd Battalion, 2nd SS-Panzer Grenadier Regiment, personal statement.
37. Confirmed Close-combat Days, 2nd SS-Panzer Grenadier Regiment LAH, War Diary.
38. Peiper's battle report in the recommendation for the award of the German Cross in Gold to Paul Guhl, 26 August 1943.
39. War Diary, 2nd SS-Panzer Grenadier Regiment LAH.
40. Sigmund Oswald, *Meine Ehre heisst Treue* (Essen: 1992). Formerly of No 13 Company, 2nd SS-Panzer Grenadier Regiment.
41. War Diary, 2nd SS-Panzer Grenadier Regiment LAH.
42. Recommendation for the award of the Knight's Cross to Jochen Peiper, 7 March 1943.
43. War Diary, 2nd SS-Panzer Grenadier Regiment LAH.
44. Ibid.
45. Peiper's battle report in the recommendation for the award of the German Cross in Gold to Paul Guhl, 26 August 1943.
46. Confirmed Close-combat Days, 2nd SS-Panzer Grenadier Regiment LAH, War Diary.
47. War Diary, 2nd SS-Panzer Grenadier Regiment LAH.
48. Divisional Order No. 8, 10 March 1943.
49. Recommendation of the award of the Knight's Cross to Rudolf Sandig, 1 April 1943.
50. Martin Säuberlich, letter 30 September 1946.
51. Heinz Glenewinkel, then of No 13 Company, 2nd SS-Panzer Grenadier Regiment, diary.
52. *Die Leibstandarte*, Vol III, Rudolf Glenewinkel.
53. War Diary, 2nd SS-Panzer Grenadier Regiment LAH.
54. Martin Saüberlich, letter 11 February 1996.
55. Martin Saüberlich letter 23 February 1996
56. Martin Saüberlich, letter 11 February 1996.
57. War Diary, 2nd SS-Panzer Grenadier Regiment LAH.
58. Oswald, *Meine Ehre heisst Treue*. Formerly of No 13 Company, 2nd SS-Panzer Grenadier Regiment.

59. *Die Leibstandarte*, Vol III, Rudolf Glenewinkel.
60. *Völkischer Beobachter*, March 1943.

Chapter Five: The Seizure of Byelgorod, 18 March 1943
1. Confirmed Close-combat Days of 2nd SS-Panzer Grenadier Regiment, LAH, War Diary.
2. War Diary, 2nd SS-Panzer Grenadier Regiment LAH.
3. Erhard Gührs, personal notes.
4. Otto Dinse, personal statement 1 May 1996.
5. Peiper's battle report in his recommendation for the award of the German Cross in Gold to Paul Guhl, 26 August 1943.
6. P. Agte, *Michael Wittmann und Tiger der LSSAH* (1993).
7. War Diary, 2nd SS-Panzer Grenadier Regiment LAH.
8. Ibid.
9. Rudolf von Ribbentrop, letter 4 October 1995.

Chapter Six: Interlude and Preparations for Kursk, 29 March–4 July 1943
1. War Diary, 2nd SS-Panzer Grenadier Regiment LAH.
2. Karl Menne, Erich Strassgschwandtner, personal information.
3. Erhard Gührs, personal information.
4. Otto Dinse, personal information 6 July 1995.
5. Bernd von Bergmann, personal information 22 May 1997.
6. Erhard Gührs, personal information.
7. Theodore Kaufman, *Germany Must Perish!* (Argyle Press: 1941): Louis Nizer, *What to Do with Germany* (1944), also published in a special edition for the US Army.
8. Casablanca conference, 14–26 January 1943.
9. Erhard Gührs, personal information.

Chapter Seven: Operation Citadel – the Kursk Offensive
1. Erhard Gührs, diary.
2. Agte, *Michael Wittmann und die Tiger der LSSAH*.
3. Dr Ernst Klink, *Gesetz des Handelns – Operation Zitadelle* (Deutsche Verl.-Aust: 1966).
4. Werner Wolff, letter to his fiancée Helga, 4 July 1943.
5. War Diary 2nd SS-Panzer Grenadier Regiment.
6. Recommendation for the award of the German Cross to Heinz Kling, 5 December 1943.
7. Erhard Gührs, diary.
8. Recomendation for the award of the German Cross to Heinz Kling, 5

December 1943.
9. Erhard Gührs, diary.
10. Hugo Kraas, letter July 1943.
11. Bernd von Bergmann, personal information 22 May 1997.
12. Confirmed Close-combat Days, 2nd SS-Panzer Grenadier Regiment.
13. Recommendation for the award of the German Cross to Heinz Kling, 5 December 1943.
14. Erich Schöbel, 7 May 1996.
15. Dr Herbert Schramm, manuscript for article *Der Siebte Tag*, 1943.

Chapter Eight: 12 July 1943 – The Death Ride of the Soviet Tanks at Prochorovka

1. Gührs, diary.
2. Gührs had been mentally overwhelmed, and did not write up his diary until 21 July 1943: 'I put my diary aside because it seemed necessary to get it all out of my system first. But I could not, it had been too much for me. Now there is some distance from it, and I can write and talk about it again.'
3. Johannes Bräuer, 16 June 1995.
4. Kurt Butenhoff, personal information 30 April 1998.
5. From the recommendation for the award of the Knight's Cross to Werner Wolff, 23 July 1943.
6. Albert Frey, *Ich wollte die Freiheit* (Munin Verlag: 1990).
7. Erhard Knöfel, 14 June 1991.
8. From the recommendation for the award of the German Cross in Gold to Paul Guhl, 26 August 1943.
9. Dr Herbert Schramme, manuscript for article *Der Siebte Tag*, 1943.
10. Recommendation for the award of the German Cross in Gold to Rudolf von Ribbentrop, 13 July 1943: OKH decided on the Knight's Cross.
11. Recommendation for the award of the German Cross in Gold to Walter Malchow, 13 July 1943
12. Gührs, diary and notes.

Chapter Nine: The Leibstandarte in Italy, 5 August – 24 October 1943

1. Gührs, diary.
2. Gührs, interview 20 July 1997.
3. Fritz Thiers, interview.
4. Werner Wolff, letters of 28 August 1943 and 30 August 1943.
5. List of awards, 2nd SS-Panzer Grenadier Regiment.
6. Gührs, interview 8 May 1997.

7. Lehmann, *Die Leibstandarte*, Vol III.

Chapter Ten: Back to the Eastern Front, 15–30 November 1943
1. Erhard Gührs.
2. War Diary, 2nd SS-Panzer Grenadier Regiment.
3. Recommendation for the award of the German Cross in Gold to Heinz Kling, 5 December 1943.
4. War Diary, 2nd SS-Panzer Grenadier Regiment.
5. List of awards, 1st SS-Panzer Division LSSAH.
6. Peiper, letter 7 April 1973.
7. Paul Guhl, interview 1 July 1995.
8. Recommendation for the award of the German Cross in Gold to Heinz Kling, 5 December 1943.
9. Recommendation for the award of the German Cross in Gold to Paul Guhl, 16 December 1943.
10. Gührs, 29 May 1997, interview 20 July 1997.
11. Peiper to Professor James Weingartner, around 1969.
12. Otto Dinse, interviews 30 April 1994, 29 April 1995 and 31 May 1996.
13. Paul Guhl, interview 1 July 1995.
14. Gührs, interview 20 July 1997.
15. Werner Wolff, 30 November 1943.
16. Willy Micheluzzi, 21 September 1995.
17. Lehmann, *Die Leibstandarte*, Vol III.
18. Wilhelm Nusshag, 18 September 1995.
19. Dr Arndt Fischer, 17 November 1995.
20. War Diary 2nd SS-Panzer Grenadier Regiment.
21. Recommendation for the award of the German Cross in Gold to Paul Guhl, 16 December 1943.
22. Paul Guhl, interview 1 July 1995.
23. Ibid.
24. Ibid.
25. Recommendation for promotion for Peiper, 28 November 1943.
26. Fritz Kosmehl, 14 July 1996.
27. Paul Guhl, interview 1 July 1995.
28. There is an entry in the divisional journal for 7 October 1943 which mentions a newly-established armoured flak platoon for the APC battalion of the LAH. None of the soldiers consulted could confirm its existence, and neither in the authorised divisional strength was a flak platoon for the APC battalion envisaged nor in the organisational structure of 1 December 1943. The explanation came to light in 2010. The

alleged flak platoon (Flakzug) was a flamethrower platoon (Flammzug). According to the order of the OKH/Chef H Rüst u BdE/AHA of 2 October 1943 a flamethrower platoon (armoured) – a platoon with medium flamethrower armoured vehicles (Sd Kfz 251/16) was set up with effect from 7 October 1943. Evidently there was a typographical error in the divisional journal. On 11 October 1943 the Leibstandarte received six flamethrower APCs from the Army Equipment Office. Three of these came to No 14 Panzer Pioneer Company of the Panzer Regiment and later to the APC battalion.

Chapter Eleven: Operation Advent and the Fighting in the USSR to March 1944

1. War diary, 2nd SS-Panzer Grenadier Regiment.
2. Recommendation for the award of the Oak Leaves to Peiper's Knight's Cross, 27 December 1943.
3. Recommendation for the award of the Knight's Cross to Paul Guhl, interview 1 July 1995.
4. Erhard Gührs, 7 September 1995.
5. Recommendation for the award of the Oak Leaves to Peiper's Knight's Cross, 27 December 1943.
6. War diary, 2nd SS-Panzer Grenadier Regiment.
7. Recommendation for the award of the Oak Leaves to Peiper's Knight's Cross, 27 December 1943.
8. Gührs, 8 May 1997.
9. P. Agte, *Michael Wittmann und die Tiger der LSSAH*.
10. War diary, 2nd SS-Panzer Grenadier Regiment.
11. Gerd Jahn, then SS-2/Lt, 2nd Battalion 1st SS-Panzer Grenadier Regiment, 8 April 1996.
12. War diary, 2nd SS-Panzer Grenadier Regiment. In place of Badyalovka it states railway station Vadyaleff.
13. Hugo Kraas, regimental commanding officer, 2nd SS-Panzer Grenadier Regiment, letter 12 December 1943.
14. Lehmann, *Die Leibstandarte*, Vol. III.
15. Friedrich W. Mellenthin, *Panzerschlachten* (Nackargemünd: 1963).
16. Otto Dinse, personal statement.
17. War diary, 2nd SS-Panzer Grenadier Regiment.
18. Paul Kurbjuhn, 'Die eiserne Särge', in *Das Schwarze Corps* (SS-official journal).
19. Hans Oeser, recorded on tape, 10 December 1997.
20. War diary, 2nd SS-Panzer Grenadier Regiment.

21. Gührs, 8 May 1997 and diary.
22. Report by Staff officer Ic LAH to XXXXVIII Panzer Corps, 20 December 1943.
23. Mellenthin, *Panzerschlachten*.
24. Erich Strassgschwandtner 29 April 1995, Tank Destruction Badges, award list, 2nd SS-Panzer Grenadier Regiment, 26 May 1994.
25. Confirmed Close-combat Days, 2nd SS-Panzer Grenadier Regiment.
26. Paul Guhl, personal interview 1 July 1995.
27. Gert Quartthammer, field-post letter 21 October 1944.
28. War diary, 2nd SS-Panzer Grenadier Regiment.
29. Bernd von Bergmann, interviews 29 April 1995, 22 May 1997.

Chapter Twelve: The Reorganisation in Flanders, April to June 1944

1. Iron Cross award list for 2nd SS-Panzer Grenadier Regiment and 1st SS-Panzer Division LAH, Soldbuch entries.
2. Award list for 2nd SS-Panzer Grenadier Regiment.
3. Gerhard Stiller, 25 March 1998.

Chapter Thirteen: Invasion: Securing the Mouth of the Scheldt, 6–17 June 1944

1. Regimental order, 2nd SS-Panzer Grenadier Regiment, 9 June 1944.
2. Luis Brandmeier, field-post letter 19 June 1944.

Chapter Fourteen: Action in Normandy, 30 June–20 August 1944

1. Paul Guhl, personal information 1 July 1995.
2. According to a report of the APC-Staffel leader, No 12 (Heavy Armoured) Company 2nd SS-Panzer Grenadier Regiment, these six tank-gun APCs were to be taken over by the 1st SS-Panzer Artillery Battalion in July 1944. They were still waiting for them long after the invasion began.
3. Traugott Schmidt, field-post letter 12 July 1944.
4. Casualty list, 2nd SS-Panzer Grenadier Regiment.
5. Rudi Knobloch, information in person 21 April 2010.
6. Karl Menne, information in person 21 April 2010.

Chapter Fifteen: Tilly-la-Campagne, Caen and Falaise to the Westwall: 25 July–November 1944

1. Gerhard Stiller, report on his operations in Normandy circa 1990.
2. Willi Pluschke, personal information 30 April 1995.
3. Erhard Gührs, personal information 20 July 1997.
4. Michael Wittmann, field-post letter 30 July 1944.

5. Dr Helmut Neumann, 17 March 1996
6. Peiper's battle report in his recommendation of mention for Wolff in the Army Honour Scroll, 2 November 1944.
7. Gerhard Stiller, 11 July 1994.
8. C.P. Stacy, *La Campagne de la Victoire* (Ottawa: 1996) in Lehmann, *Die Leibstandarte*, Vol IV/I.
9. Gührs, 27 December 1997.
10. Fritz Kraemer, SS-Gruppenführer und Generalleunant der Waffen-SS, 17 November 1945 Ethint 24.
11. Gührs, 27 December 1997.
12. Georg Preuss in Lehmann, *Die Leibstandarte*, Vol IV/I. Reinecken aged 19 died on 23 August 1944 in Military Hospital 613.
13. Dr Helmut Neumann, 17 March 1996.
14. Gührs, 27 December 1997.
15. Otto Dinse, personal information 30 April 1995.
16. Franz Steineck, personal file.
17. Helmut Feldvoss, letter 23 November 1994.
18. Volksbund Deutsche Kriegsgräberfürsorge, 13 October 1996.
19. Battle report, Kampfgruppe Rink, 22 October 1994, authored by SS-Hauptsturmführer Rink.
20. Heinrich Kahlen, 7 June 1990, Helga Wolff, 30 May 1994.

Chapter Sixteen: The Führer-Escort Company, the Gold Clasp and Preparing for the Ardennes

1. Dr Helmut Neumann, 1 December 1995.
2. Rudi Knobloch, 12 March 1995
3. Details of awards for 2nd SS-Panzer Grenadier Regiment.
4. 1st SS-Panzer Division LAH to OKH, PA/P5 1.Staffel, Berlin, 27 November 1944 re request for Close-combat Clasp in silver and gold for two officers.
5. List of awards, 1st SS-Panzer Division.
6. Jochen Peiper 1975/76.

Chapter Seventeen: The Ardennes Offensive, 16–24 December 1944

1. Rudi Knobloch, personal information 2 March 2010.
2. Heinz Tomhardt, statement in the Malmédy trial, 1946.
3. Peiper, 22 February 1959.
4. Recommendation for the award to Peiper of the Swords to the Oak Leaves of the Knight's Cross, 26 December 1944.
5. Ibid.

6. Werner Sternebeck, report on the Ardennes offensive.
7. Peiper, in his recommendation for the award of the Knight's Cross to Georg Preuss, 28 December 1944.
8. Rudi Knobloch, personal information 21 April 2010.
9. Peiper, in his recommendation for a mention for Karl Übler in the Honour Scroll of the German Army, 28 December 1944.
10. Dr Helmut Neumann, 1 December 1995.
11. Werner Sternebeck, report on the Ardennes offensive.
12. Wolfgang Richter, 5 March 1996.
13. Rudi Rayer, 26 April 1947.
14. Dr Hans Hennecke, 14 March 1996.
15. Werner Poetschke, in the recommendation for a mention for Erich Strelow in the Honour Scroll of the German Army, 28 December 1944.
16. Peiper, statement in the Malmédy trail: Wm Gilbert, 10 September 1948 et al.
17. Erich Strassgschwandtner, 18 December 1995.
18. Karl-Heinz Fetzer, 13 July 1997.
19. Erich Strassgschwandtner, 18 December 1995.
20. Peiper, 22 February 1959.

Chapter Eighteen: Transfer to Hungary, January–February 1945
1. Erich Strassgschwandtner, 18 February 1995.
2. Peiper, recommendation for award of Knight's Cross to Preuss, 28 December 1944.

Chapter Nineteen: Operation South Wind, 17–24 February 1945, and the Retreat from Hungary
1. Günther Borchers, diary, SS-2/Lt No 9 Company, 1st SS-Panzer Regiment.
2. Diefenthal, quoted in Ralf Tiemann, *Die Leibstandarte*, Vol IV/2.
3. Peiper, 6 January 1958.
4. Diefenthal, quoted in Ralf Tiemann, *Die Leibstandarte*, Vol IV/2.
5. Günther Wagner.
6. Kindler's Soldbuch: confirmation from Sepp Dietrich, 17 July 1953, first mention of the Close-combat Clasp in gold in recommendation award of Knight's Cross for Preuss, 28 December 1944.
7. Confirmed by Georg Preuss, 9 February 1988, and several statements from Rudi Knobloch.

Chapter Twenty: The Fighting on Reich Soil, 1 April–8 May 1945
1. War diary, Fahnenjunkerbataillon/War Academy, Wiener Neustadt.

2. Soldbuch, Werner Kindler, letter from Sepp Dietrich to Georg Preuss, 7 July 1953.
3. Heinz Meier, 14 December 1995.
4. Heinz Meier, 29 July 1995.
5. Letter from Georg Preuss, 9 February 1988: statement by Rudi Knobloch, 2010.
6. The Close-combat Clasp in gold, the German Cross in Gold and the promotion of Preuss were confirmed on affidavit by, amongst others, Dietrich Ziemssen, 16 July 1953 and Sepp Dietrich, 17 July 1953, letters from Georg Preuss, 16 February 1987, 9 February 1988. As a result of the surprise discontinuation of the award no more entries were made in the Soldbuch.
7. Letters from Günther Janzen, 5 July 1995, Paul Zwigart, 31 March 1996, statements by several former battalion members.
8. American Instruction on Occupation, ICG 106, April 1945 quoted in *Die Welt*, 4 July 1994.
9. Walter Lehn, 24 October 1995.
10. Erich Strassgschwandtner, 21 October 1995.